絶対絶望少女

Danganronpa Another Episode:
Ultra Despair Girls

1

Manga By
HAJIME TOUYA

Created By
SPIKE CHUNSOFT

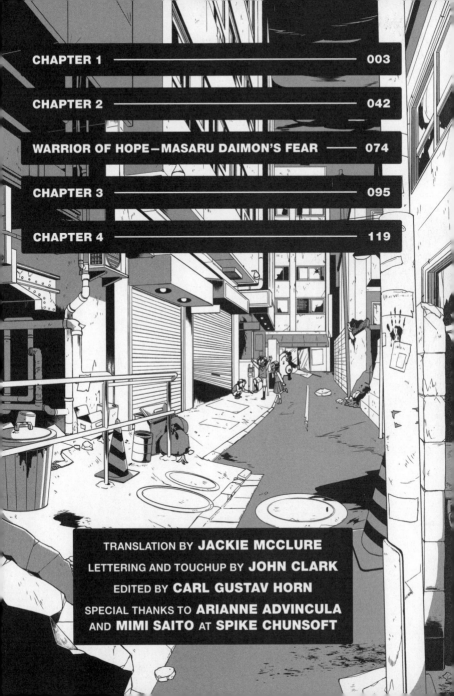

TRANSLATION BY **JACKIE MCCLURE**

LETTERING AND TOUCHUP BY **JOHN CLARK**

EDITED BY **CARL GUSTAV HORN**

SPECIAL THANKS TO **ARIANNE ADVINCULA**
AND **MIMI SAITO** AT **SPIKE CHUNSOFT**

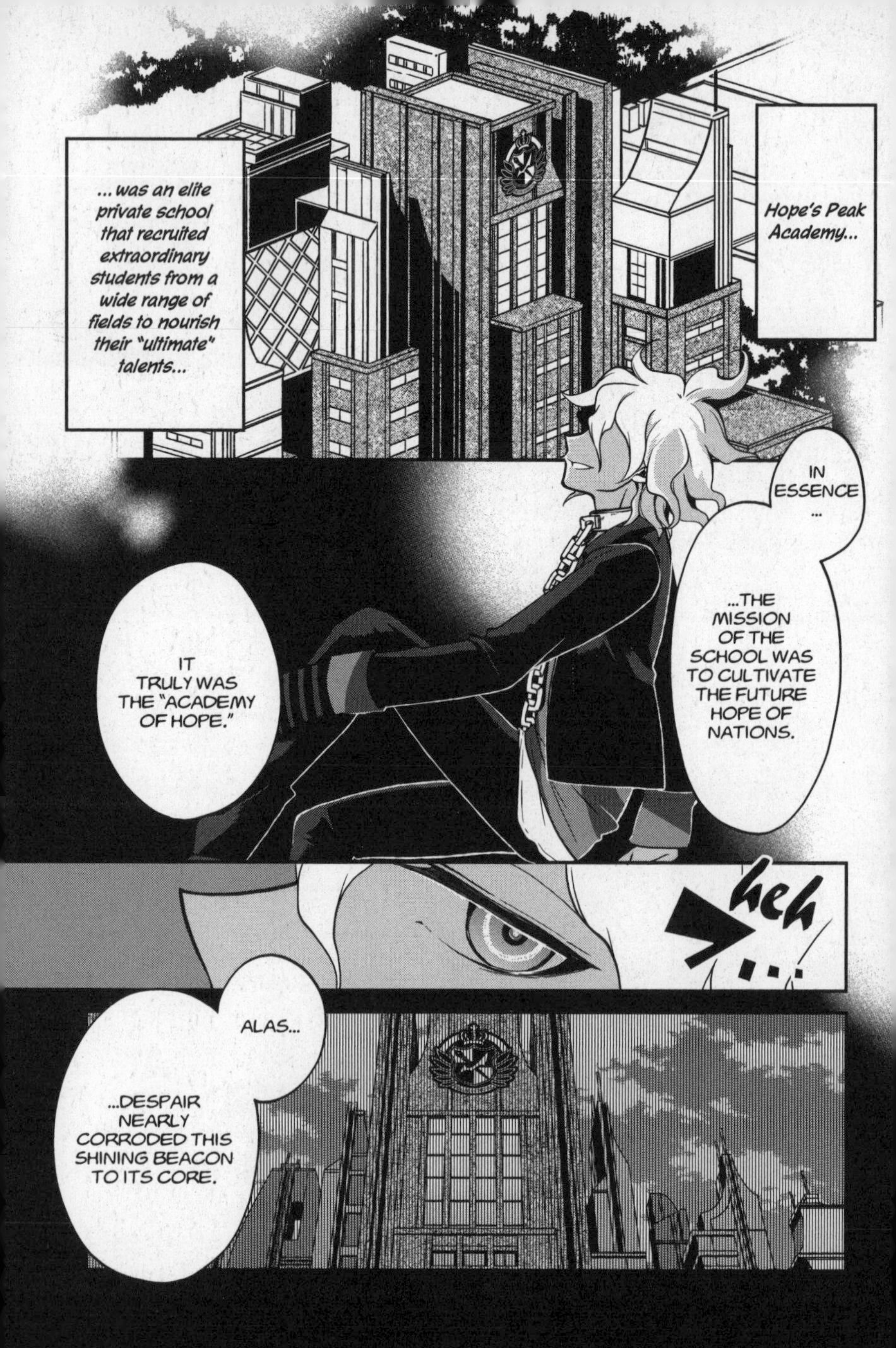
Hope's Peak Academy...
... was an elite private school that recruited extraordinary students from a wide range of fields to nourish their "ultimate" talents...
IN ESSENCE ...
...THE MISSION OF THE SCHOOL WAS TO CULTIVATE THE FUTURE HOPE OF NATIONS.
IT TRULY WAS THE "ACADEMY OF HOPE."
heh...
ALAS...
...DESPAIR NEARLY CORRODED THIS SHINING BEACON TO ITS CORE.

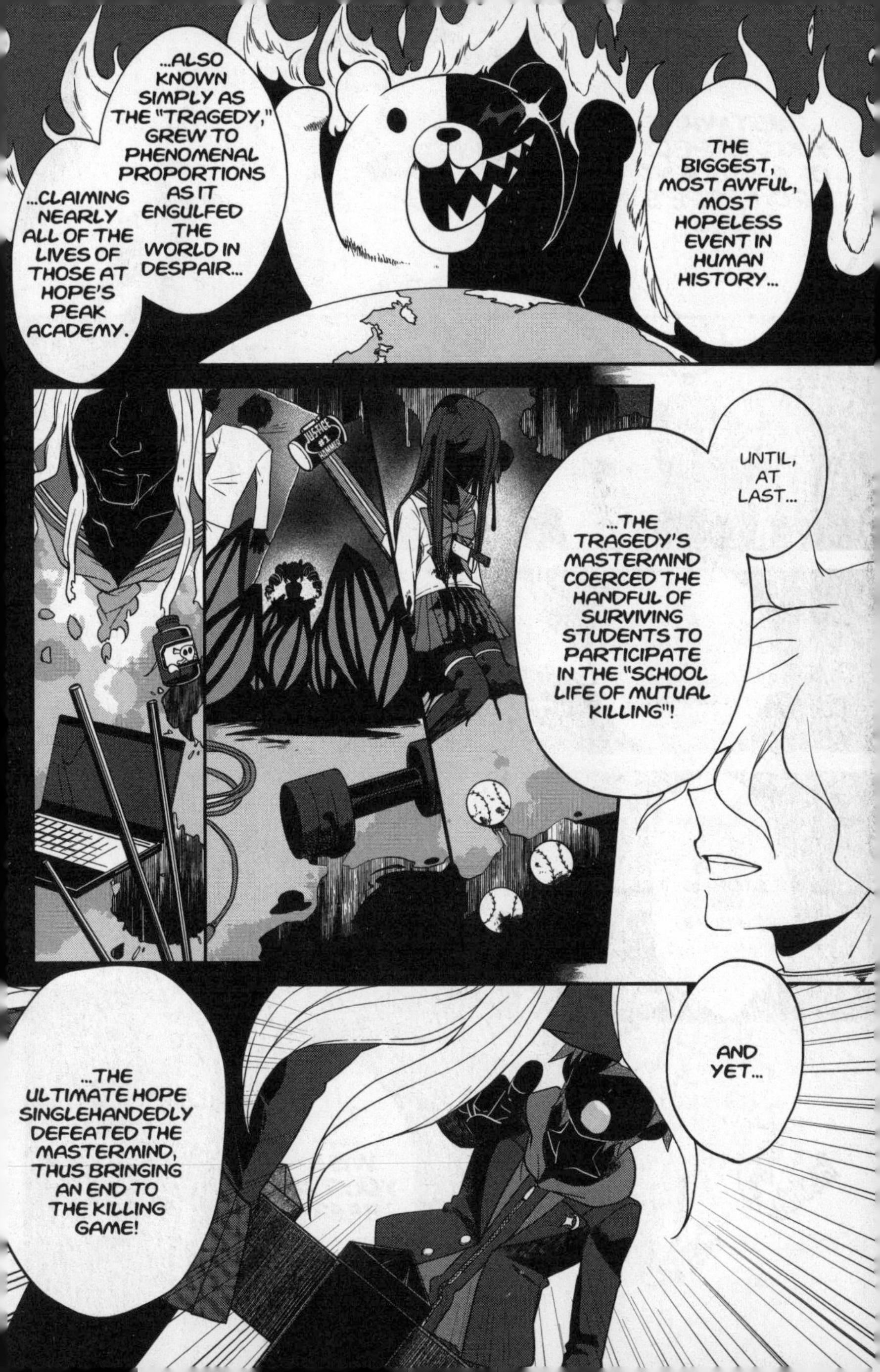
THE BIGGEST, MOST AWFUL, MOST HOPELESS EVENT IN HUMAN HISTORY...
...ALSO KNOWN SIMPLY AS THE "TRAGEDY," GREW TO PHENOMENAL PROPORTIONS AS IT ENGULFED THE WORLD IN DESPAIR...
...CLAIMING NEARLY ALL OF THE LIVES OF THOSE AT HOPE'S PEAK ACADEMY.
UNTIL, AT LAST...
...THE TRAGEDY'S MASTERMIND COERCED THE HANDFUL OF SURVIVING STUDENTS TO PARTICIPATE IN THE "SCHOOL LIFE OF MUTUAL KILLING"!
AND YET...
...THE ULTIMATE HOPE SINGLEHANDEDLY DEFEATED THE MASTERMIND, THUS BRINGING AN END TO THE KILLING GAME!

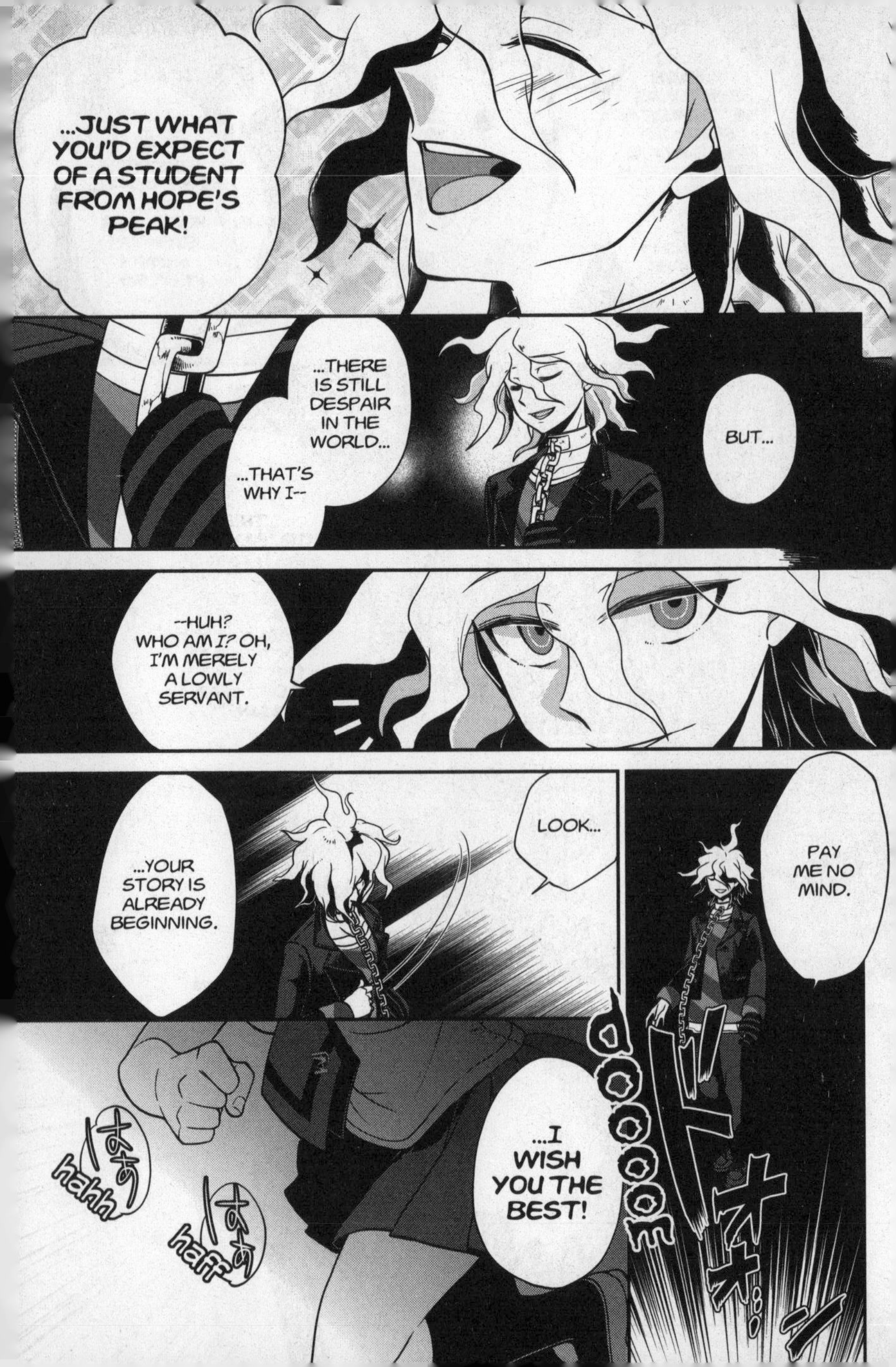
...JUST WHAT YOU'D EXPECT OF A STUDENT FROM HOPE'S PEAK!
BUT...
...THERE IS STILL DESPAIR IN THE WORLD...
...THAT'S WHY I--
--HUH? WHO AM I? OH, I'M MERELY A LOWLY SERVANT.
PAY ME NO MIND.
LOOK...
...YOUR STORY IS ALREADY BEGINNING.
ドーオオ...ン
DOOOOOM
...I WISH YOU THE BEST!
はあ haff
はあ hahh

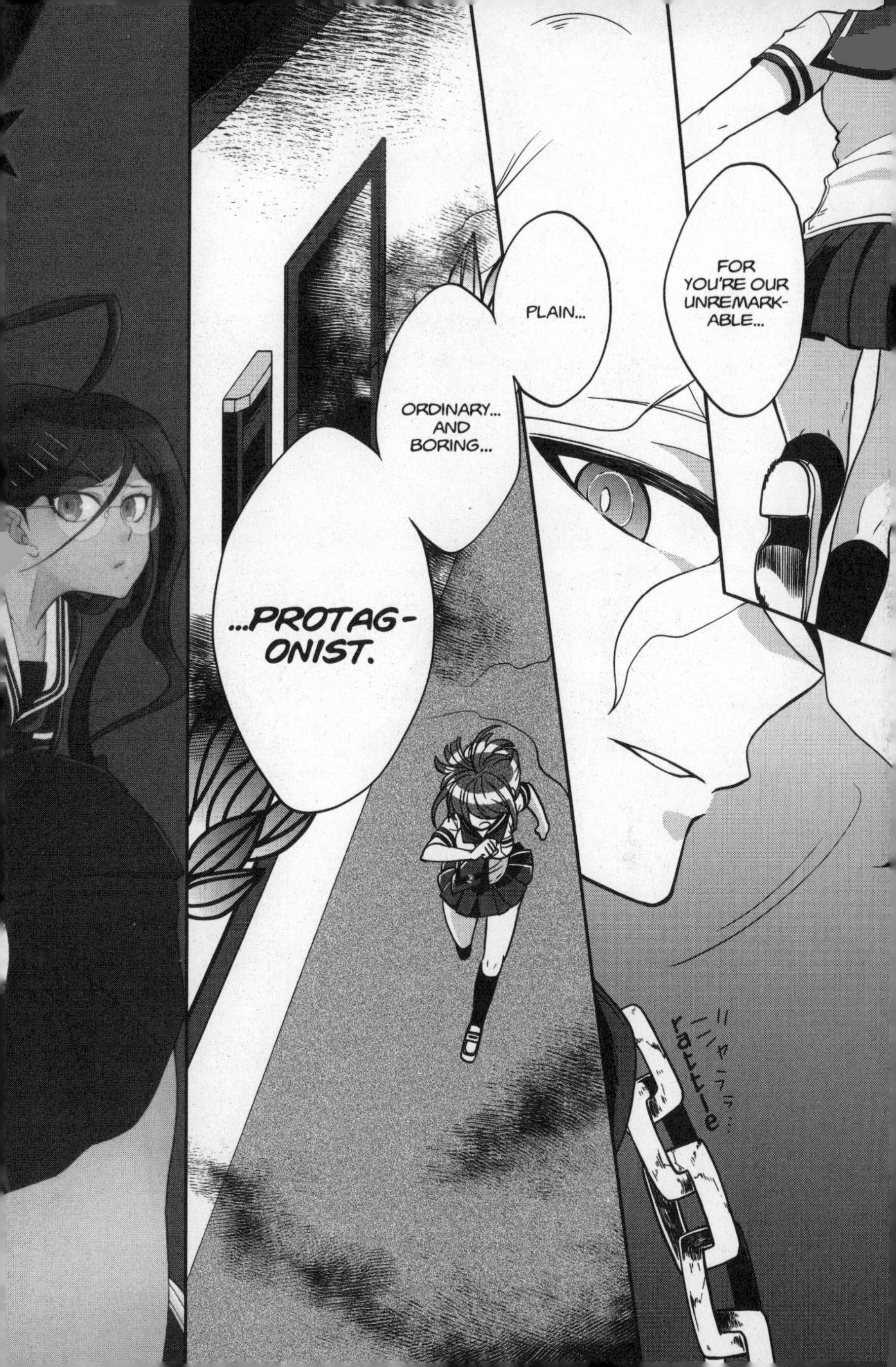
FOR YOU'RE OUR UNREMARKABLE...
PLAIN...
ORDINARY... AND BORING...
...PROTAGONIST.
rattle

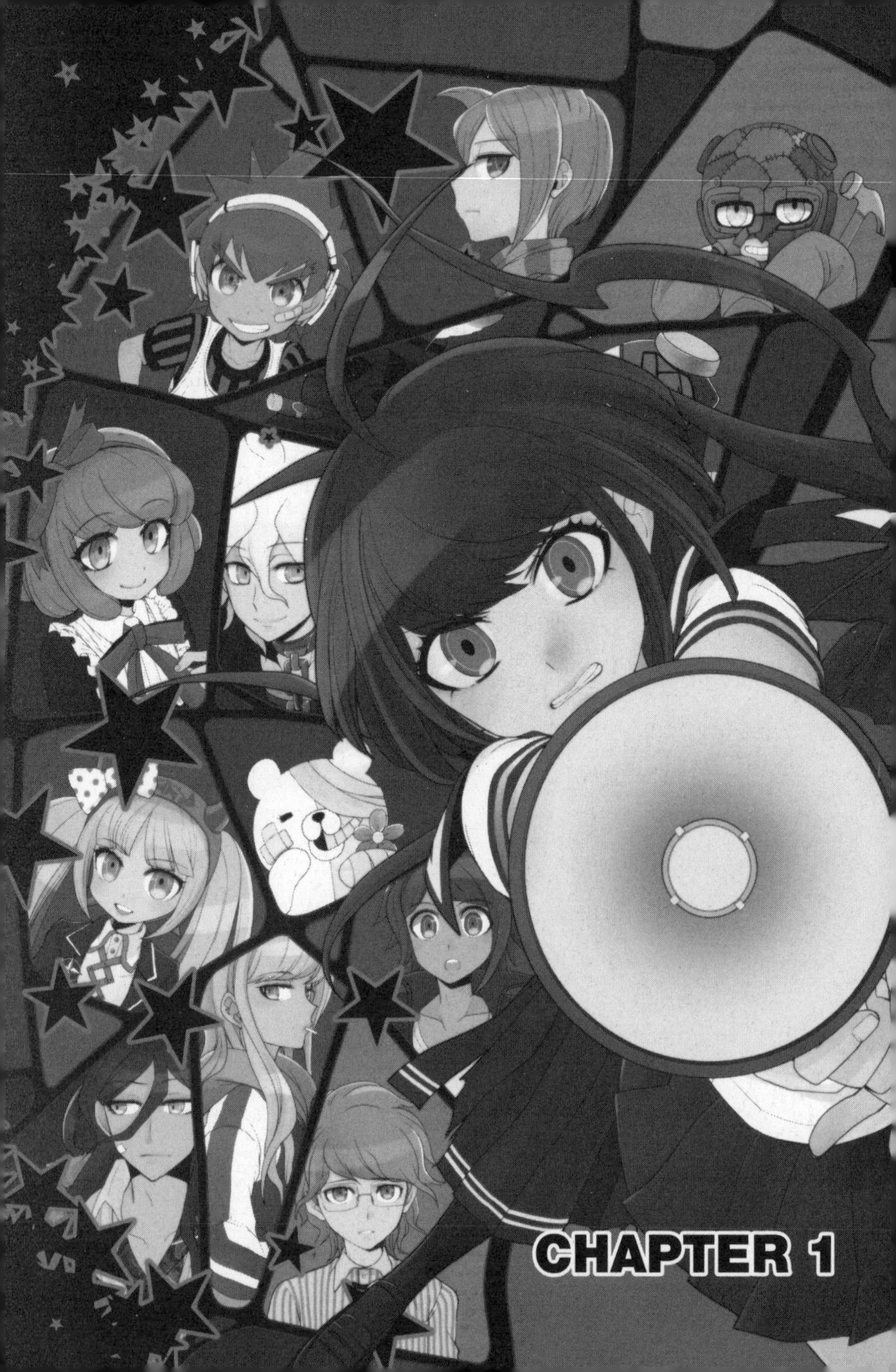
CHAPTER 1

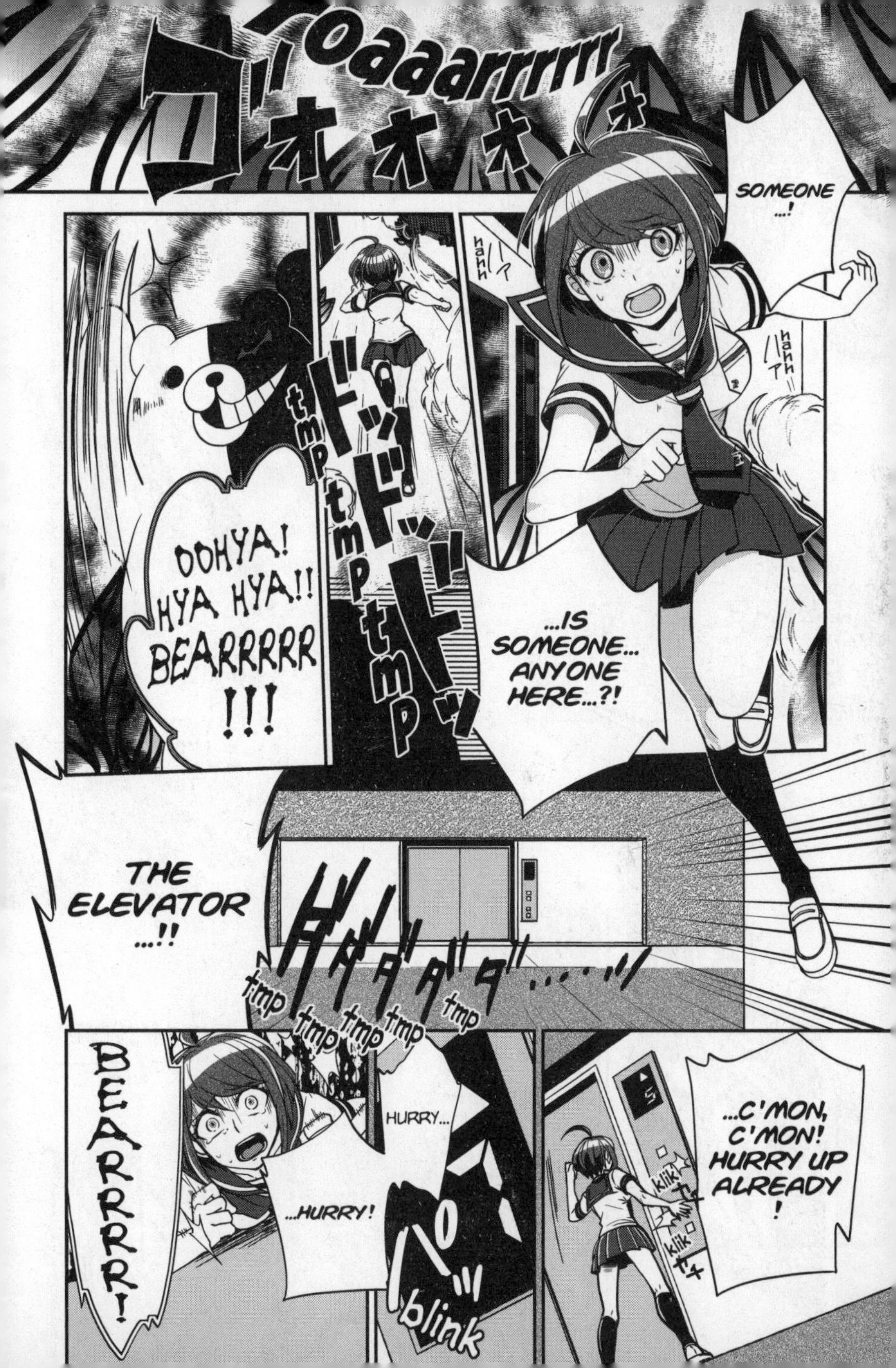
Oaaarrrrrr
ゴオオオオ
SOMEONE ...!
hahh
ハァ
hahh
ハァ
...IS SOMEONE... ANYONE HERE...?!
tmp tmp tmp tmp
OOHYA! HYA HYA!! BEARRRRR !!!
THE ELEVATOR ...!!
tmp tmp tmp tmp tmp
...C'MON, C'MON! HURRY UP ALREADY!
klik
klik
HURRY...
...HURRY!
blink
BEARRRRR!

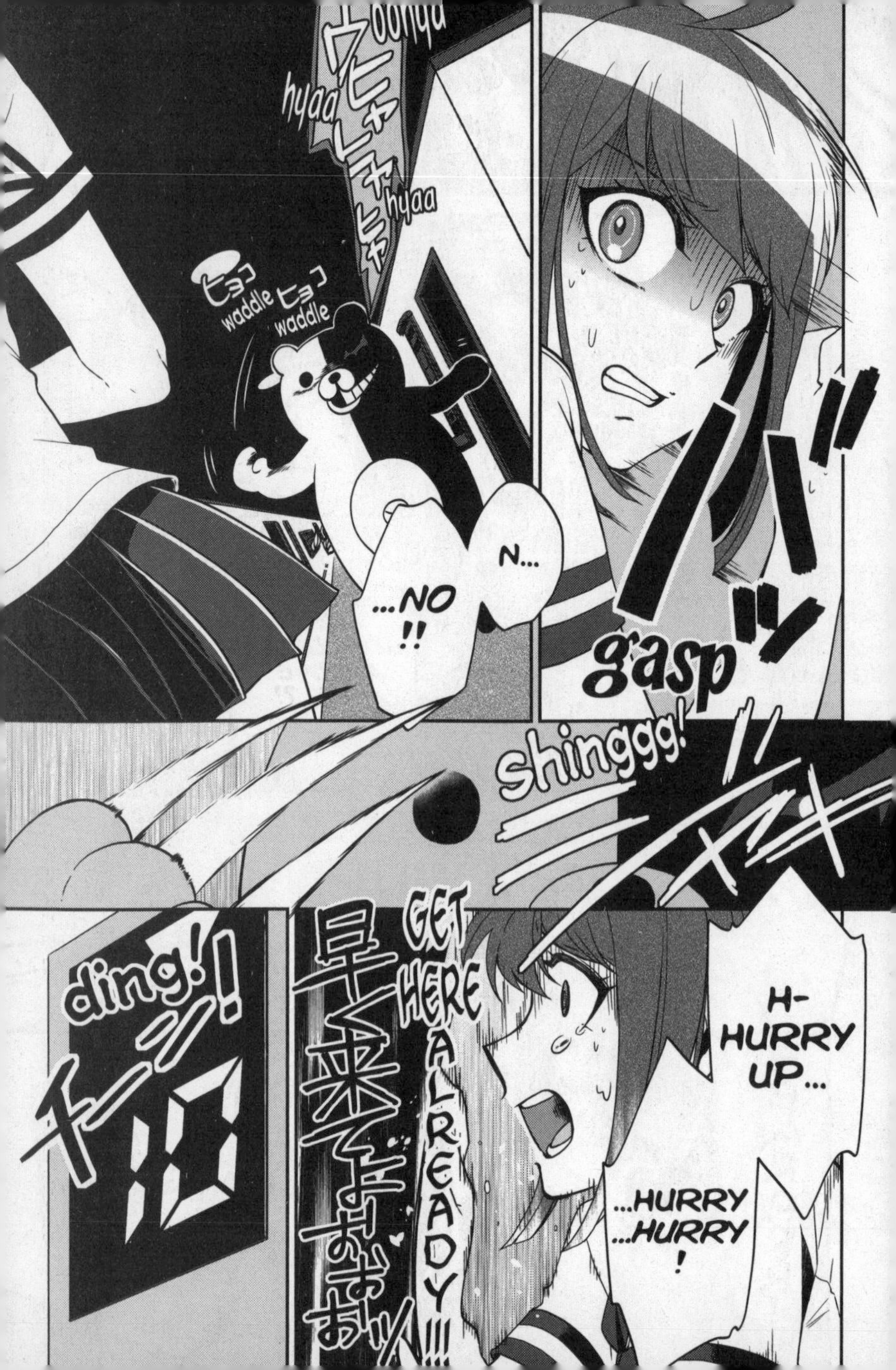
gasp
ウヒャヒャヒャ
hyaa
hyaa
ヒョコ ヒョコ
waddle waddle
N...
...NO !!
shinggg!
H- HURRY UP...
...HURRY ...HURRY !
早く来てよおおおおっ
GET HERE ALREADY!!!
チーン
ding!!

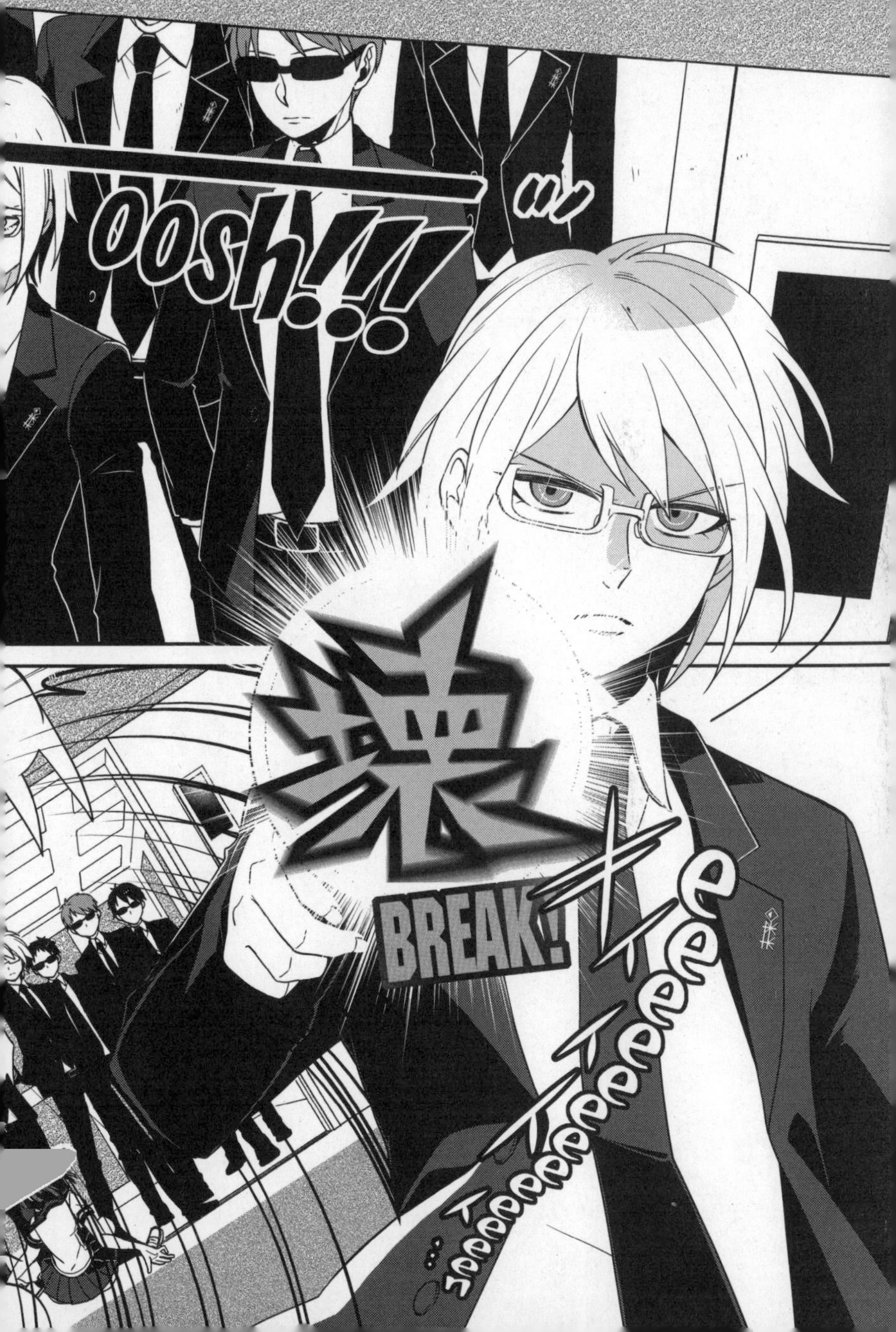
oosh!!!
BREAK!

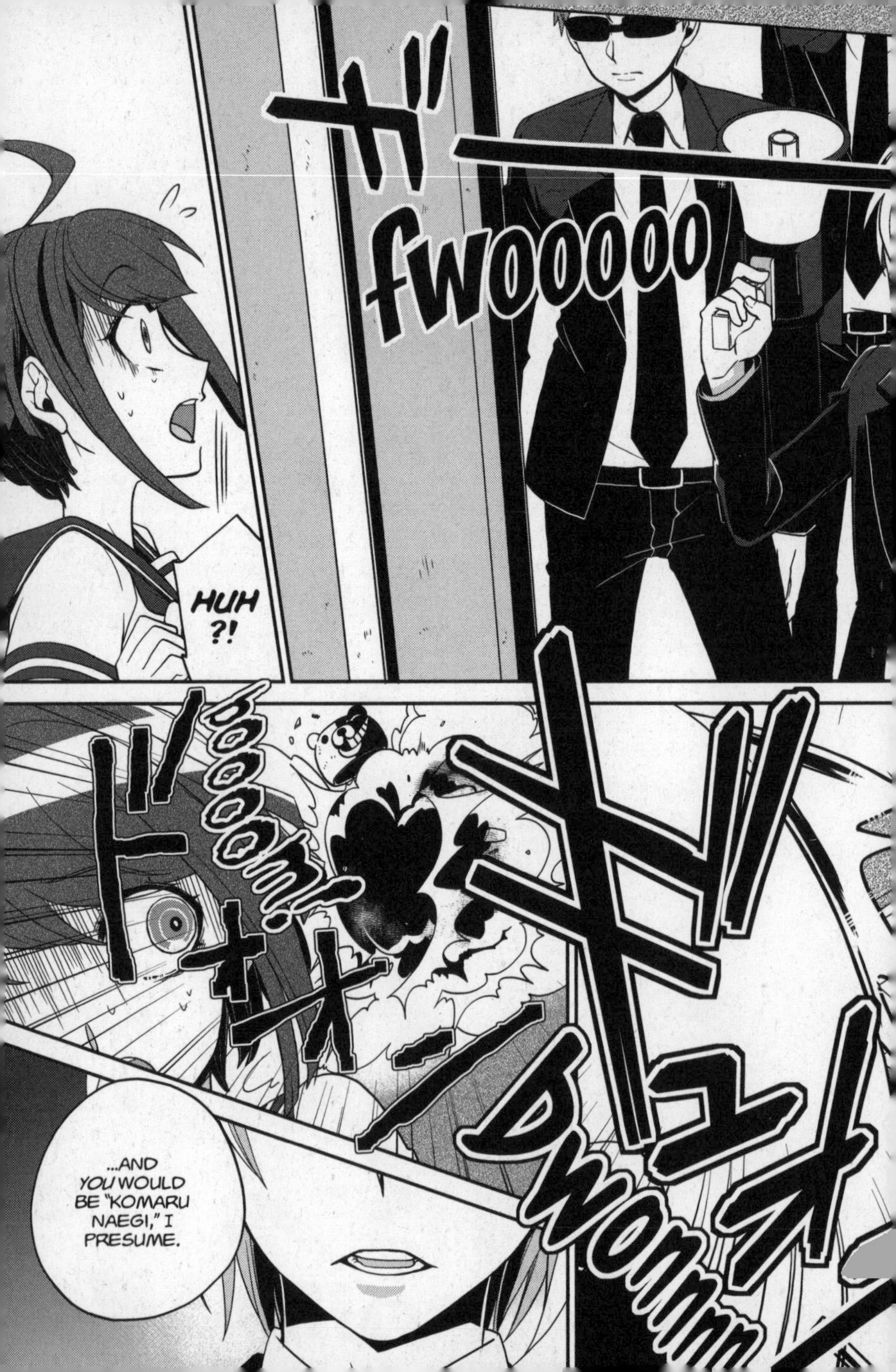
fwooooo
HUH ?!
DWOMMM
booooom!
...AND YOU WOULD BE "KOMARU NAEGI," I PRESUME.

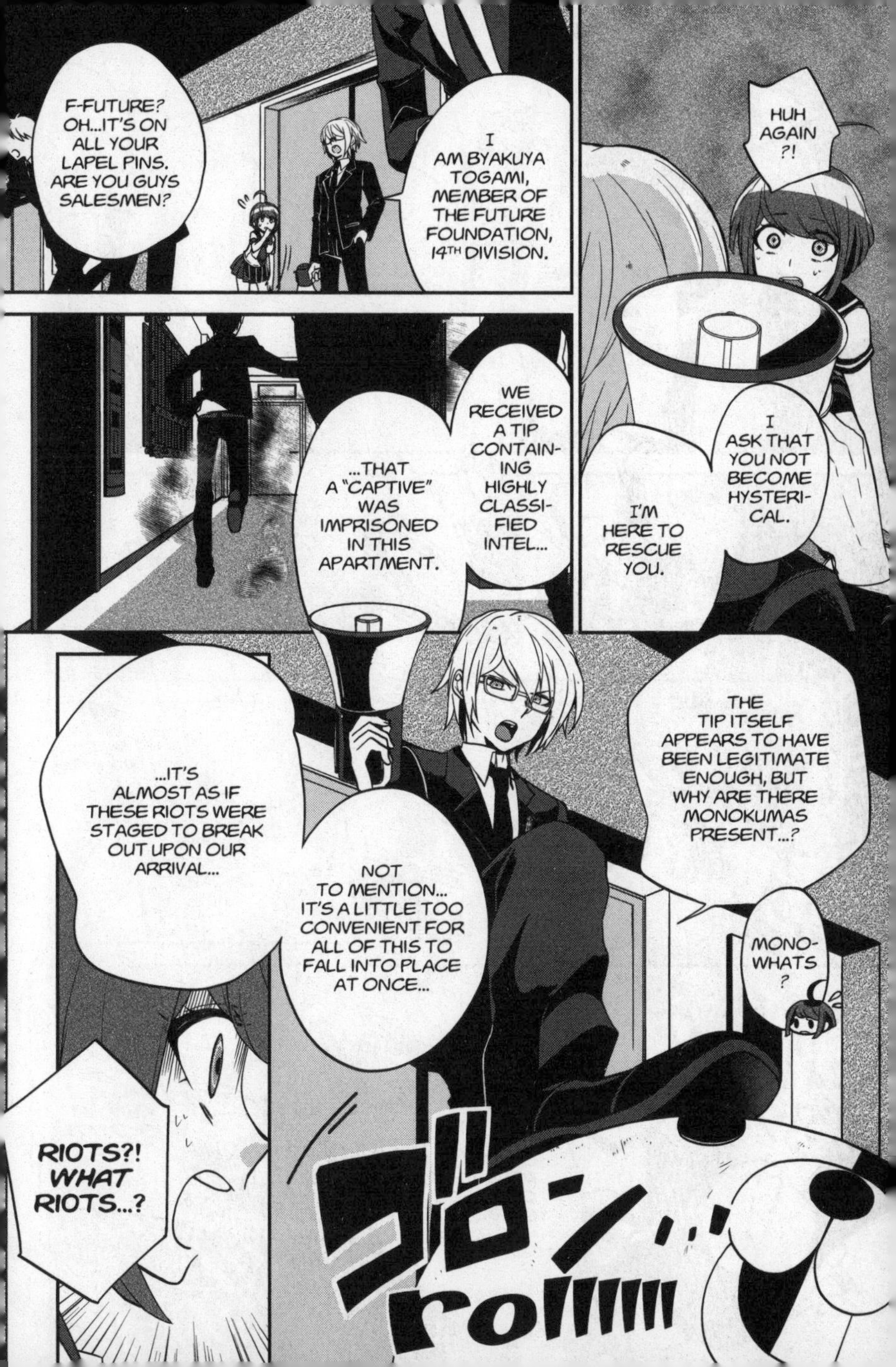
HUH AGAIN ?!
I ASK THAT YOU NOT BECOME HYSTERICAL.
I'M HERE TO RESCUE YOU.
I AM BYAKUYA TOGAMI, MEMBER OF THE FUTURE FOUNDATION, 14TH DIVISION.
F-FUTURE? OH...IT'S ON ALL YOUR LAPEL PINS. ARE YOU GUYS SALESMEN?
WE RECEIVED A TIP CONTAINING HIGHLY CLASSIFIED INTEL...
...THAT A "CAPTIVE" WAS IMPRISONED IN THIS APARTMENT.
THE TIP ITSELF APPEARS TO HAVE BEEN LEGITIMATE ENOUGH, BUT WHY ARE THERE MONOKUMAS PRESENT...?
MONO-WHATS?
NOT TO MENTION... IT'S A LITTLE TOO CONVENIENT FOR ALL OF THIS TO FALL INTO PLACE AT ONCE...
...IT'S ALMOST AS IF THESE RIOTS WERE STAGED TO BREAK OUT UPON OUR ARRIVAL...
RIOTS?! WHAT RIOTS...?
rollllll

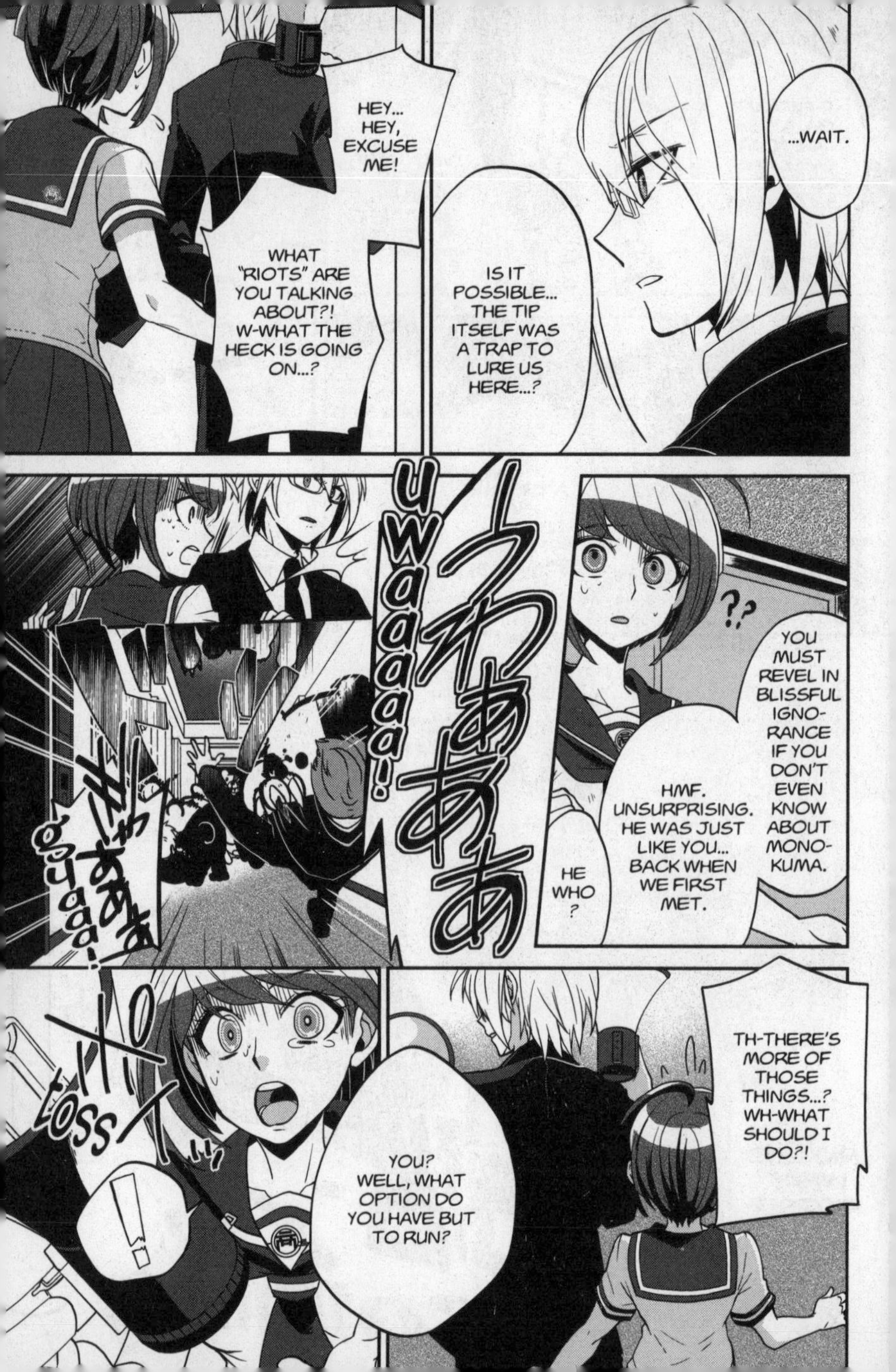
...WAIT.
IS IT POSSIBLE... THE TIP ITSELF WAS A TRAP TO LURE US HERE...?
HEY... HEY, EXCUSE ME!
WHAT "RIOTS" ARE YOU TALKING ABOUT?! W-WHAT THE HECK IS GOING ON...?
??
YOU MUST REVEL IN BLISSFUL IGNO-RANCE IF YOU DON'T EVEN KNOW ABOUT MONO-KUMA.
HMF. UNSURPRISING. HE WAS JUST LIKE YOU... BACK WHEN WE FIRST MET.
HE WHO?
うわあああ
UWAAAAAA!
ぎゃあああ
GYAAA!
TH-THERE'S MORE OF THOSE THINGS...? WH-WHAT SHOULD I DO?!
YOU? WELL, WHAT OPTION DO YOU HAVE BUT TO RUN?
ポイ
TOSS
!

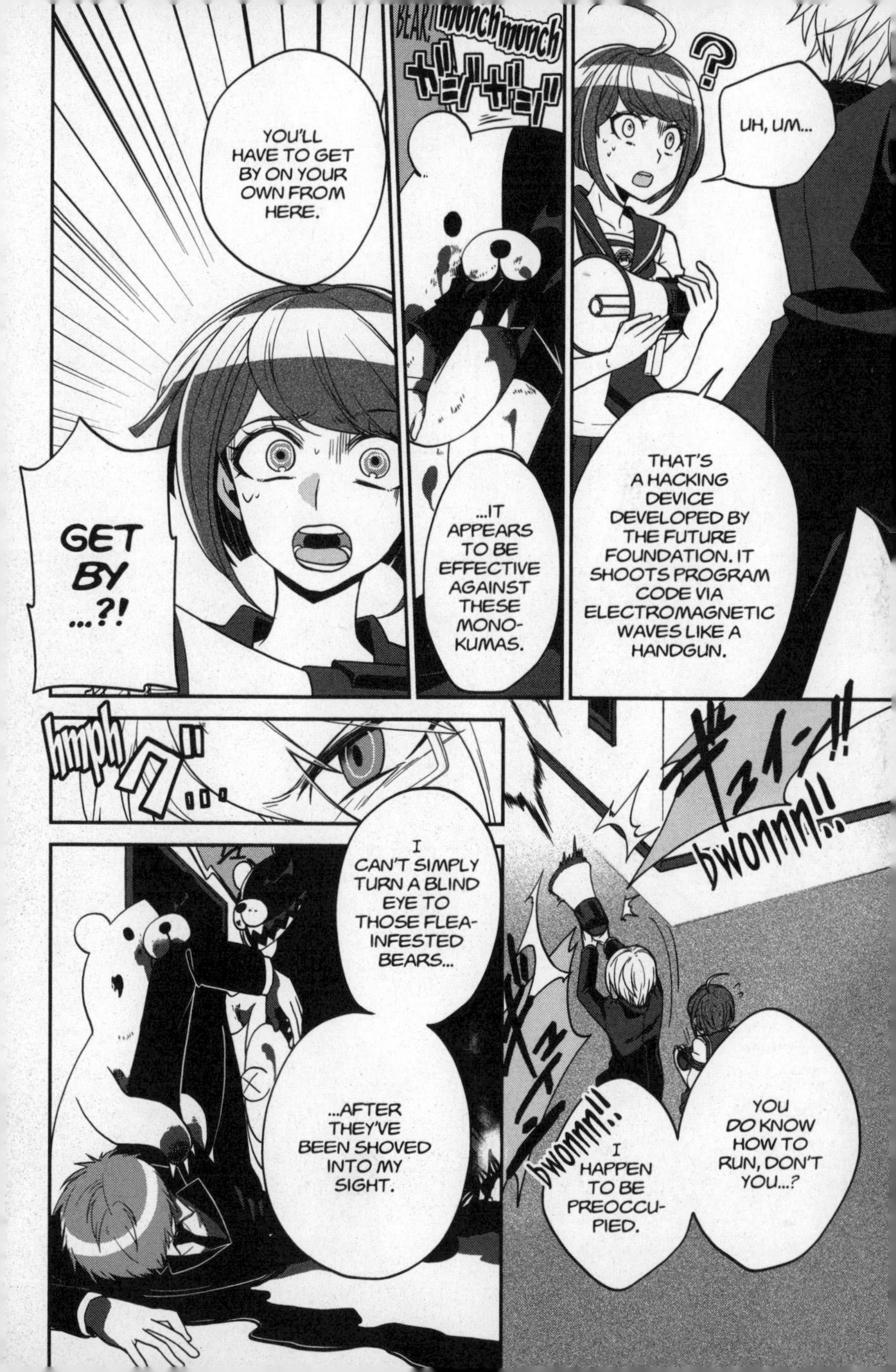

?
UH, UM...
THAT'S A HACKING DEVICE DEVELOPED BY THE FUTURE FOUNDATION. IT SHOOTS PROGRAM CODE VIA ELECTROMAGNETIC WAVES LIKE A HANDGUN.
BEAR!
munch munch
...IT APPEARS TO BE EFFECTIVE AGAINST THESE MONO-KUMAS.
YOU'LL HAVE TO GET BY ON YOUR OWN FROM HERE.
GET BY ...?!
bwonnn!!
YOU DO KNOW HOW TO RUN, DON'T YOU...?
I HAPPEN TO BE PREOCCU-PIED.
bwonnn!!
hmph
I CAN'T SIMPLY TURN A BLIND EYE TO THOSE FLEA-INFESTED BEARS...
...AFTER THEY'VE BEEN SHOVED INTO MY SIGHT.

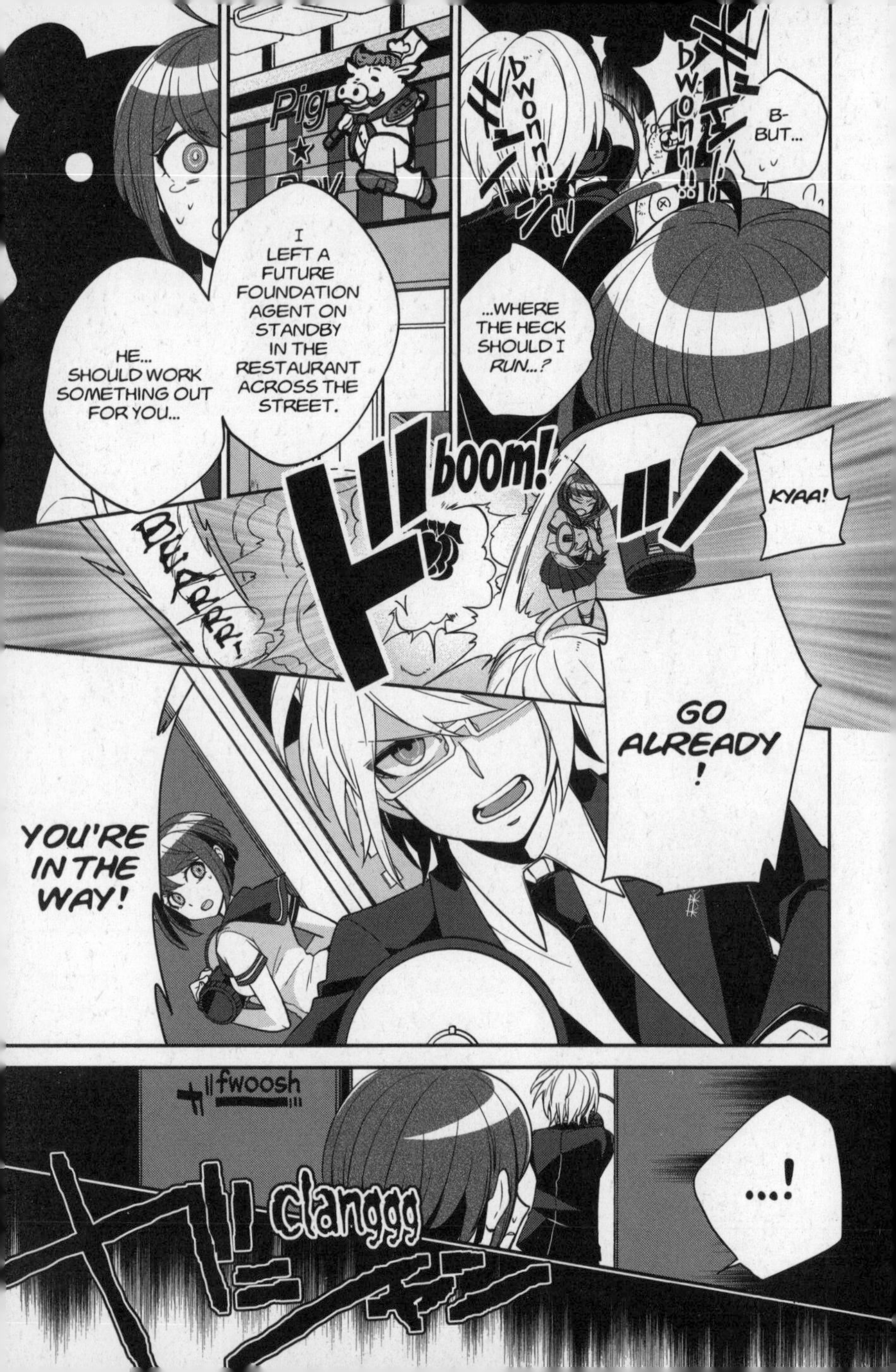
DWONN!!
DWONN!!
B-BUT...
...WHERE THE HECK SHOULD I RUN...?
Pig
I LEFT A FUTURE FOUNDATION AGENT ON STANDBY IN THE RESTAURANT ACROSS THE STREET.
HE... SHOULD WORK SOMETHING OUT FOR YOU...
KYAA!
boom!
BWARRR!
GO ALREADY!
YOU'RE IN THE WAY!
...!
fwoosh
clanggg

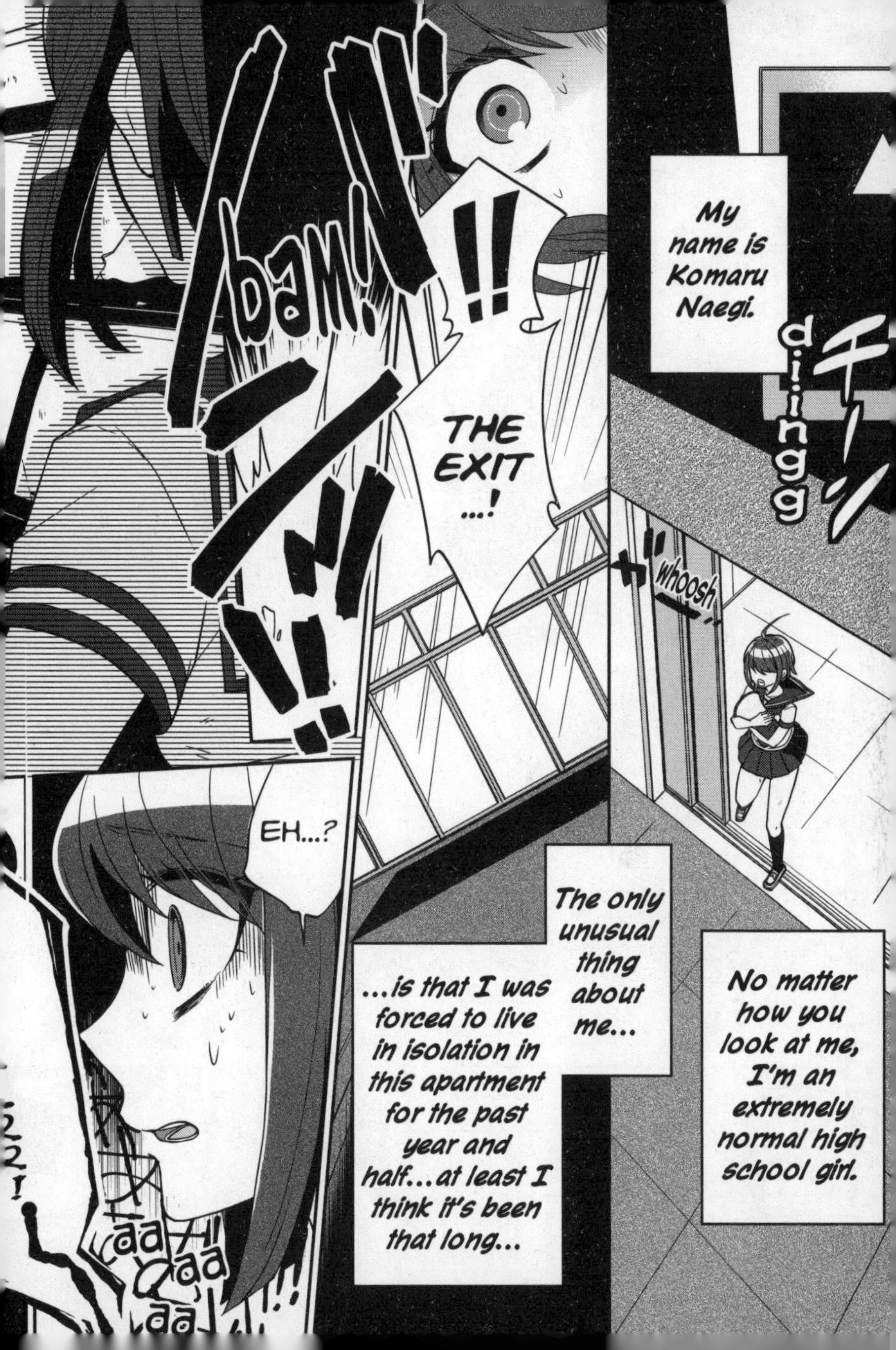

My name is Komaru Naegi.
diingg
whoosh
No matter how you look at me, I'm an extremely normal high school girl.
The only unusual thing about me...
...is that I was forced to live in isolation in this apartment for the past year and half...at least I think it's been that long...
bam!!
THE EXIT ...!
EH...?

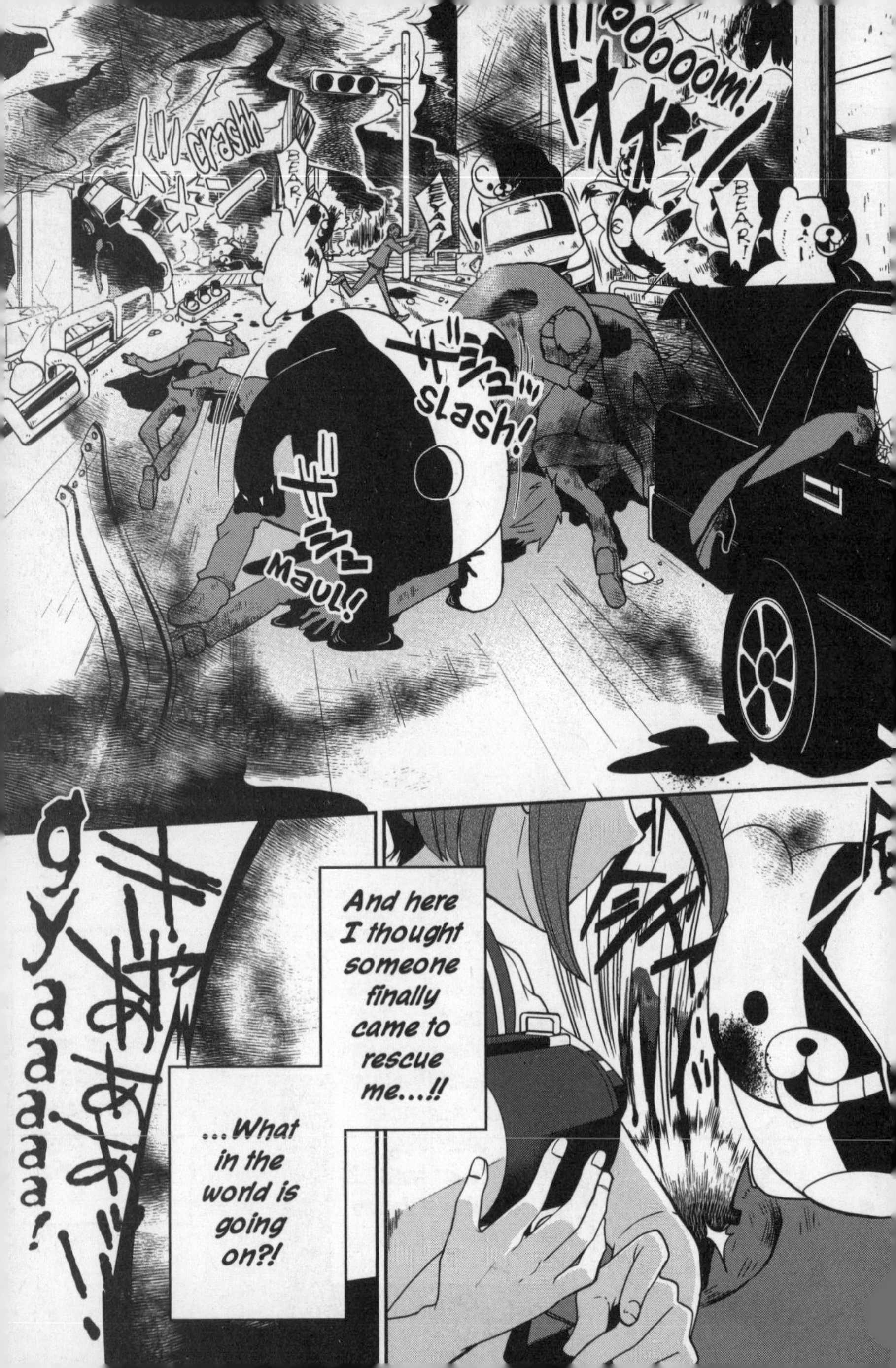
BOOOOOM!
BEAR!
BEAR!
EEYAA!
crashh
BEAR!
SLASH!
MAUL!
And here I thought someone finally came to rescue me...!!
...What in the world is going on?!
gyaaaaa!

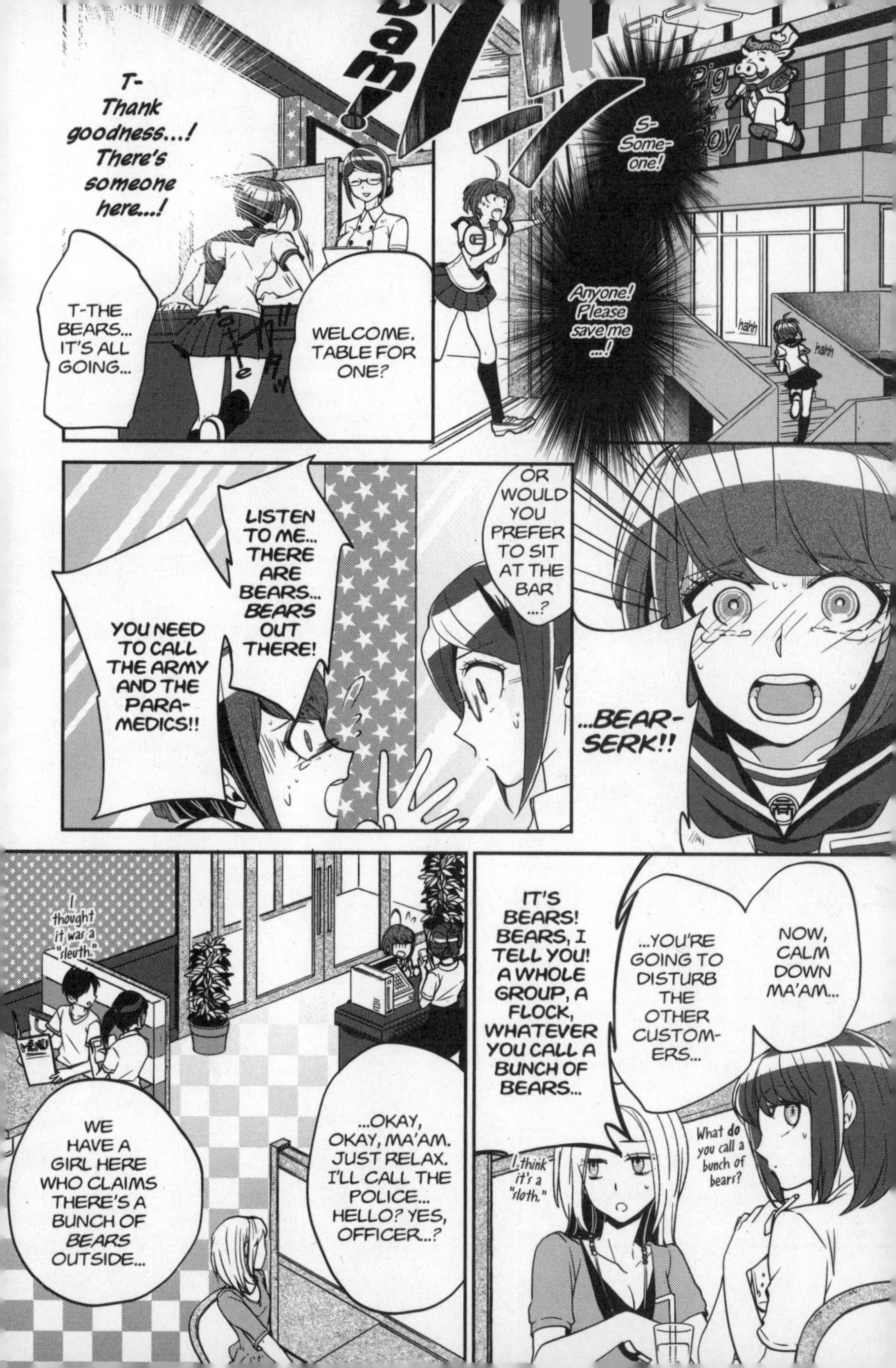
hahh
hahh
Anyone! Please save me ...!
Bam!
S-Someone!
WELCOME. TABLE FOR ONE?
T-Thank goodness...! There's someone here...!
T-THE BEARS... IT'S ALL GOING...
OR WOULD YOU PREFER TO SIT AT THE BAR ...?
...BEAR-SERK!!
LISTEN TO ME... THERE ARE BEARS... BEARS OUT THERE!
YOU NEED TO CALL THE ARMY AND THE PARA-MEDICS!!
NOW, CALM DOWN MA'AM...
...YOU'RE GOING TO DISTURB THE OTHER CUSTOM-ERS...
IT'S BEARS! BEARS, I TELL YOU! A WHOLE GROUP, A FLOCK, WHATEVER YOU CALL A BUNCH OF BEARS...
What do you call a bunch of bears?
I think it's a "sloth."
...OKAY, OKAY, MA'AM. JUST RELAX. I'LL CALL THE POLICE... HELLO? YES, OFFICER...?
WE HAVE A GIRL HERE WHO CLAIMS THERE'S A BUNCH OF BEARS OUTSIDE...
I thought it was a "sleuth."
MENU
Pig Boy

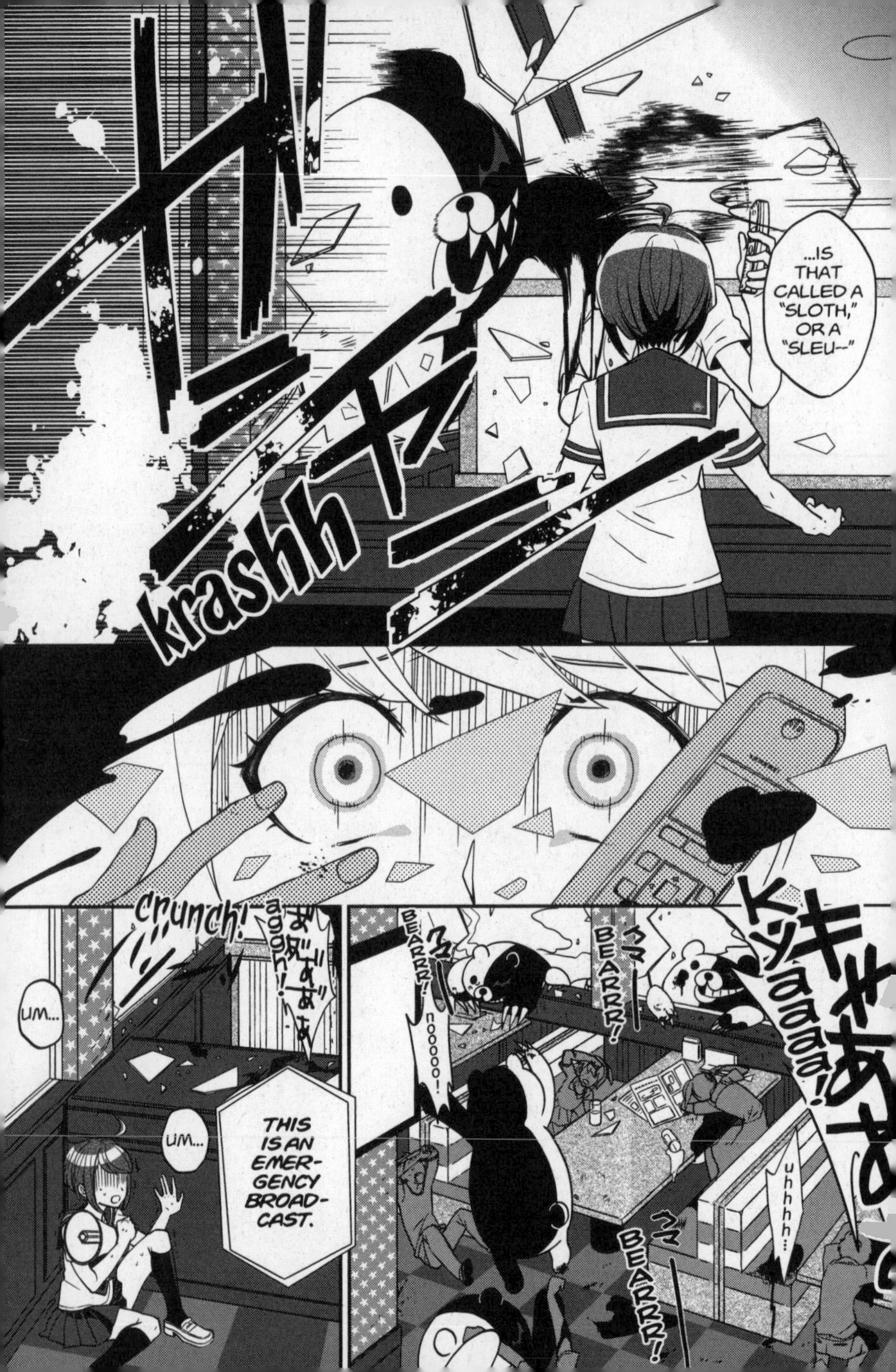
...IS THAT CALLED A "SLOTH," OR A "SLEU--"
krashh
kyaaaaa!
BEARRR!
BEARRR!
nooooo!
uhhhh...
BEARRR!
crunch!
aggh!
um...
um...
THIS IS AN EMERGENCY BROADCAST.

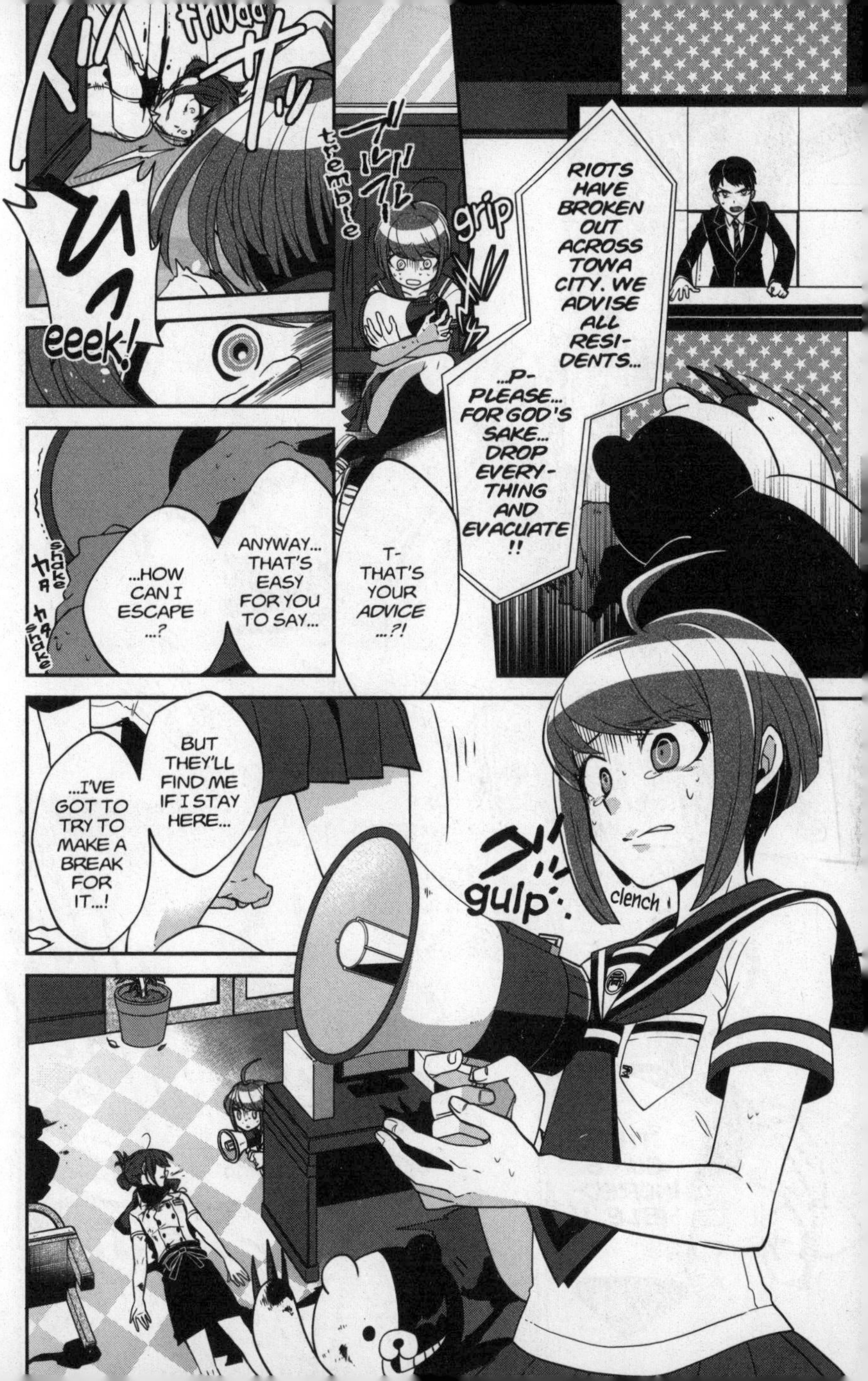
RIOTS HAVE BROKEN OUT ACROSS TOWA CITY. WE ADVISE ALL RESIDENTS...
...P-PLEASE... FOR GOD'S SAKE... DROP EVERYTHING AND EVACUATE!!
tremble
grip
T-THAT'S YOUR ADVICE...?!
ANYWAY... THAT'S EASY FOR YOU TO SAY...
thud
eeek!
shake shake
...HOW CAN I ESCAPE...?
gulp
clench
BUT THEY'LL FIND ME IF I STAY HERE...
...I'VE GOT TO TRY TO MAKE A BREAK FOR IT...!

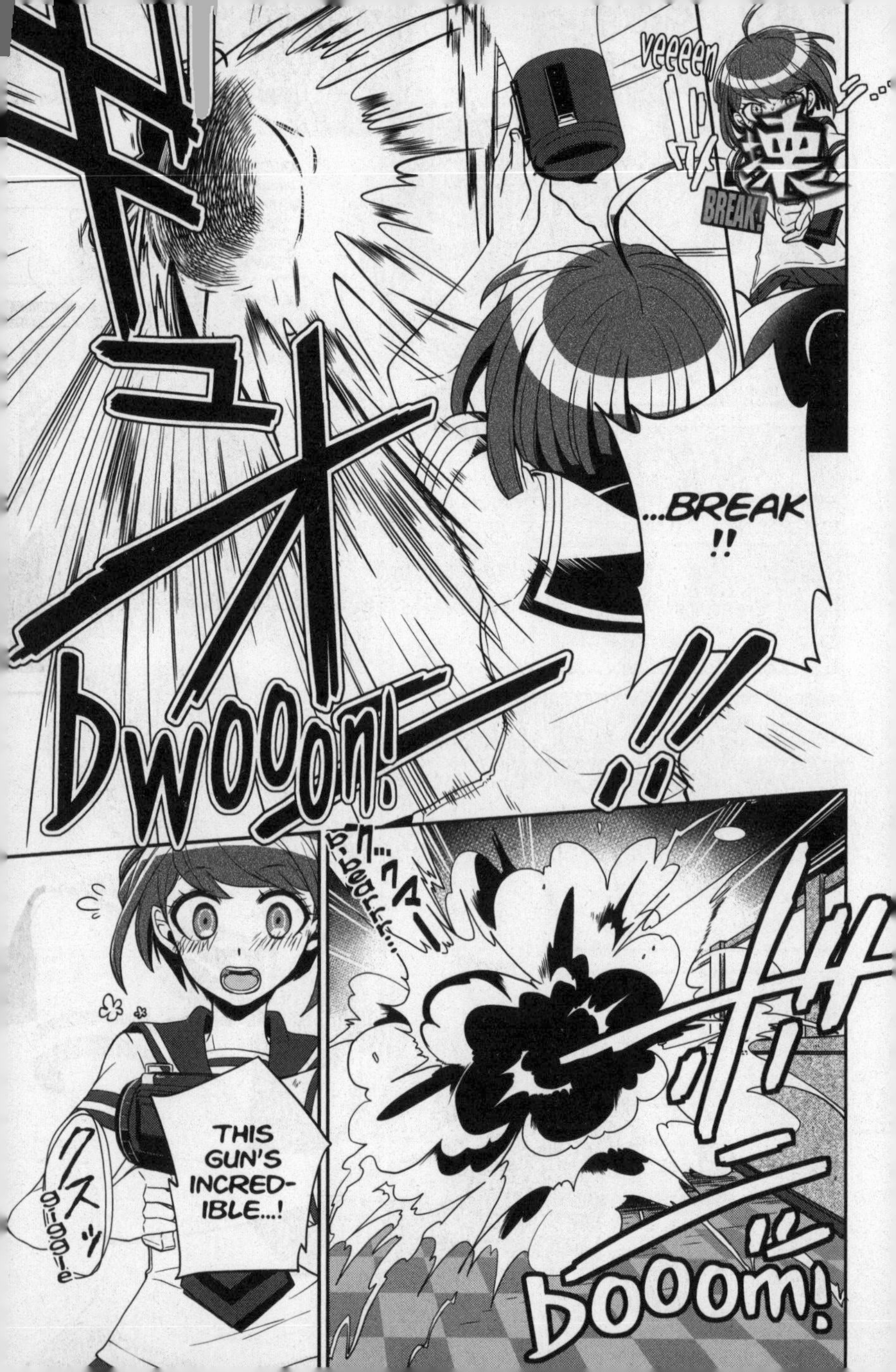
veeeen
BREAK!
...BREAK !!
bwooon!
booom!
THIS GUN'S INCREDIBLE...!
giggle

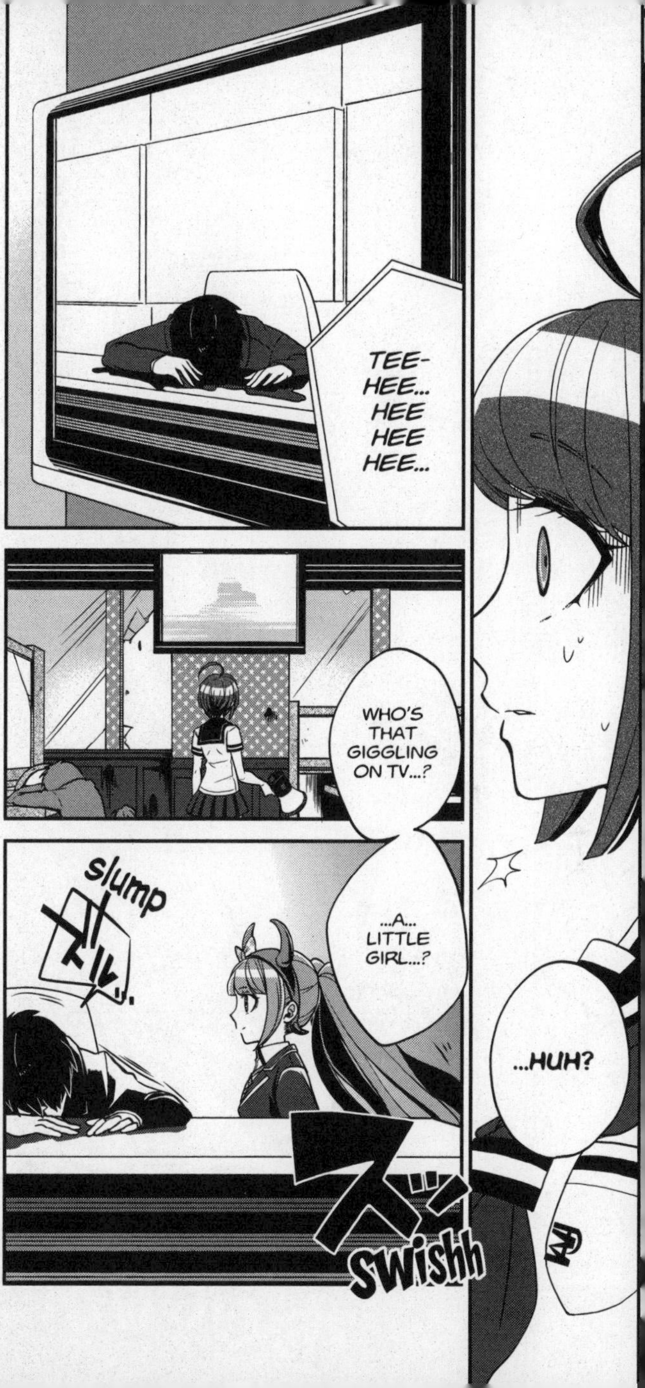
...HUH?
TEE-HEE... HEE HEE HEE...
WHO'S THAT GIGGLING ON TV...?
...A... LITTLE GIRL...?
slump
SWISHH

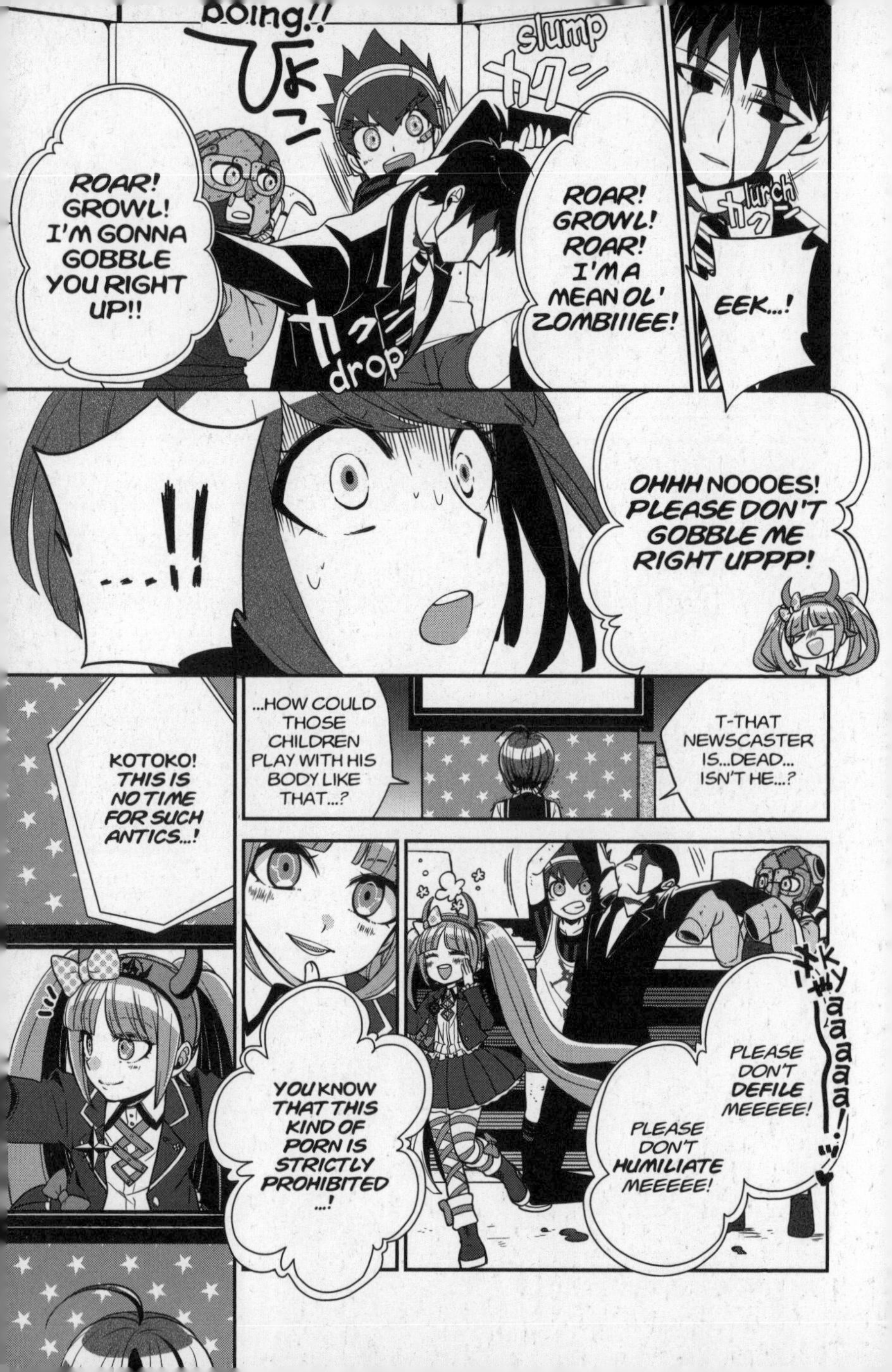
lurch
EEK...!
boing!!
slump
ROAR! GROWL! ROAR! I'M A MEAN OL' ZOMBIIIEE!
ROAR! GROWL! I'M GONNA GOBBLE YOU RIGHT UP!!
drop
OHHH NOOOES! PLEASE DON'T GOBBLE ME RIGHT UPPP!
...!!
T-THAT NEWSCASTER IS...DEAD... ISN'T HE...?
...HOW COULD THOSE CHILDREN PLAY WITH HIS BODY LIKE THAT...?
KOTOKO! THIS IS NO TIME FOR SUCH ANTICS...!
kyaaaaaaa!!
PLEASE DON'T DEFILE MEEEEE!
PLEASE DON'T HUMILIATE MEEEEE!
YOU KNOW THAT THIS KIND OF PORN IS STRICTLY PROHIBITED...!

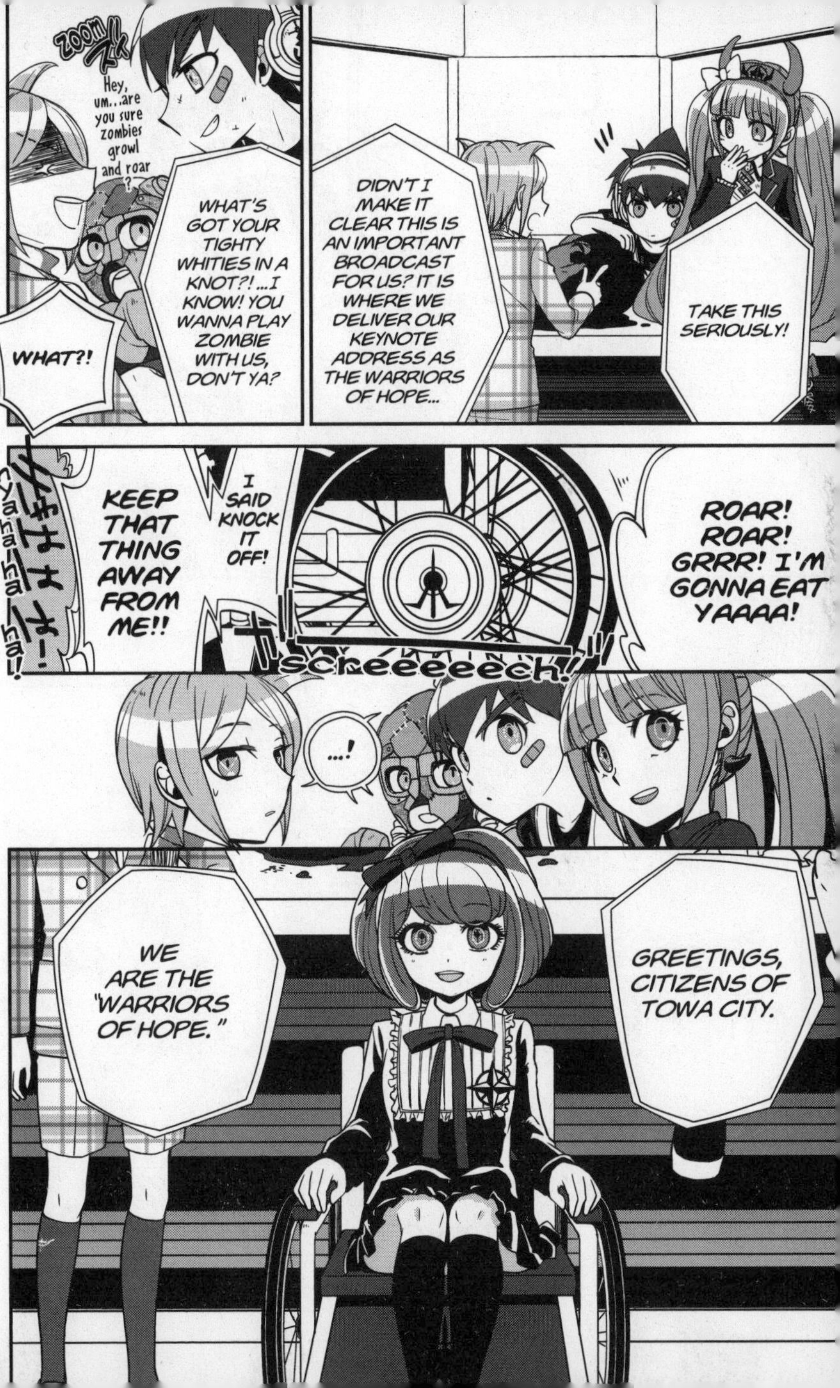
DIDN'T I MAKE IT CLEAR THIS IS AN IMPORTANT BROADCAST FOR US? IT IS WHERE WE DELIVER OUR KEYNOTE ADDRESS AS THE WARRIORS OF HOPE...
TAKE THIS SERIOUSLY!
ZOOM!!
WHAT'S GOT YOUR TIGHTY WHITIES IN A KNOT?! ...I KNOW! YOU WANNA PLAY ZOMBIE WITH US, DON'T YA?
Hey, um...are you sure zombies growl and roar?
WHAT?!
ROAR! ROAR! GRRR! I'M GONNA EAT YAAAA!
I SAID KNOCK IT OFF!
KEEP THAT THING AWAY FROM ME!!
screeeeeech!!
nyahahaha!
...!
GREETINGS, CITIZENS OF TOWA CITY.
WE ARE THE "WARRIORS OF HOPE."

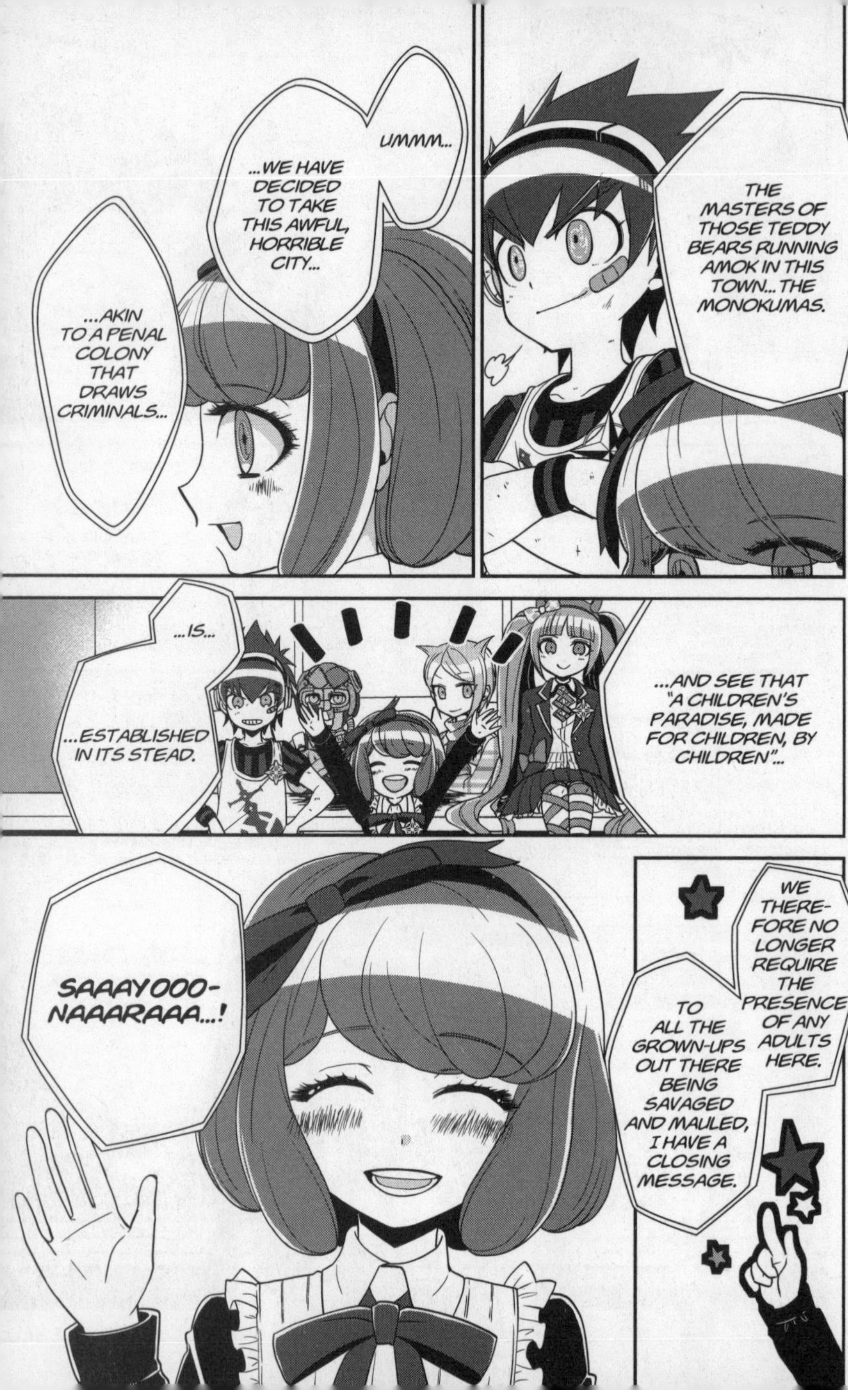
THE MASTERS OF THOSE TEDDY BEARS RUNNING AMOK IN THIS TOWN... THE MONOKUMAS.
UMMM...
...WE HAVE DECIDED TO TAKE THIS AWFUL, HORRIBLE CITY...
...AKIN TO A PENAL COLONY THAT DRAWS CRIMINALS...
...AND SEE THAT "A CHILDREN'S PARADISE, MADE FOR CHILDREN, BY CHILDREN"...
...IS...
...ESTABLISHED IN ITS STEAD.
WE THEREFORE NO LONGER REQUIRE THE PRESENCE OF ANY ADULTS HERE.
TO ALL THE GROWN-UPS OUT THERE BEING SAVAGED AND MAULED, I HAVE A CLOSING MESSAGE.
SAAAYOOO-NAAARAAA...!

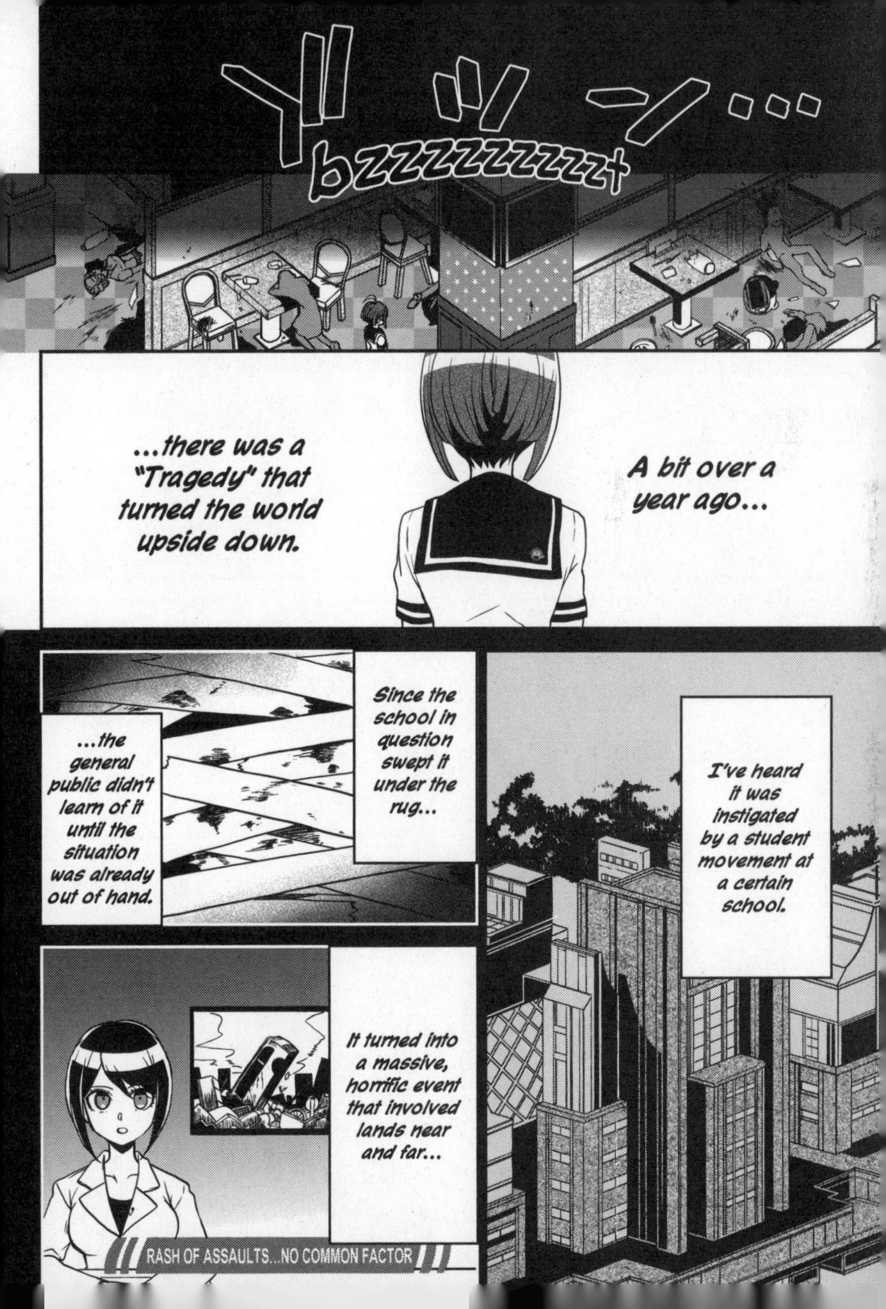
ゾッーン…
bzzzzzzzzzzt
A bit over a year ago...
...there was a "Tragedy" that turned the world upside down.
I've heard it was instigated by a student movement at a certain school.
Since the school in question swept it under the rug...
...the general public didn't learn of it until the situation was already out of hand.
It turned into a massive, horrific event that involved lands near and far...
RASH OF ASSAULTS...NO COMMON FACTOR

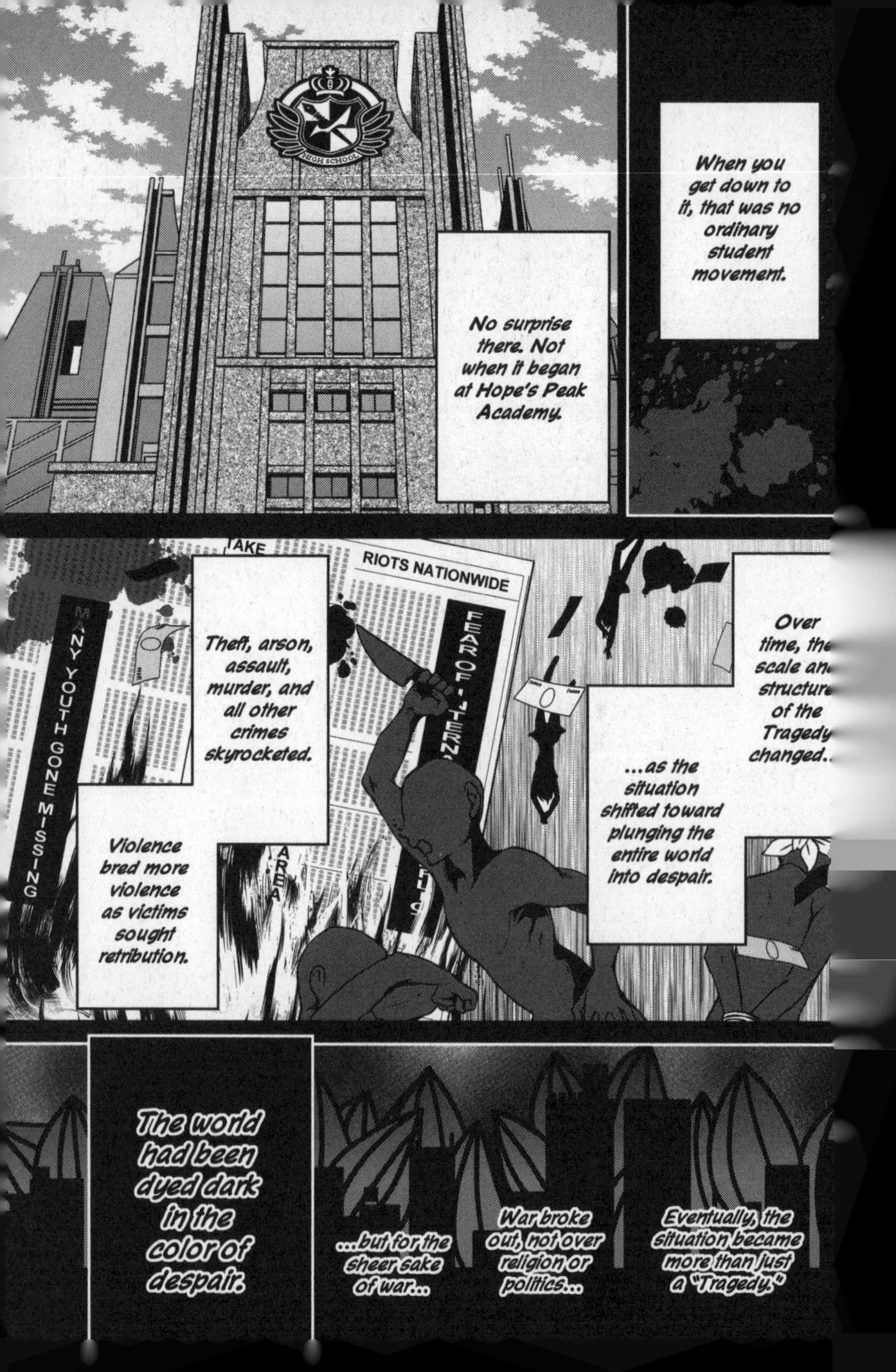

HIGH SCHOOL
When you get down to it, that was no ordinary student movement.
No surprise there. Not when it began at Hope's Peak Academy.
Over time, the scale an structure of the Traged changed..
...as the situation shifted toward plunging the entire world into despair.
RIOTS NATIONWIDE
Theft, arson, assault, murder, and all other crimes skyrocketed.
MANY YOUTH GONE MISSING
Violence bred more violence as victims sought retribution.
Eventually, the situation became more than just a "Tragedy."
War broke out, not over religion or politics...
...but for the sheer sake of war...
The world had been dyed dark in the color of despair.

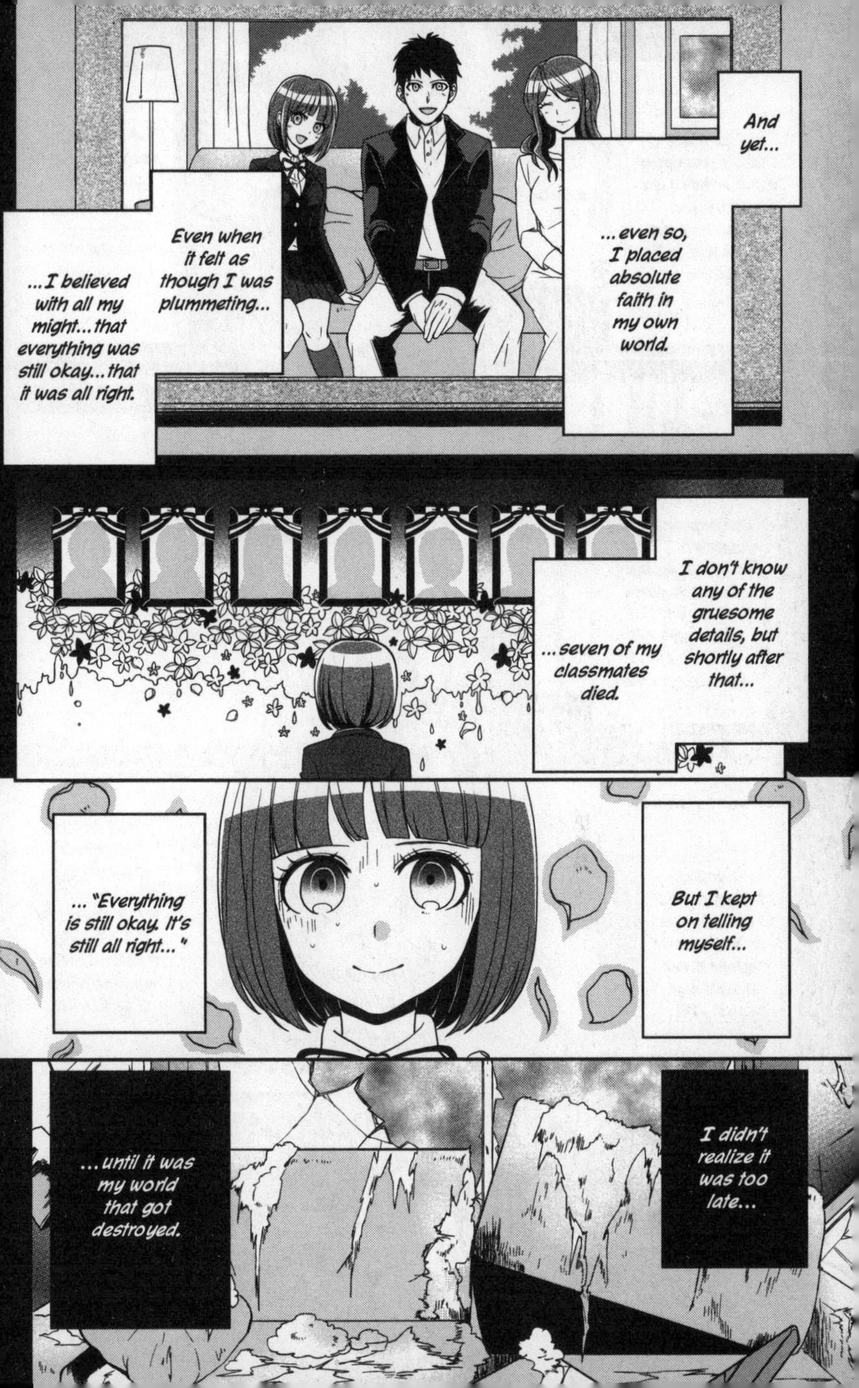
And yet...
...even so, I placed absolute faith in my own world.
Even when it felt as though I was plummeting...
...I believed with all my might...that everything was still okay...that it was all right.
I don't know any of the gruesome details, but shortly after that...
...seven of my classmates died.
But I kept on telling myself...
... "Everything is still okay. It's still all right..."
I didn't realize it was too late...
...until it was my world that got destroyed.

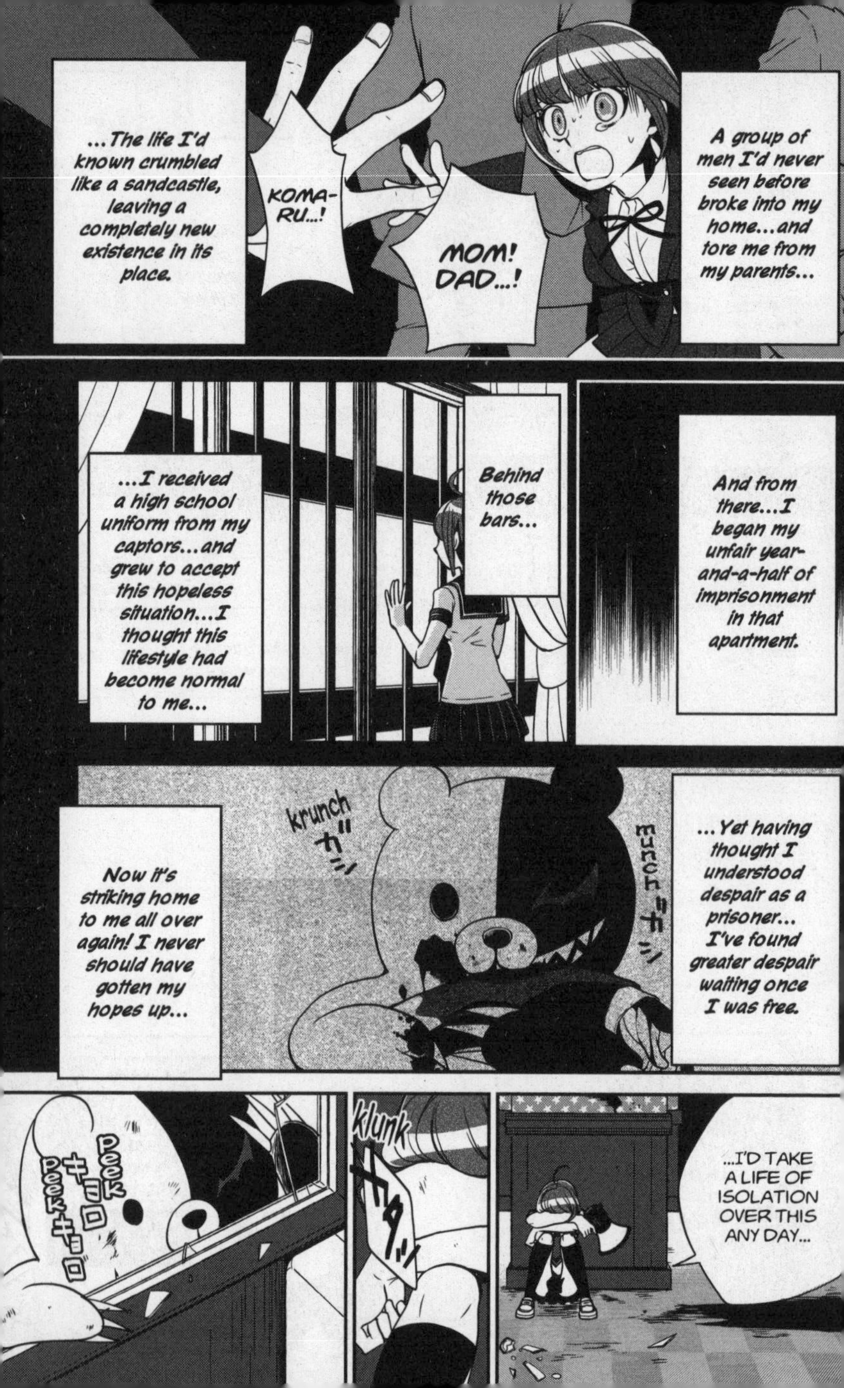
A group of men I'd never seen before broke into my home...and tore me from my parents...
MOM! DAD...!
KOMA-RU...!
...The life I'd known crumbled like a sandcastle, leaving a completely new existence in its place.
And from there...I began my unfair year-and-a-half of imprisonment in that apartment.
Behind those bars...
...I received a high school uniform from my captors...and grew to accept this hopeless situation...I thought this lifestyle had become normal to me...
...Yet having thought I understood despair as a prisoner... I've found greater despair waiting once I was free.
munch
krunch
Now it's striking home to me all over again! I never should have gotten my hopes up...
...I'D TAKE A LIFE OF ISOLATION OVER THIS ANY DAY...
klunk
peek
peek

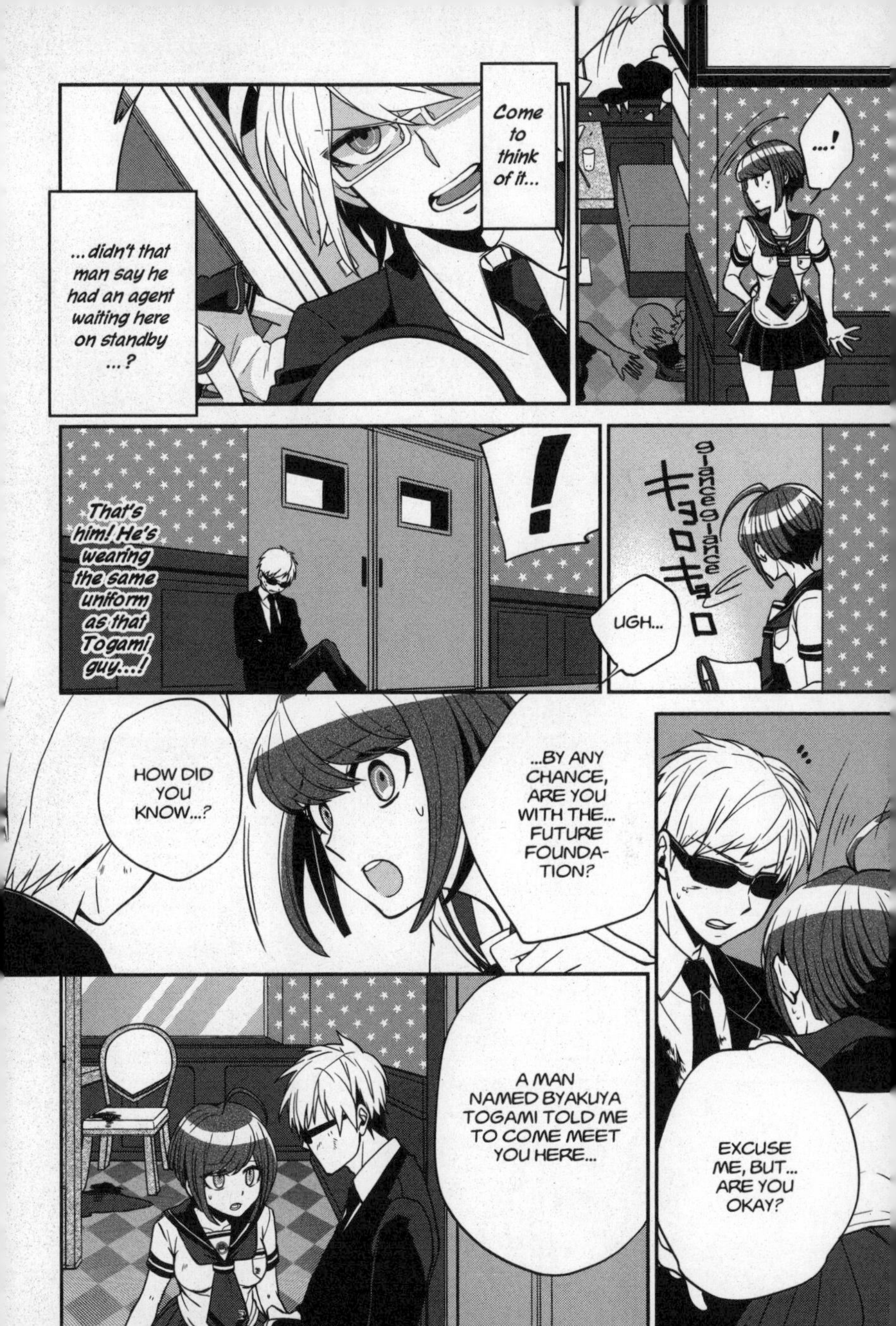
...!
Come to think of it...
...didn't that man say he had an agent waiting here on standby ...?
glance glance
UGH...
!
That's him! He's wearing the same uniform as that Togami guy...!
...
EXCUSE ME, BUT... ARE YOU OKAY?
...BY ANY CHANCE, ARE YOU WITH THE... FUTURE FOUNDATION?
HOW DID YOU KNOW...?
A MAN NAMED BYAKUYA TOGAMI TOLD ME TO COME MEET YOU HERE...

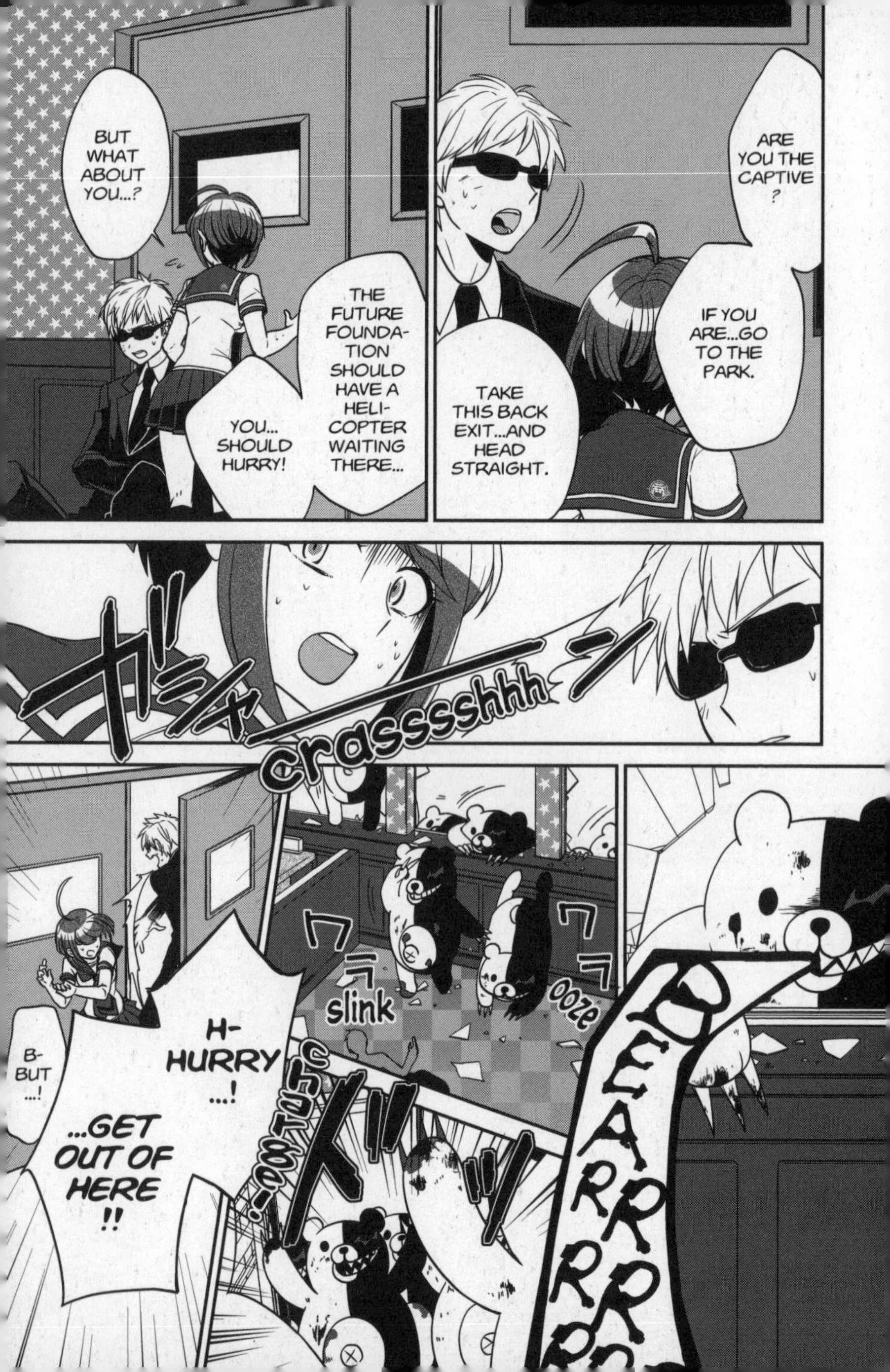
ARE YOU THE CAPTIVE?
IF YOU ARE...GO TO THE PARK.
TAKE THIS BACK EXIT...AND HEAD STRAIGHT.
THE FUTURE FOUNDATION SHOULD HAVE A HELICOPTER WAITING THERE...
YOU... SHOULD HURRY!
BUT WHAT ABOUT YOU...?
crasssshhh
BEARRRR
slink
ooze
H-HURRY...!
...GET OUT OF HERE!!
B-BUT...!

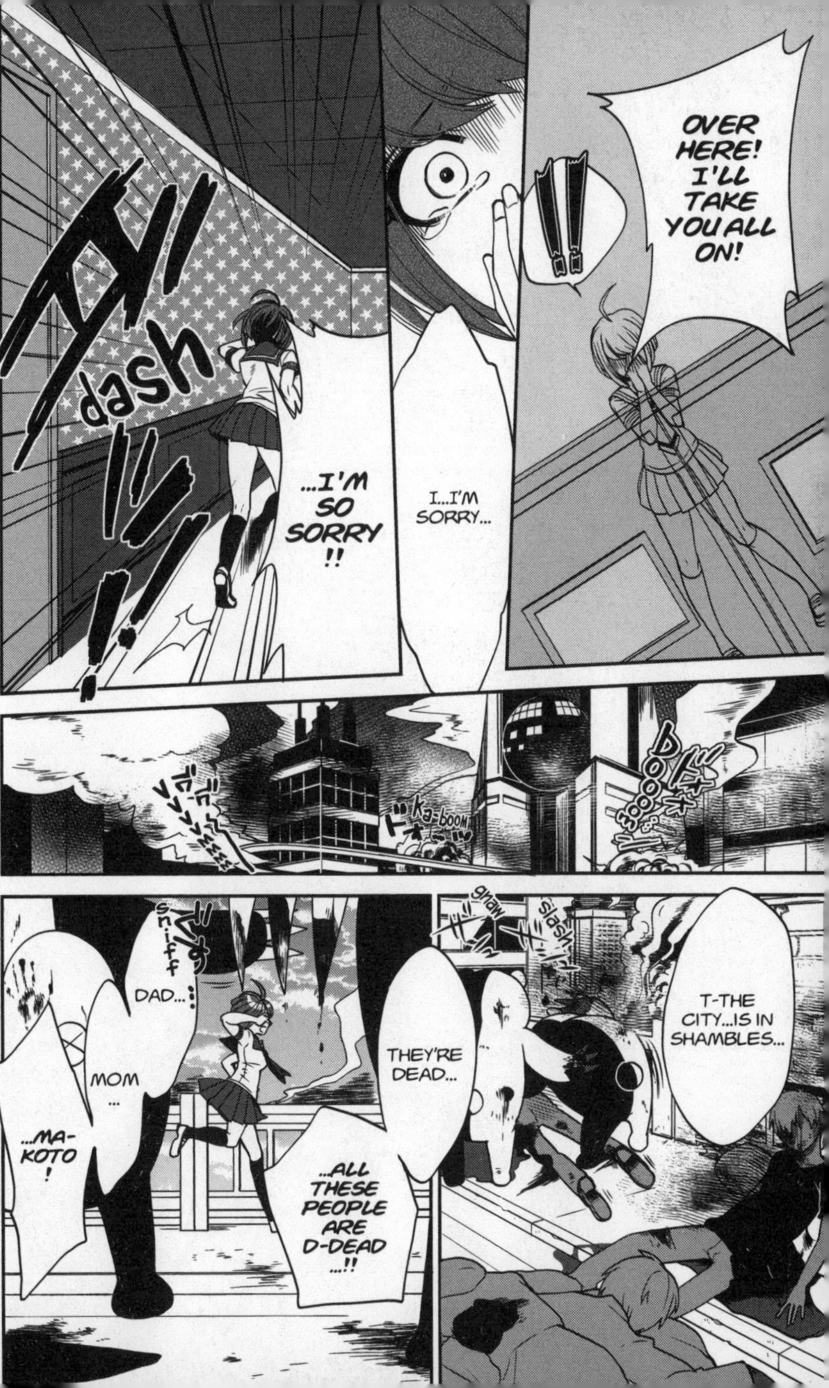
OVER HERE! I'LL TAKE YOU ALL ON!
!!
I...I'M SORRY...
...I'M SO SORRY!!
dash
Dooom
ka-boom
T-THE CITY...IS IN SHAMBLES...
slash
gnaw
THEY'RE DEAD...
...ALL THESE PEOPLE ARE D-DEAD...!!
sniff
DAD...
MOM...
...MA-KOTO!

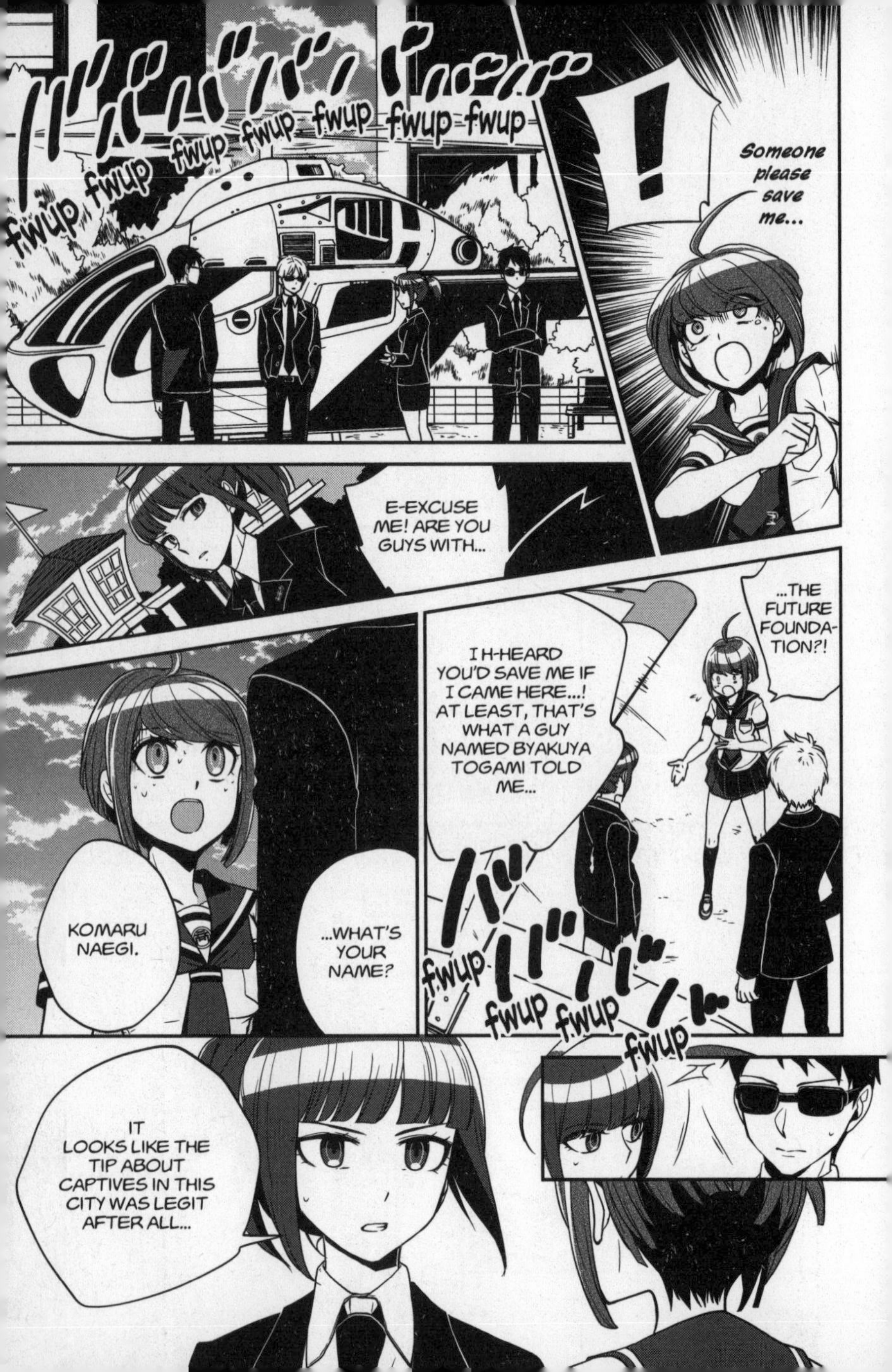
!
Someone please save me...
fwup fwup fwup fwup fwup fwup fwup
E-EXCUSE ME! ARE YOU GUYS WITH...
...THE FUTURE FOUNDA-TION?!
I H-HEARD YOU'D SAVE ME IF I CAME HERE...! AT LEAST, THAT'S WHAT A GUY NAMED BYAKUYA TOGAMI TOLD ME...
fwup fwup fwup fwup
...WHAT'S YOUR NAME?
KOMARU NAEGI.
IT LOOKS LIKE THE TIP ABOUT CAPTIVES IN THIS CITY WAS LEGIT AFTER ALL...

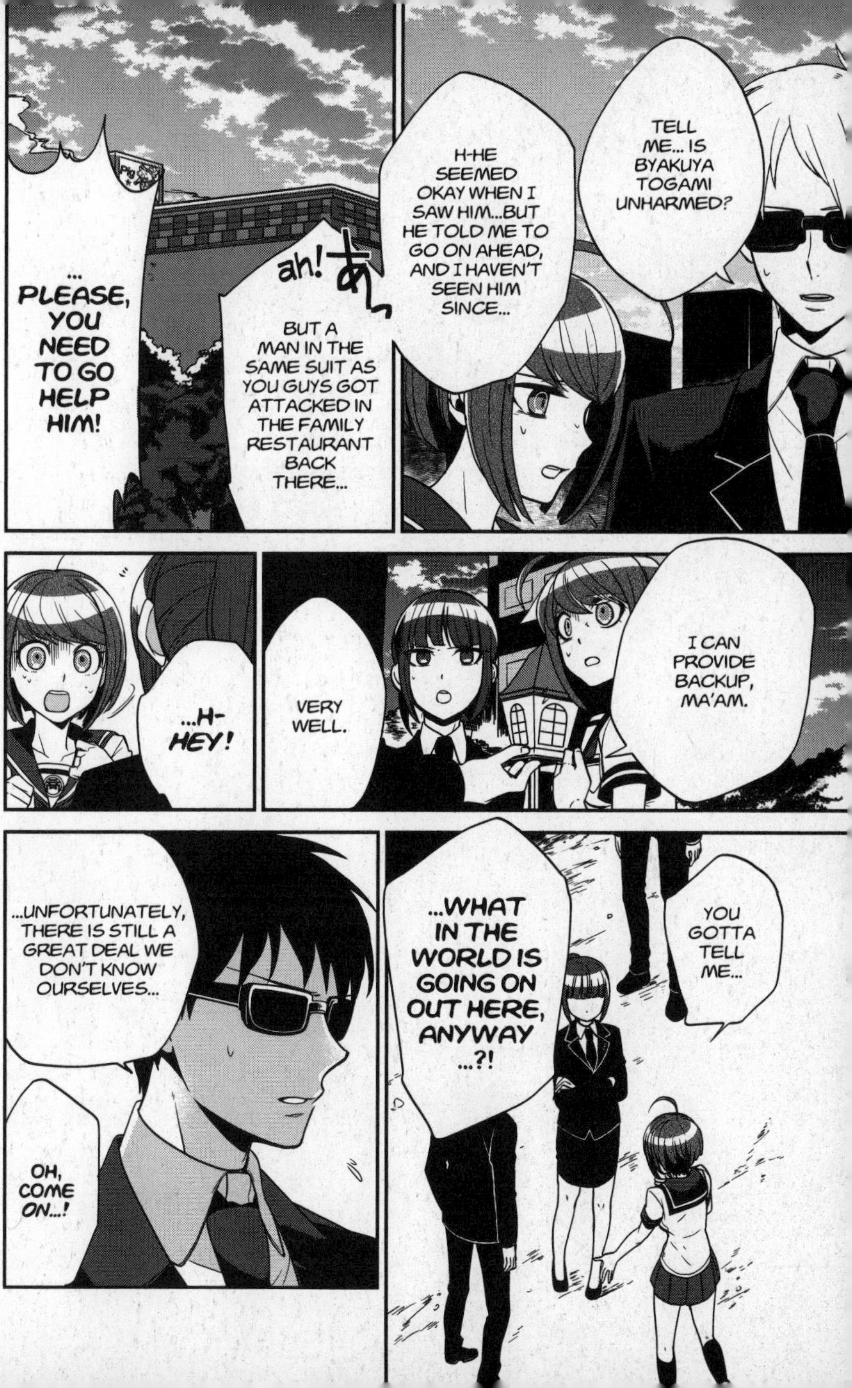
TELL ME... IS BYAKUYA TOGAMI UNHARMED?
H-HE SEEMED OKAY WHEN I SAW HIM...BUT HE TOLD ME TO GO ON AHEAD, AND I HAVEN'T SEEN HIM SINCE...
ah! あ
BUT A MAN IN THE SAME SUIT AS YOU GUYS GOT ATTACKED IN THE FAMILY RESTAURANT BACK THERE...
... PLEASE, YOU NEED TO GO HELP HIM!
I CAN PROVIDE BACKUP, MA'AM.
VERY WELL.
...H- HEY!
YOU GOTTA TELL ME...
...WHAT IN THE WORLD IS GOING ON OUT HERE, ANYWAY ...?!
...UNFORTUNATELY, THERE IS STILL A GREAT DEAL WE DON'T KNOW OURSELVES...
OH, COME ON...!

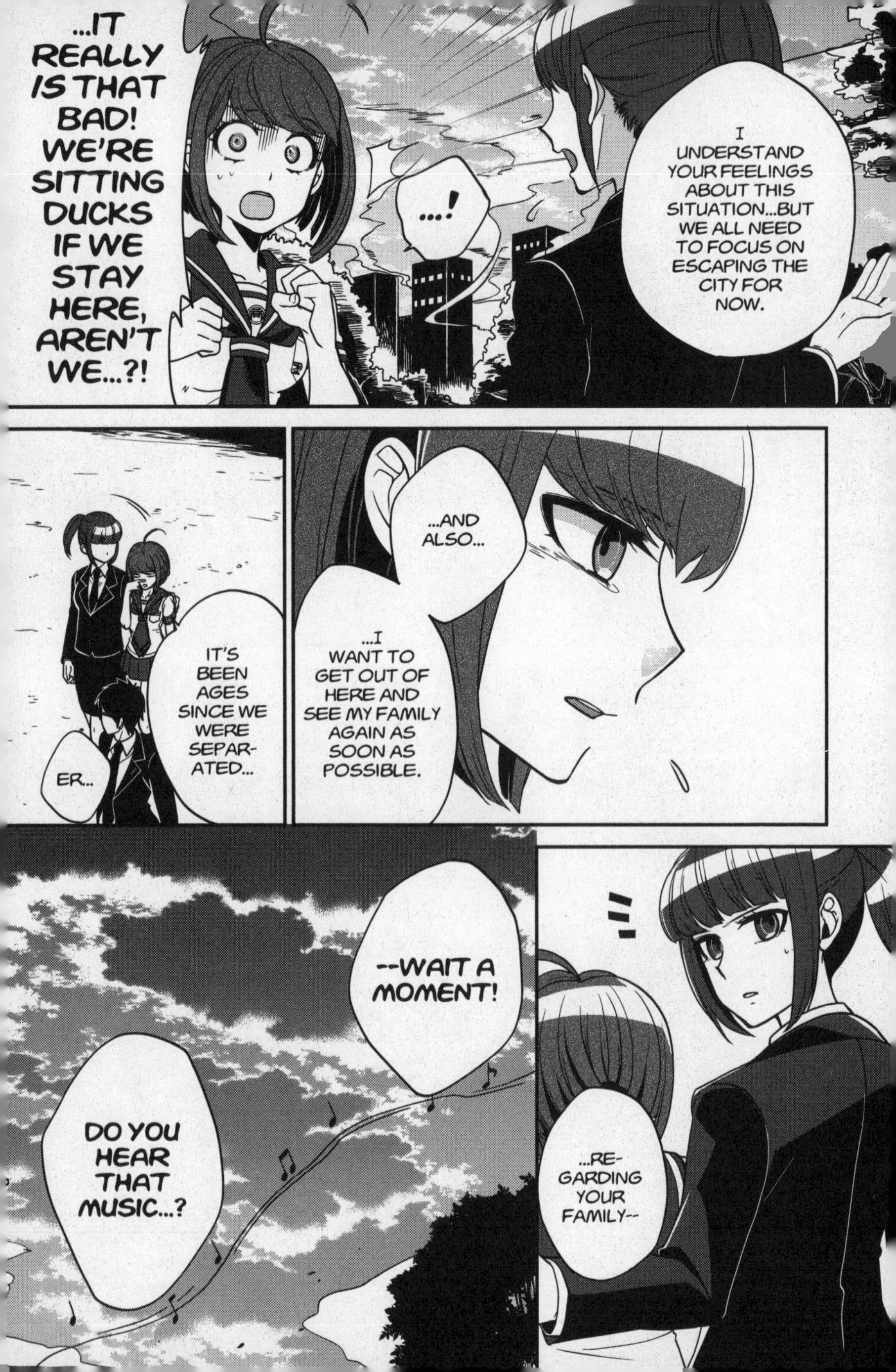
I UNDERSTAND YOUR FEELINGS ABOUT THIS SITUATION...BUT WE ALL NEED TO FOCUS ON ESCAPING THE CITY FOR NOW.
...!
...IT REALLY IS THAT BAD! WE'RE SITTING DUCKS IF WE STAY HERE, AREN'T WE...?!
...AND ALSO...
...I WANT TO GET OUT OF HERE AND SEE MY FAMILY AGAIN AS SOON AS POSSIBLE.
IT'S BEEN AGES SINCE WE WERE SEPAR-ATED...
ER...
...RE-GARDING YOUR FAMILY--
--WAIT A MOMENT!
DO YOU HEAR THAT MUSIC...?

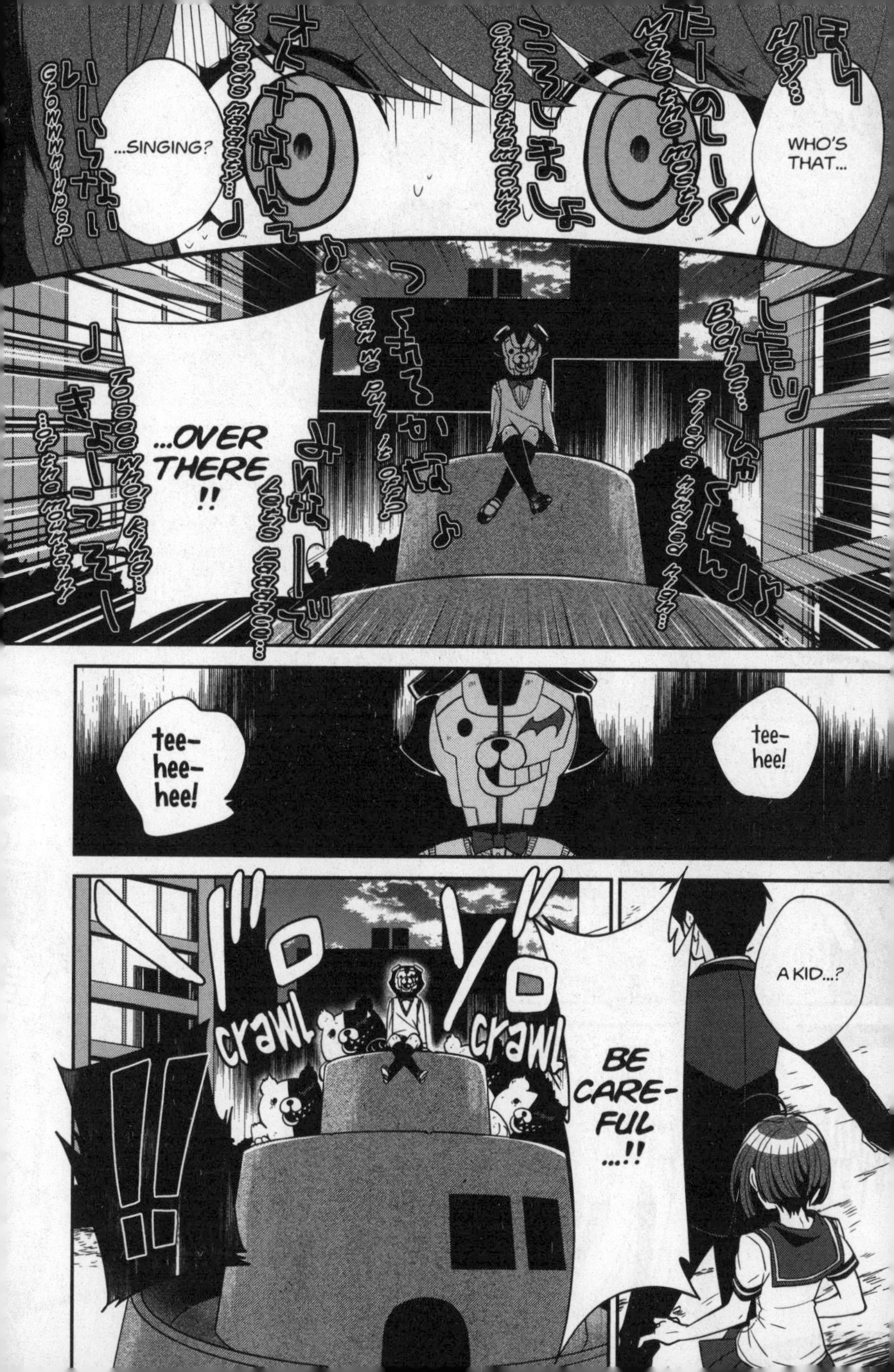
WHO'S THAT...
ほ～い
Hey...
た～のしく
Make the most!
ころしましょ
Cutting them down!
オトナなんて♪
No needs aaaany...♪
い～らない
Growwwwn-ups?
...SINGING?
したい♪
Bodies...
ひゃくにん♪♪
Piled a hundred high...
つくれるかな♪
Can we pull it off?
みんな～で
Let's race...
...OVER THERE!!
きょ～って～
To see who's king...
...of the mountain!
tee-hee!
tee-hee-hee!
A KID...?
BE CAREFUL...!!
ゾロ
crawl
ゾロ
crawl
!!

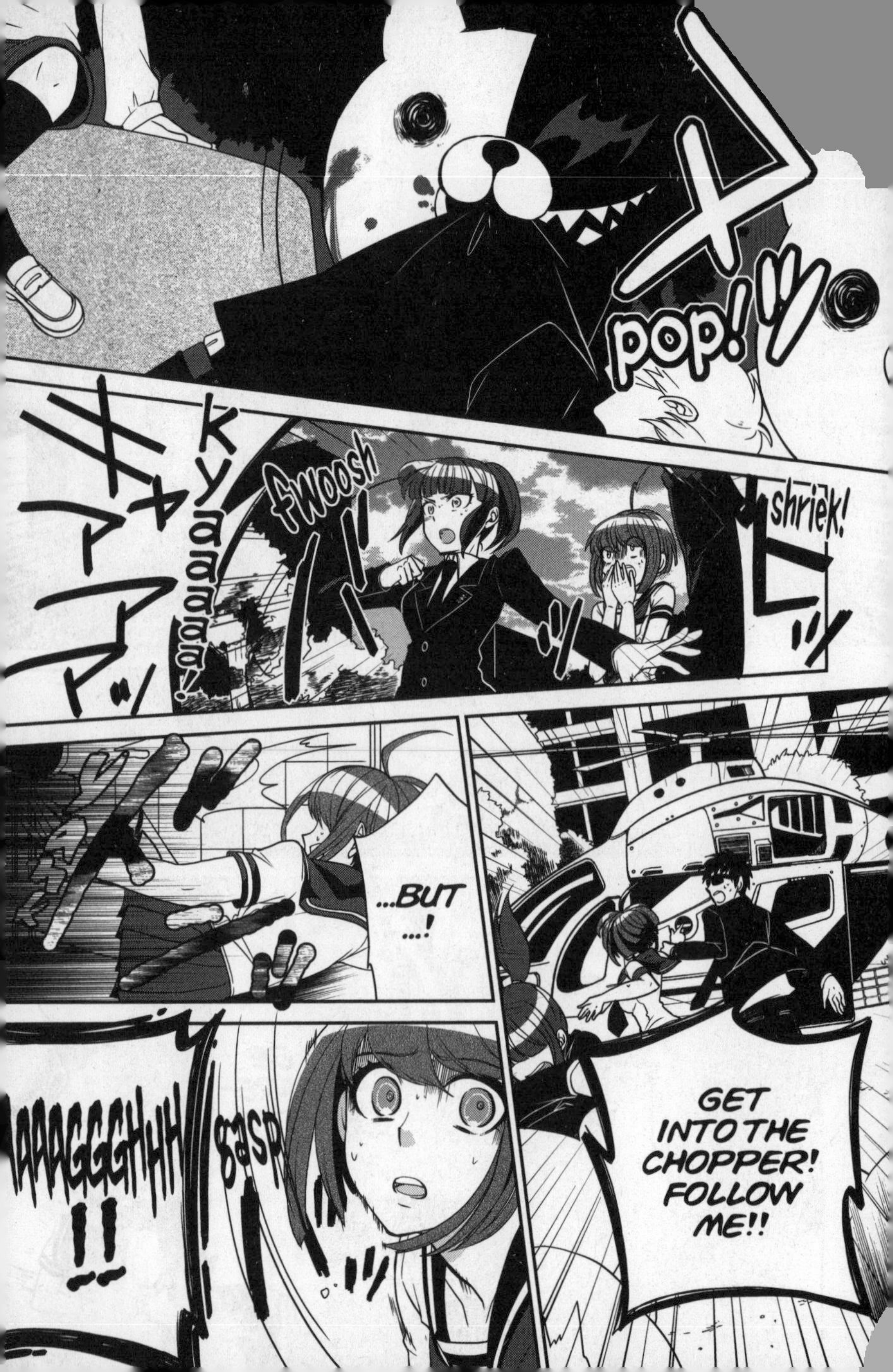
POP!
shriek!
fwoosh
Kyaaaaaaaa!!
...BUT ...!
GET INTO THE CHOPPER! FOLLOW ME!!
gasp
AAAAGGGHHH!!

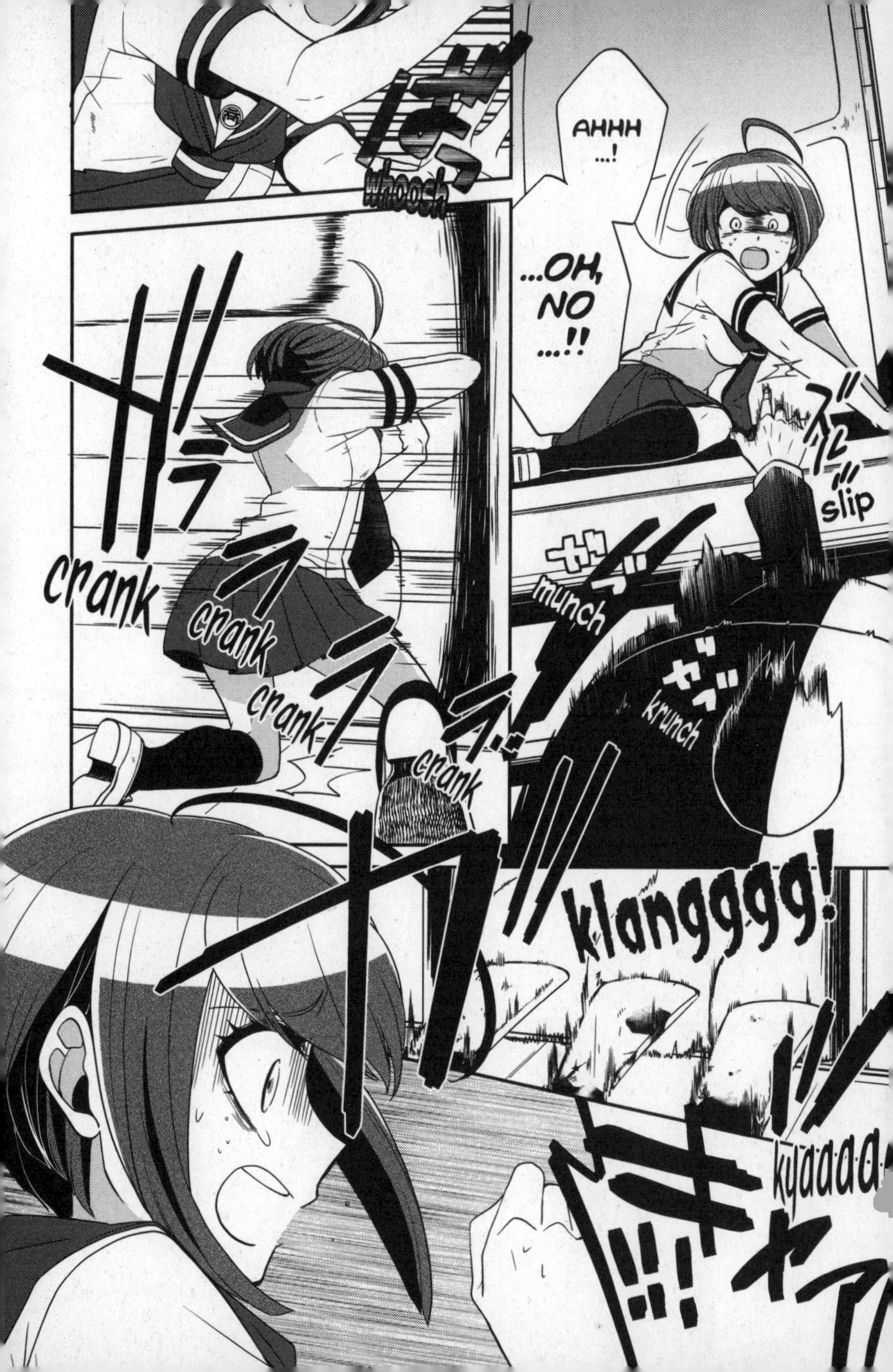
AHHH ...!
...OH, NO ...!!
slip
munch
krunch
whoosh
crank
crank
crank
crank
klangggg!
kyaaaa

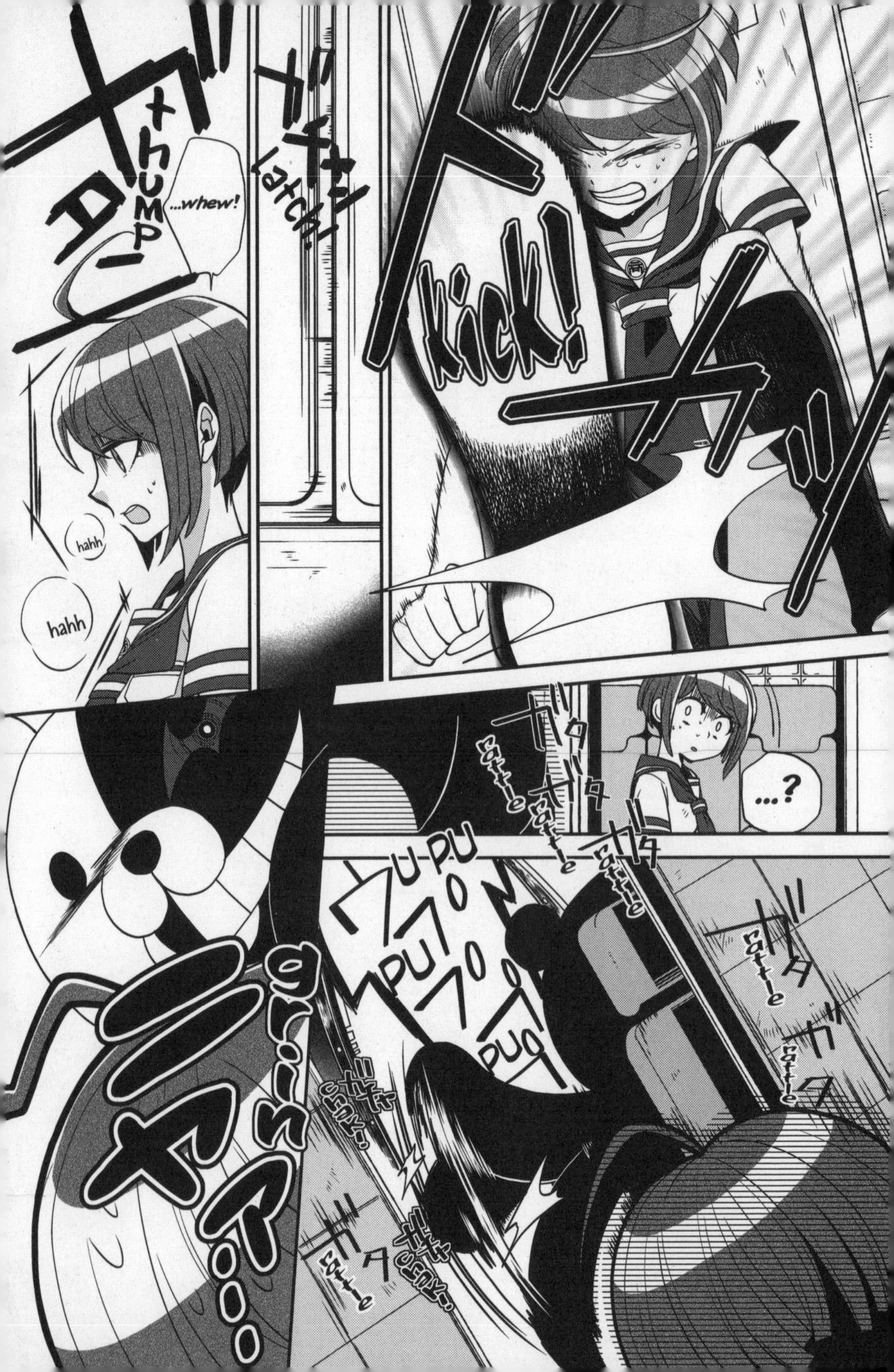
kick!
latch!
thump
...whew!
hahh
hahh
rattle
rattle
...?
rattle
rattle
rattle
UPUPUPU
creak!
creak!
rattle
grin...

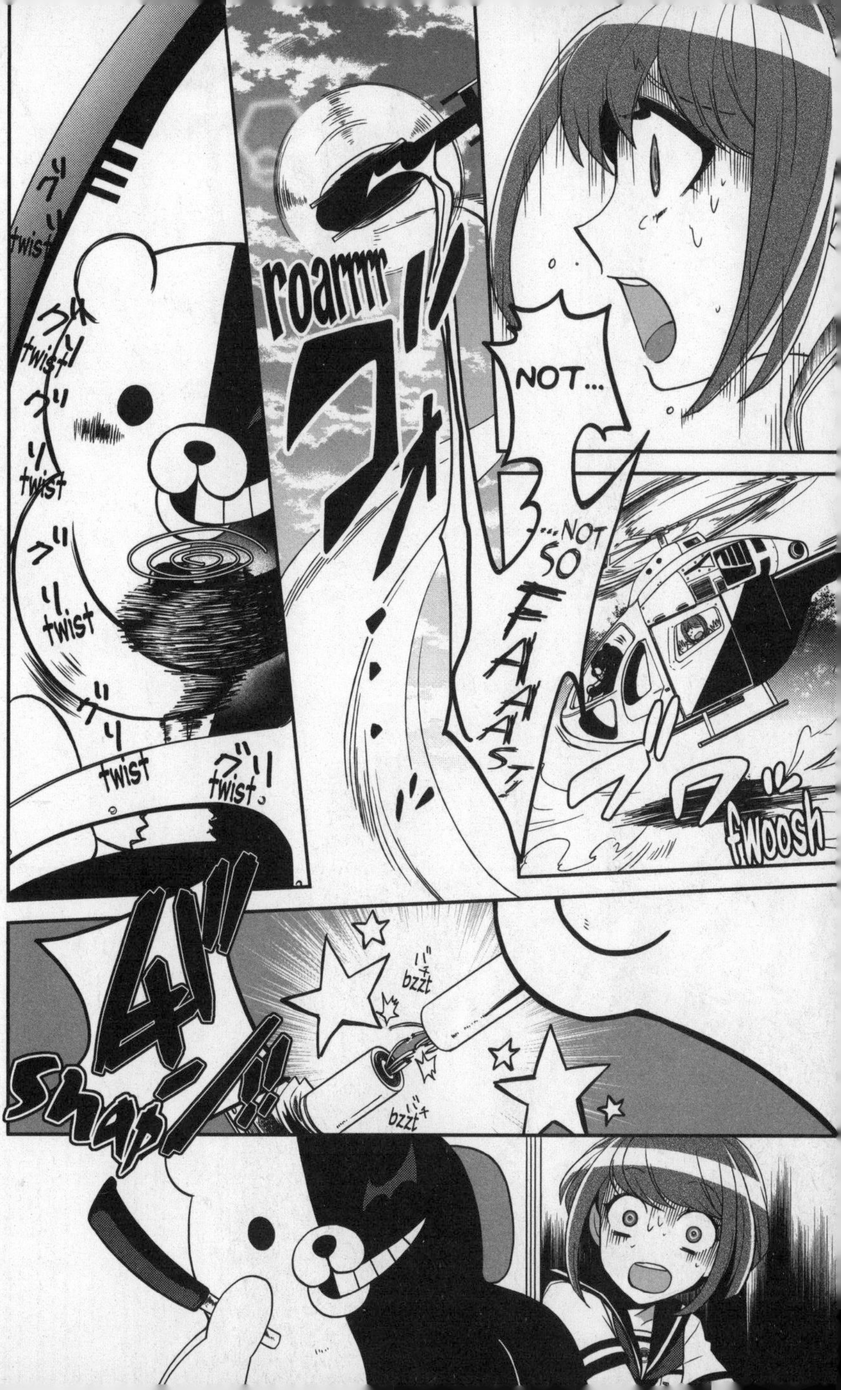

NOT...
...NOT SO FAAAAST!
fwoosh
roarrrr
グリ twist
グリ twist
グリ twist
グリ twist
グリ twist
グリ twist
グリ twist
bzzt
bzzt
Snap!!

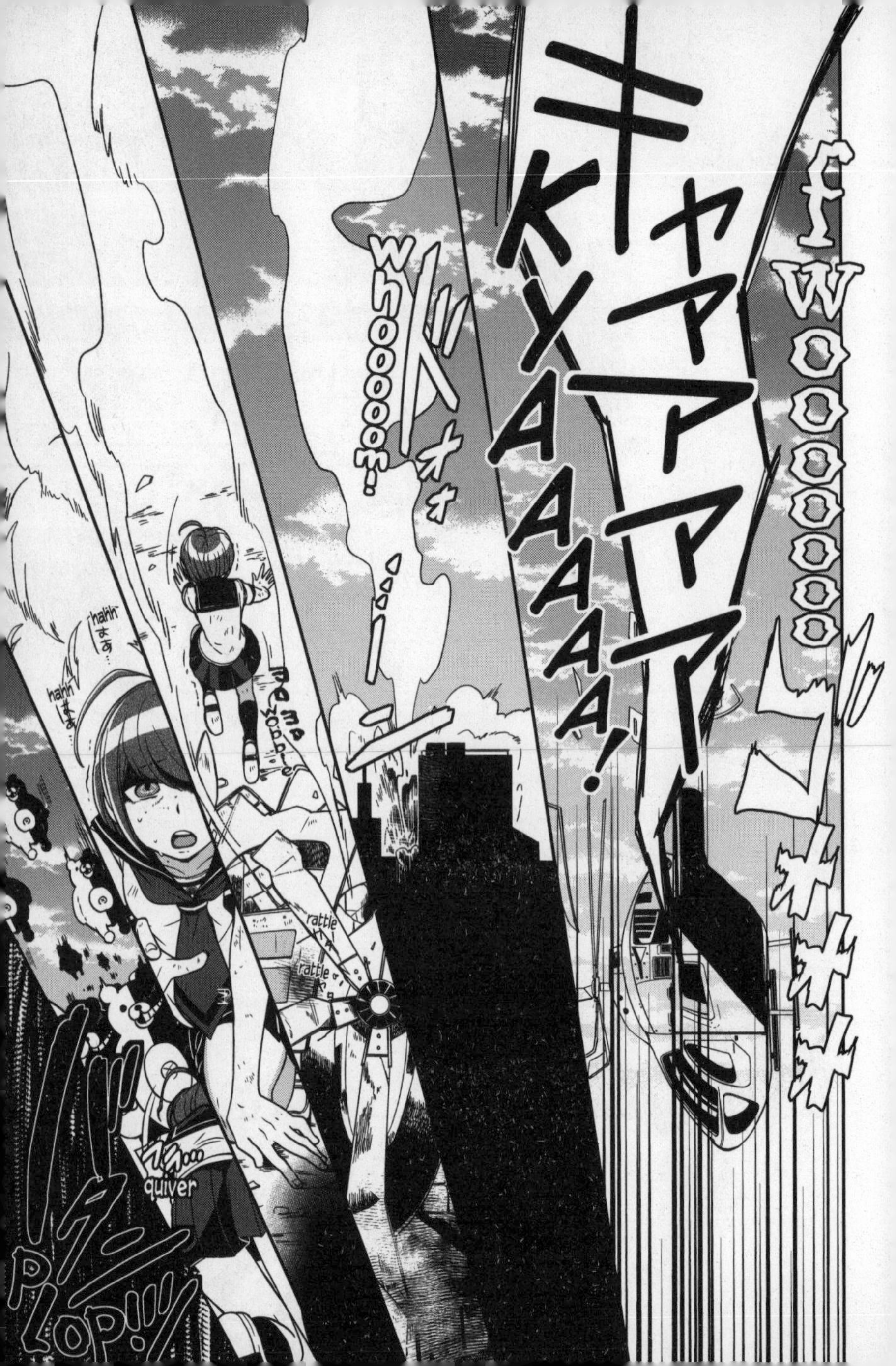
FWOOOOOOOOM
ゴオオオ
KYAAAAAA!
キャアアアアアー
whoooooom!
ドォォォー
wobble
rattle
rattle
hahh
ますす…
hahh
ますす…
quiver
PLOP!!!

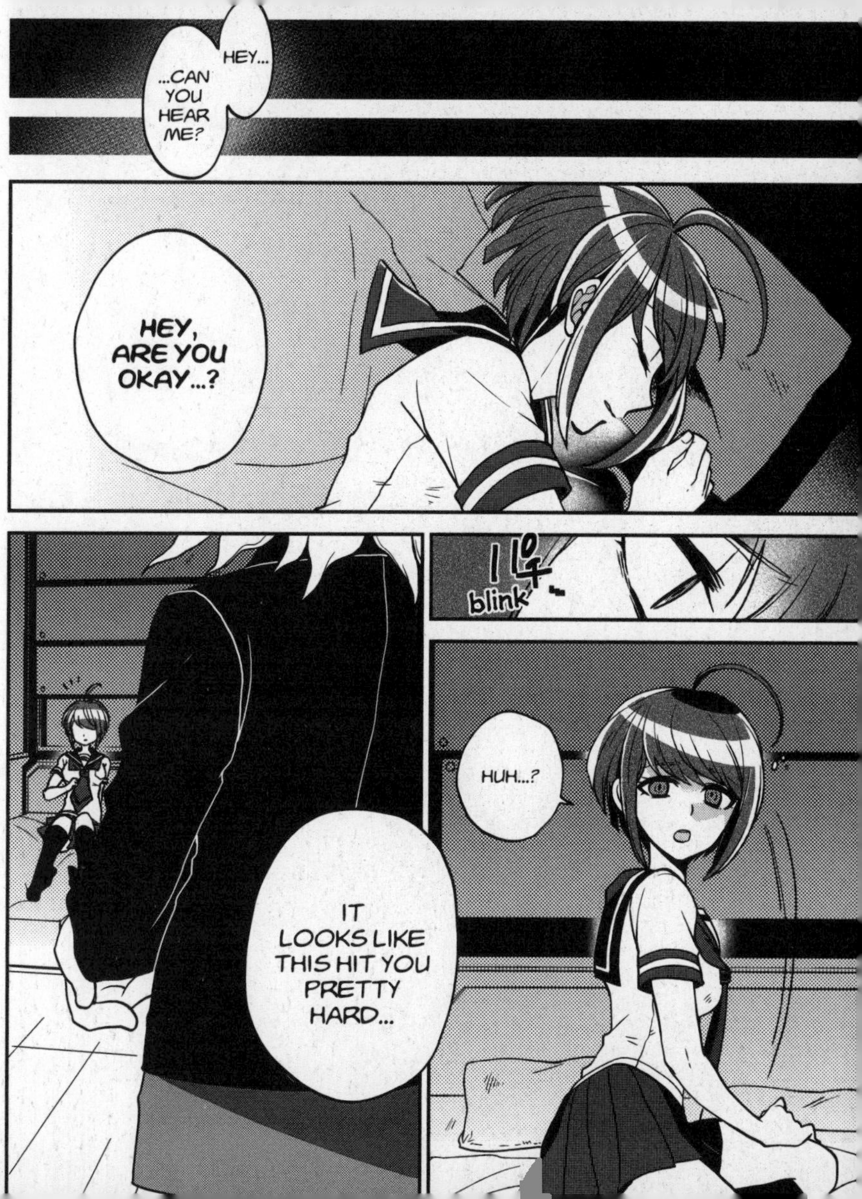
HEY...
...CAN YOU HEAR ME?
HEY, ARE YOU OKAY...?
blink
HUH...?
IT LOOKS LIKE THIS HIT YOU PRETTY HARD...

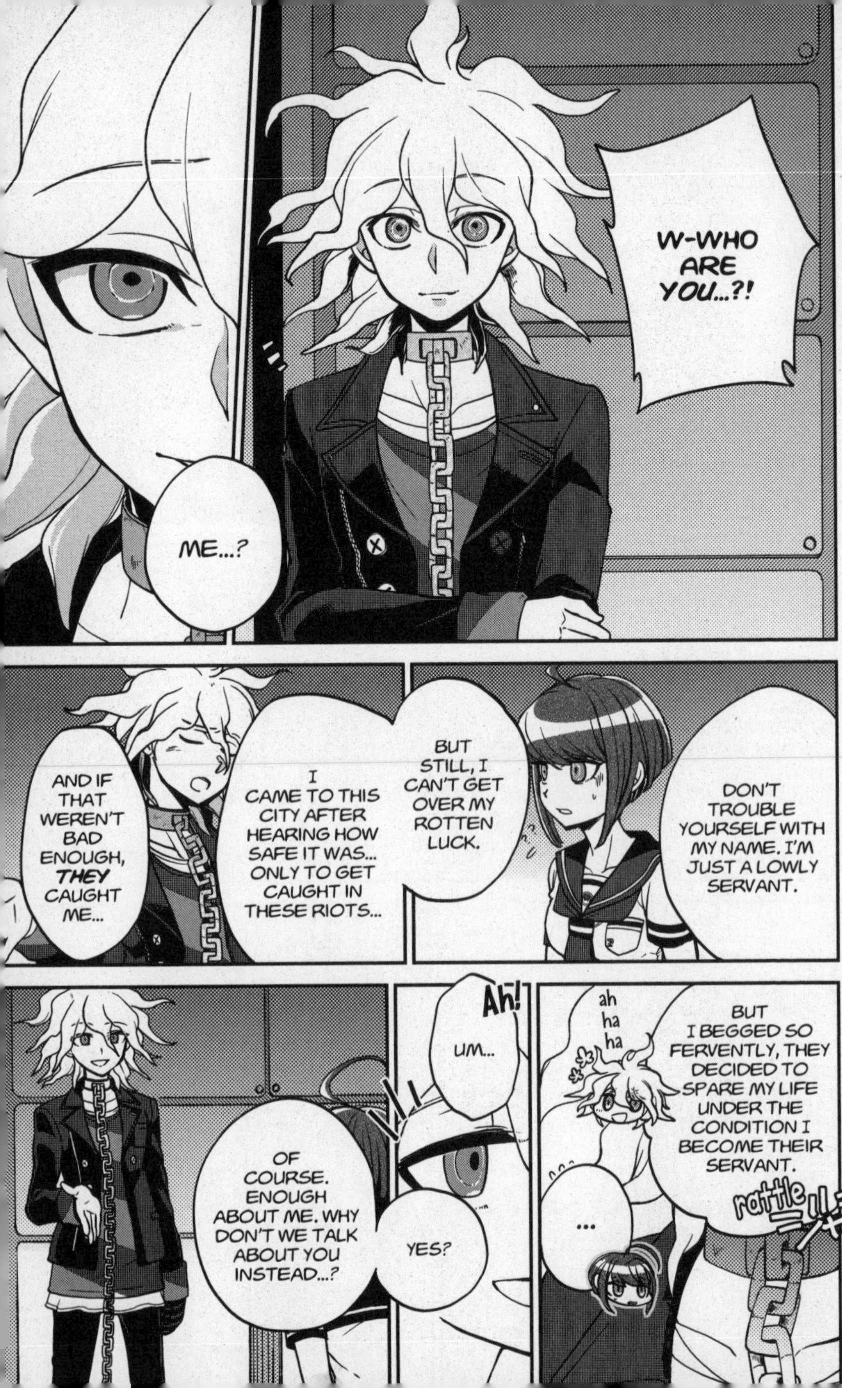
W-WHO ARE YOU...?!
ME...?
DON'T TROUBLE YOURSELF WITH MY NAME. I'M JUST A LOWLY SERVANT.
BUT STILL, I CAN'T GET OVER MY ROTTEN LUCK.
I CAME TO THIS CITY AFTER HEARING HOW SAFE IT WAS... ONLY TO GET CAUGHT IN THESE RIOTS...
AND IF THAT WEREN'T BAD ENOUGH, THEY CAUGHT ME...
ah ha ha
BUT I BEGGED SO FERVENTLY, THEY DECIDED TO SPARE MY LIFE UNDER THE CONDITION I BECOME THEIR SERVANT.
rattle
...
Ah!
UM...
YES?
OF COURSE. ENOUGH ABOUT ME. WHY DON'T WE TALK ABOUT YOU INSTEAD...?

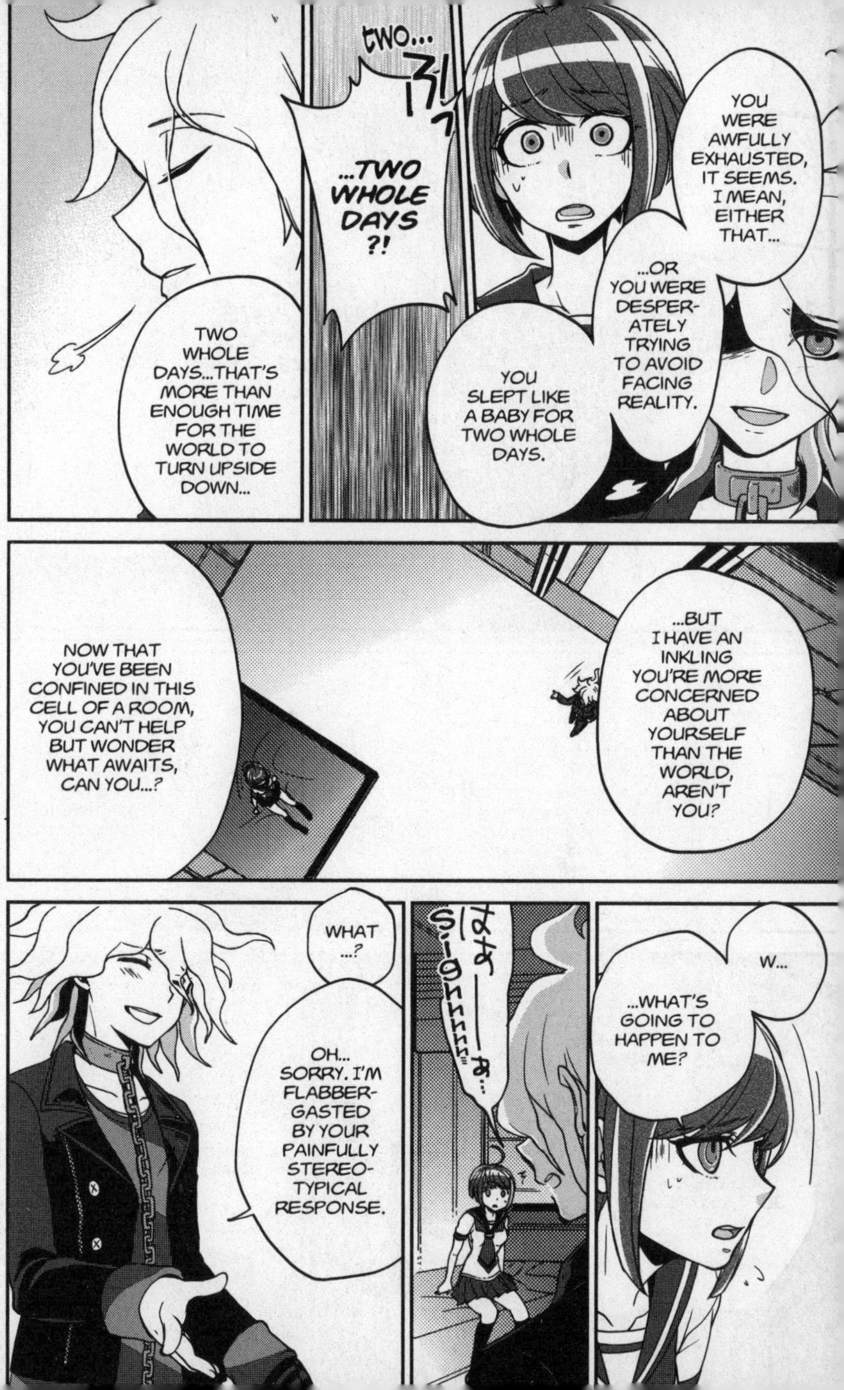

YOU WERE AWFULLY EXHAUSTED, IT SEEMS. I MEAN, EITHER THAT...
...OR YOU WERE DESPERATELY TRYING TO AVOID FACING REALITY.
YOU SLEPT LIKE A BABY FOR TWO WHOLE DAYS.
TWO...
...TWO WHOLE DAYS ?!
TWO WHOLE DAYS...THAT'S MORE THAN ENOUGH TIME FOR THE WORLD TO TURN UPSIDE DOWN...
...BUT I HAVE AN INKLING YOU'RE MORE CONCERNED ABOUT YOURSELF THAN THE WORLD, AREN'T YOU?
NOW THAT YOU'VE BEEN CONFINED IN THIS CELL OF A ROOM, YOU CAN'T HELP BUT WONDER WHAT AWAITS, CAN YOU...?
W...
...WHAT'S GOING TO HAPPEN TO ME?
はぁ——あ…
sighhhhh...
WHAT ...?
OH... SORRY. I'M FLABBERGASTED BY YOUR PAINFULLY STEREOTYPICAL RESPONSE.

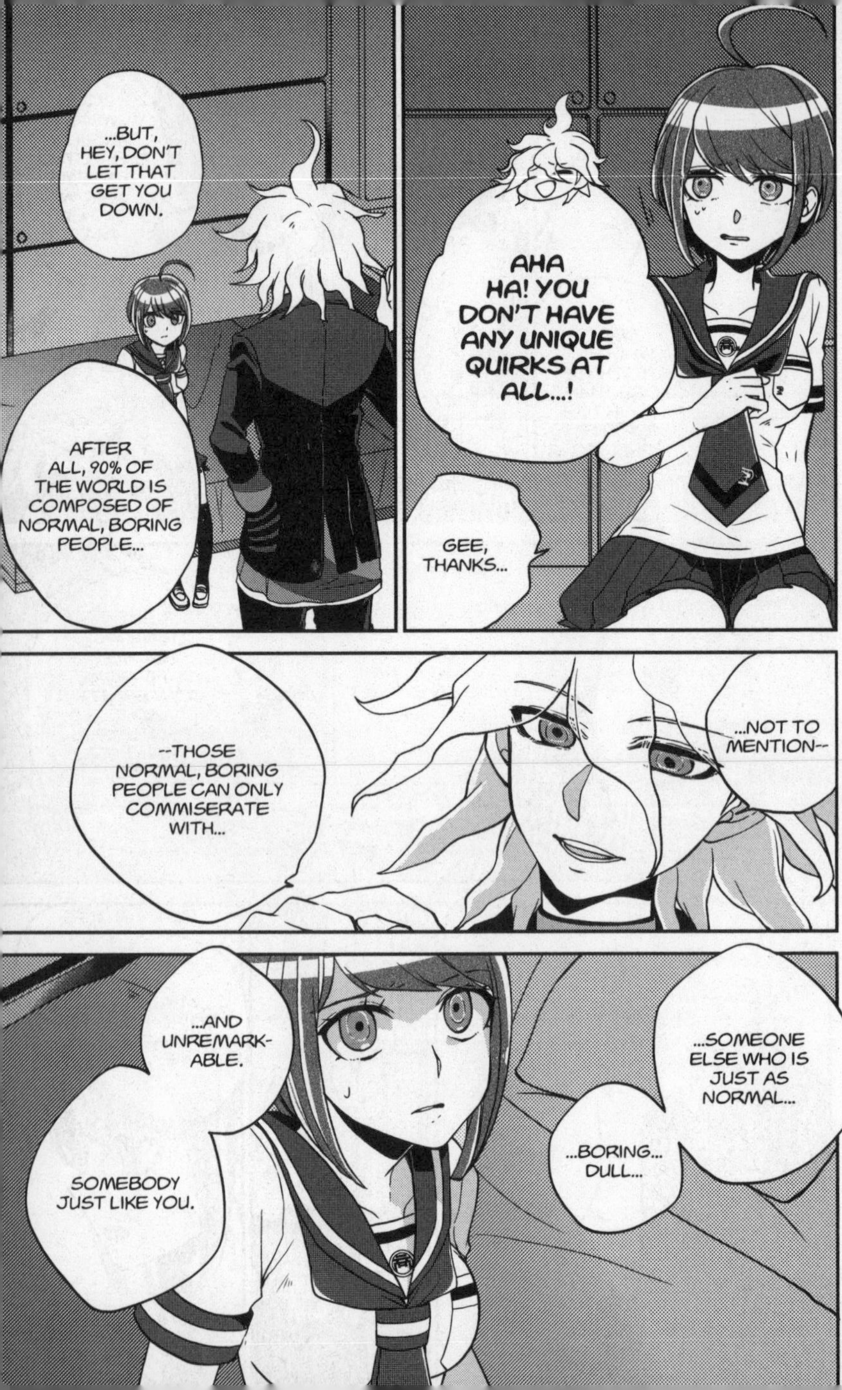
AHA HA! YOU DON'T HAVE ANY UNIQUE QUIRKS AT ALL...!
GEE, THANKS...
...BUT, HEY, DON'T LET THAT GET YOU DOWN.
AFTER ALL, 90% OF THE WORLD IS COMPOSED OF NORMAL, BORING PEOPLE...
...NOT TO MENTION--
--THOSE NORMAL, BORING PEOPLE CAN ONLY COMMISERATE WITH...
...SOMEONE ELSE WHO IS JUST AS NORMAL...
...BORING... DULL...
...AND UNREMARK-ABLE.
SOMEBODY JUST LIKE YOU.

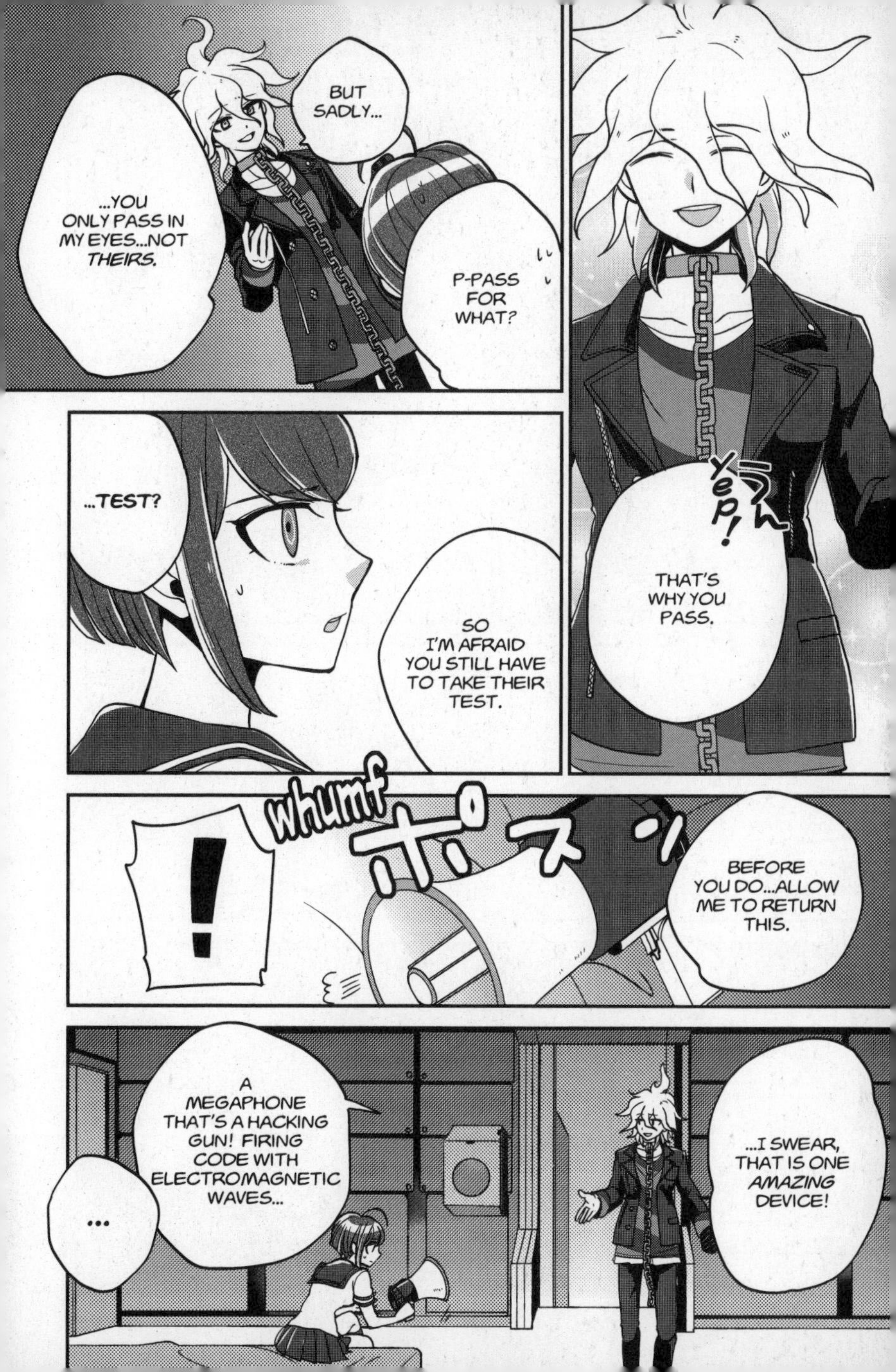
うん
Yep!
THAT'S WHY YOU PASS.
P-PASS FOR WHAT?
BUT SADLY...
...YOU ONLY PASS IN MY EYES...NOT *THEIRS.*
SO I'M AFRAID YOU STILL HAVE TO TAKE THEIR TEST.
...TEST?
BEFORE YOU DO...ALLOW ME TO RETURN THIS.
ポスッ
whumf
!
...I SWEAR, THAT IS ONE *AMAZING* DEVICE!
A MEGAPHONE THAT'S A HACKING GUN! FIRING CODE WITH ELECTROMAGNETIC WAVES...
...

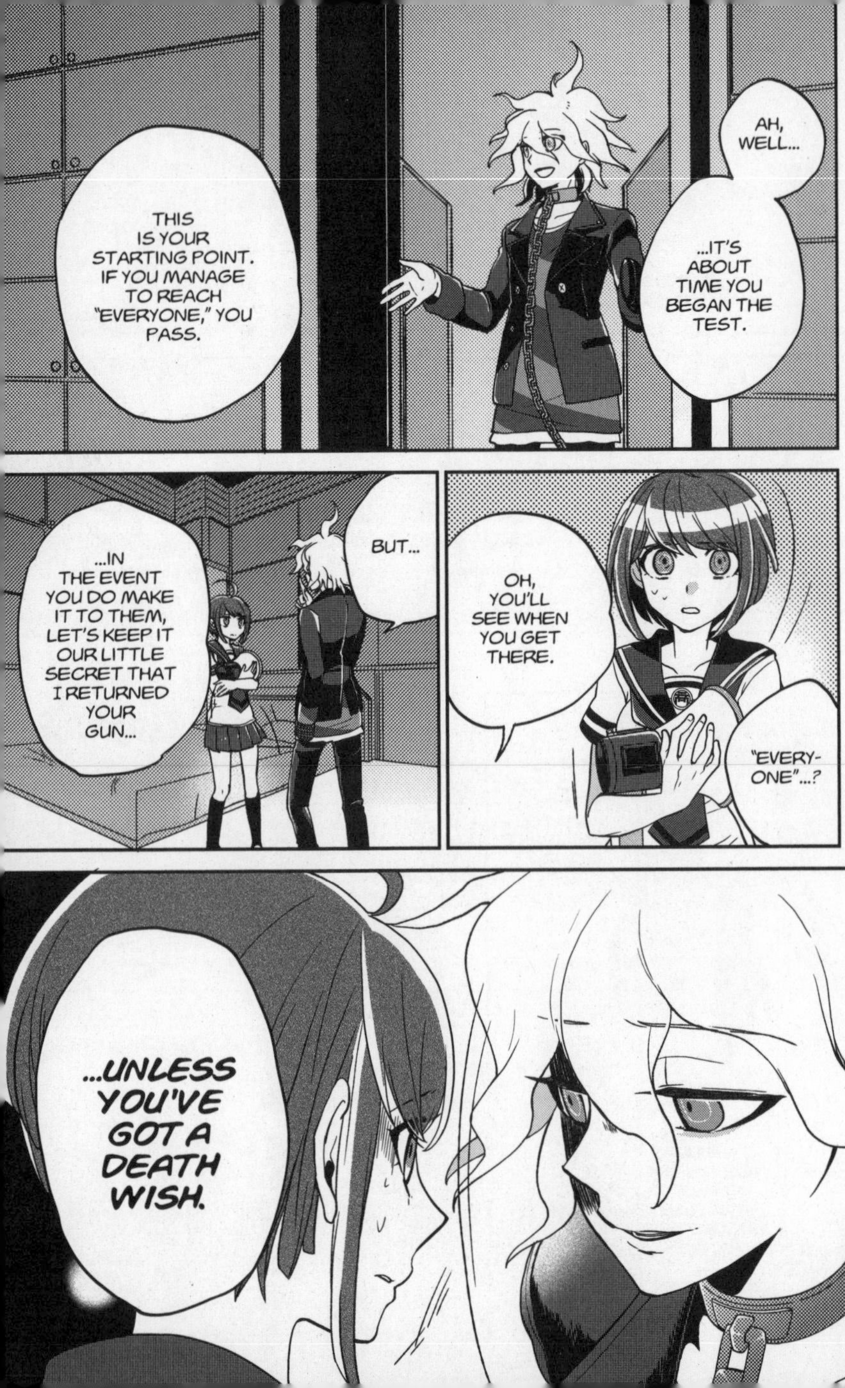
AH, WELL...
...IT'S ABOUT TIME YOU BEGAN THE TEST.
THIS IS YOUR STARTING POINT. IF YOU MANAGE TO REACH "EVERYONE," YOU PASS.
"EVERY-ONE"...?
OH, YOU'LL SEE WHEN YOU GET THERE.
BUT...
...IN THE EVENT YOU DO MAKE IT TO THEM, LET'S KEEP IT OUR LITTLE SECRET THAT I RETURNED YOUR GUN...
...UNLESS YOU'VE GOT A DEATH WISH.

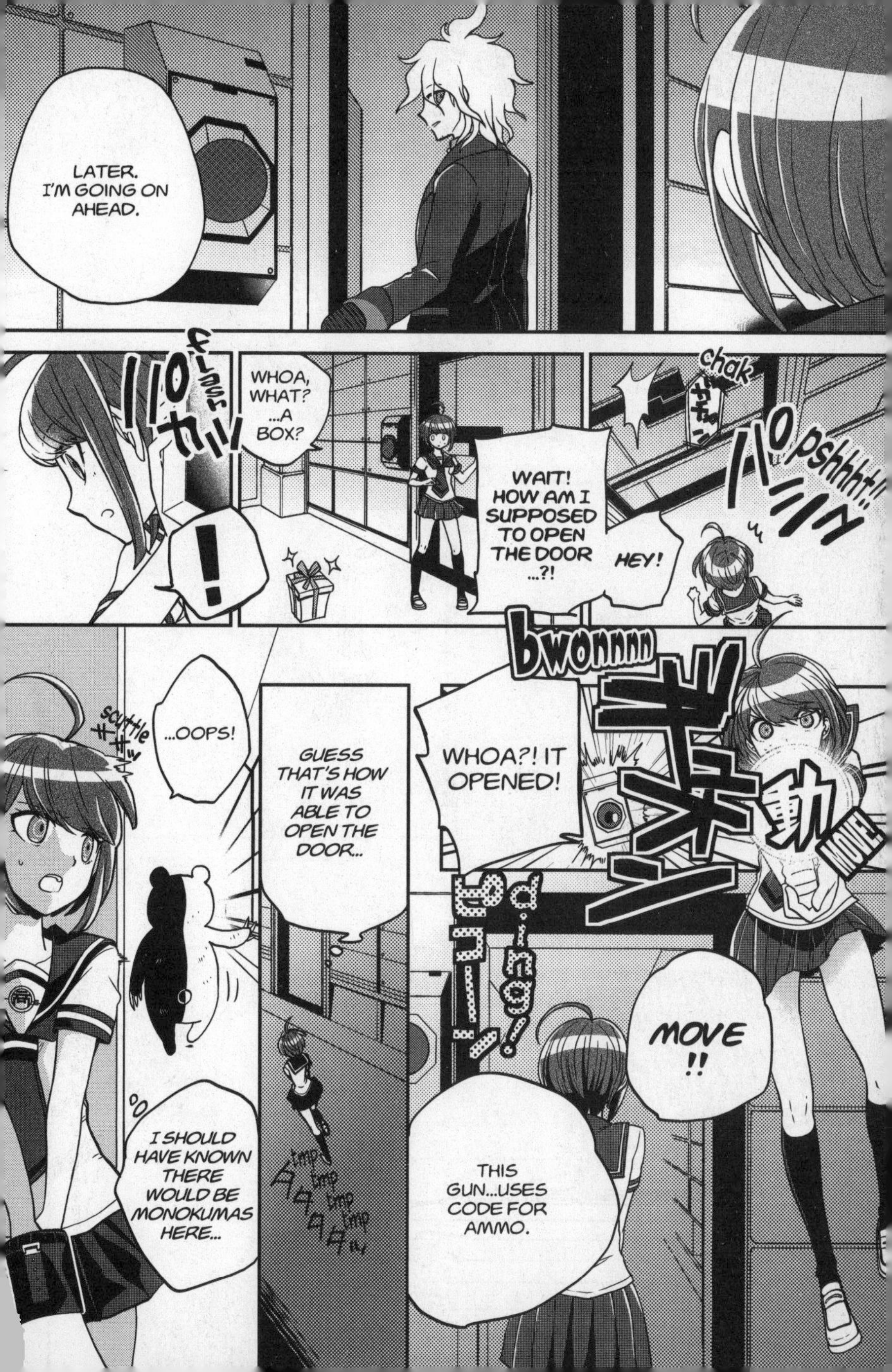
LATER. I'M GOING ON AHEAD.
chak
pshhht!!
HEY!
WAIT! HOW AM I SUPPOSED TO OPEN THE DOOR ...?!
WHOA, WHAT? ...A BOX?
flash
!
bwonnnn
MOVE
WHOA?! IT OPENED!
ping!
MOVE !!
THIS GUN...USES CODE FOR AMMO.
GUESS THAT'S HOW IT WAS ABLE TO OPEN THE DOOR...
tmp tmp tmp tmp
scuttle
...OOPS!
I SHOULD HAVE KNOWN THERE WOULD BE MONOKUMAS HERE...

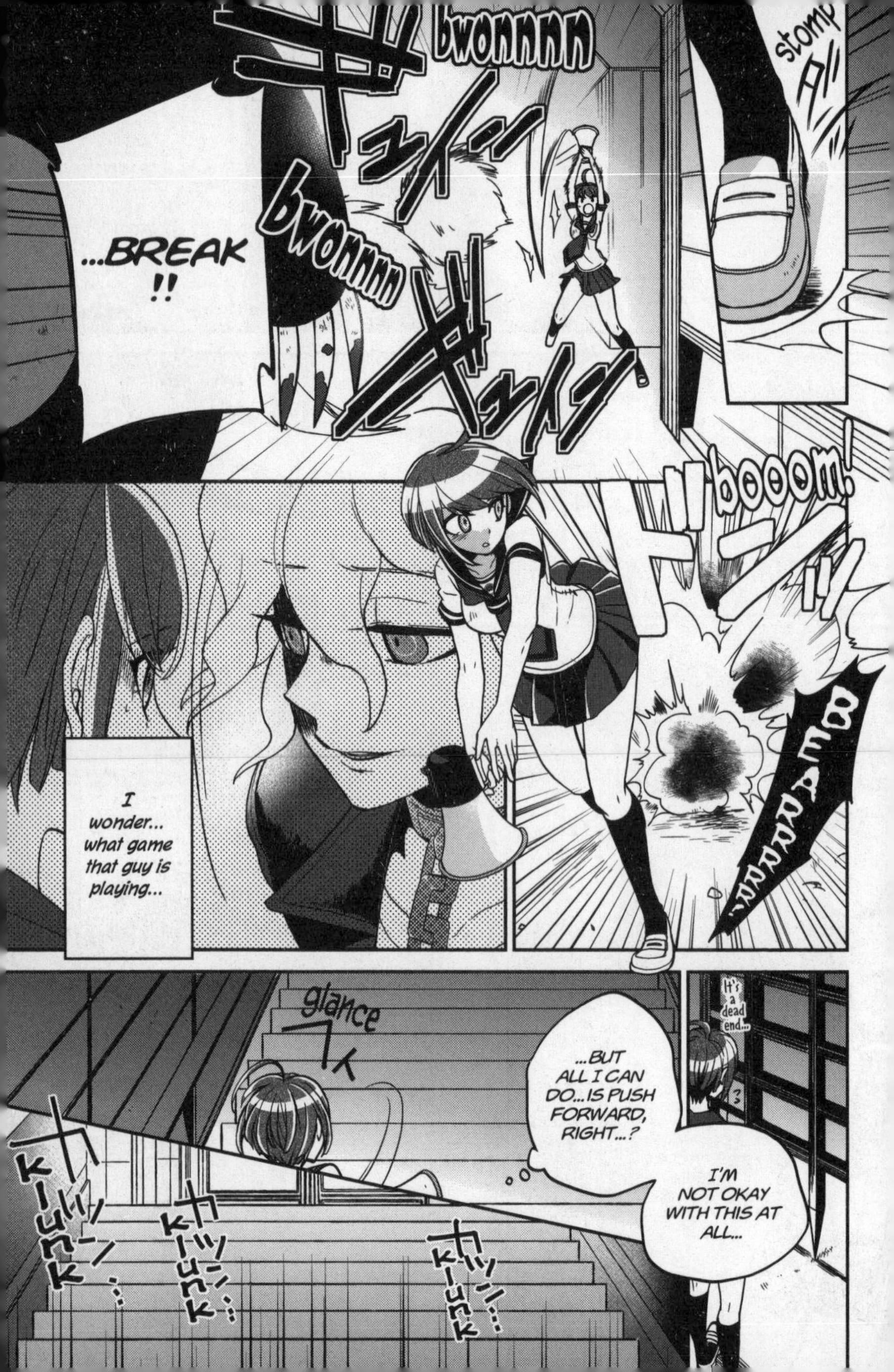
stomp
bwonnnn
bwonnnn
...BREAK !!
booom!
BEARRRRRR...
I wonder... what game that guy is playing...
It's a dead end...
glance
...BUT ALL I CAN DO...IS PUSH FORWARD, RIGHT...?
I'M NOT OKAY WITH THIS AT ALL...
klunk...
klunk...
klunk...

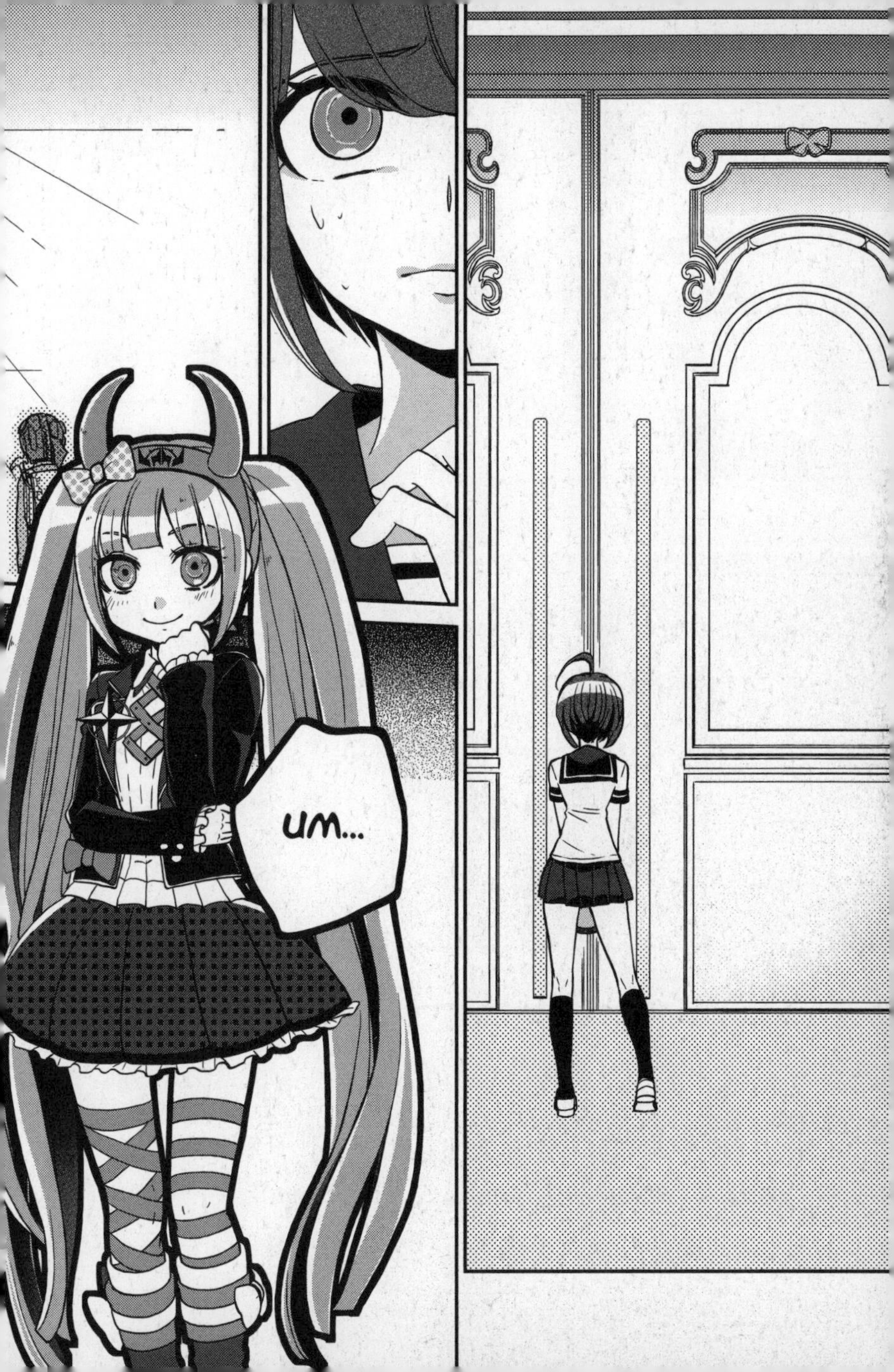
UM...

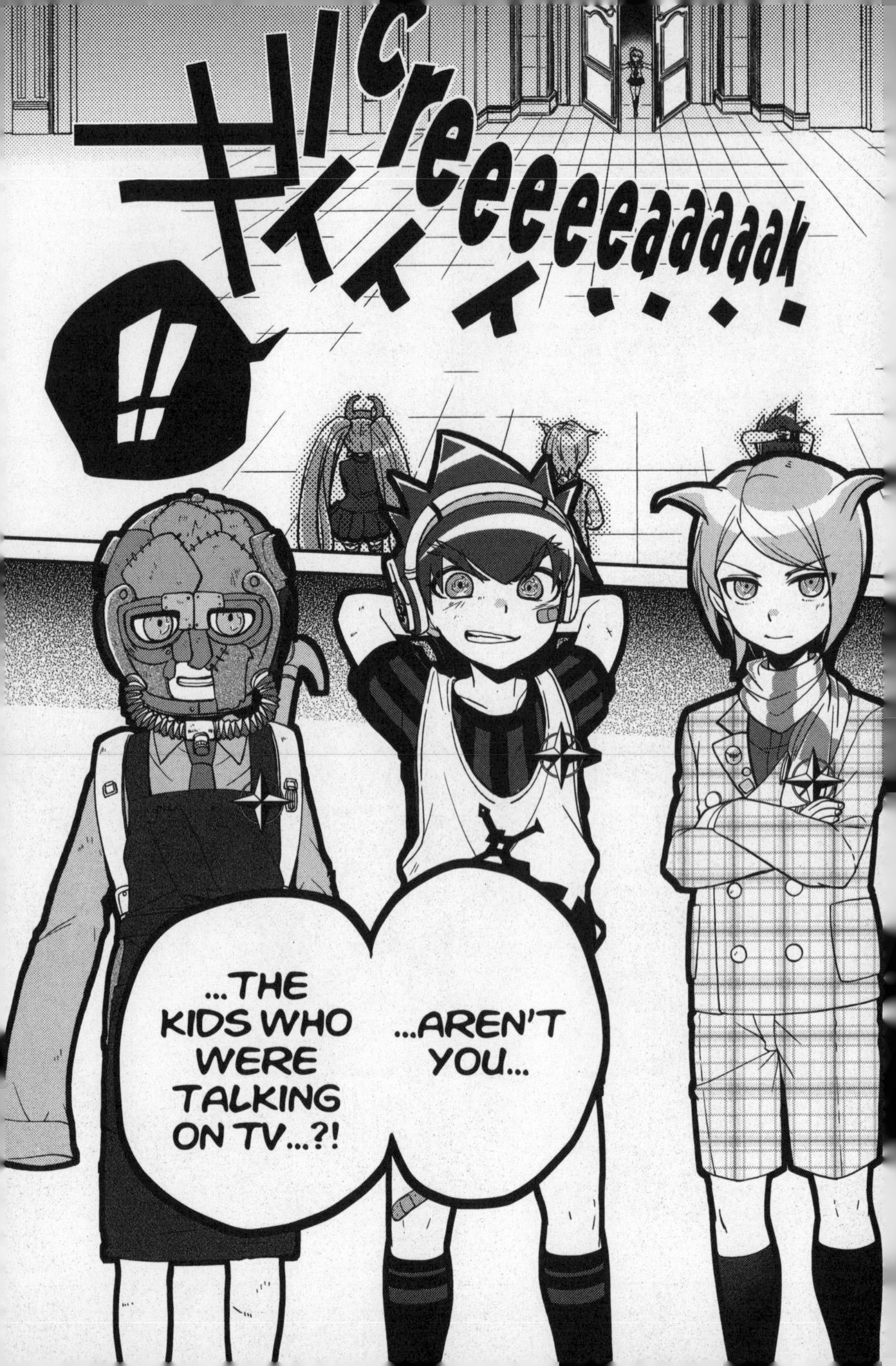
Creeeeeaaaaak...
!!
...THE KIDS WHO WERE TALKING ON TV...?!
...AREN'T YOU...

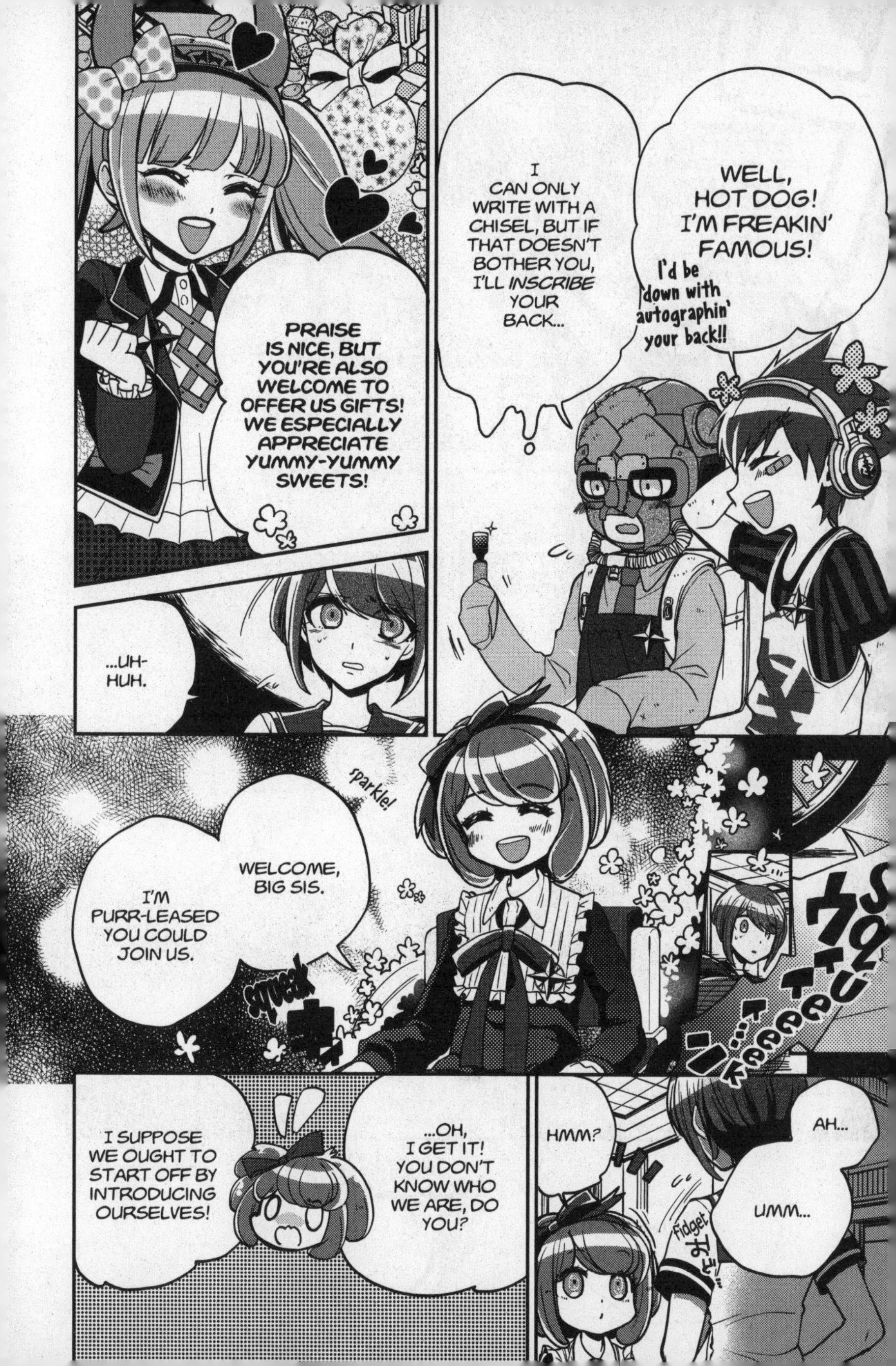
WELL, HOT DOG! I'M FREAKIN' FAMOUS!
I'd be down with autographin' your back!!
I CAN ONLY WRITE WITH A CHISEL, BUT IF THAT DOESN'T BOTHER YOU, I'LL *INSCRIBE* YOUR BACK...
PRAISE IS NICE, BUT YOU'RE ALSO WELCOME TO OFFER US GIFTS! WE ESPECIALLY APPRECIATE YUMMY-YUMMY SWEETS!
...UH-HUH.
sparkle!
WELCOME, BIG SIS.
I'M PURR-LEASED YOU COULD JOIN US.
squeak
AH...
HMM?
UMM...
fidget
...OH, I GET IT! YOU DON'T KNOW WHO WE ARE, DO YOU?
I SUPPOSE WE OUGHT TO START OFF BY INTRODUCING OURSELVES!

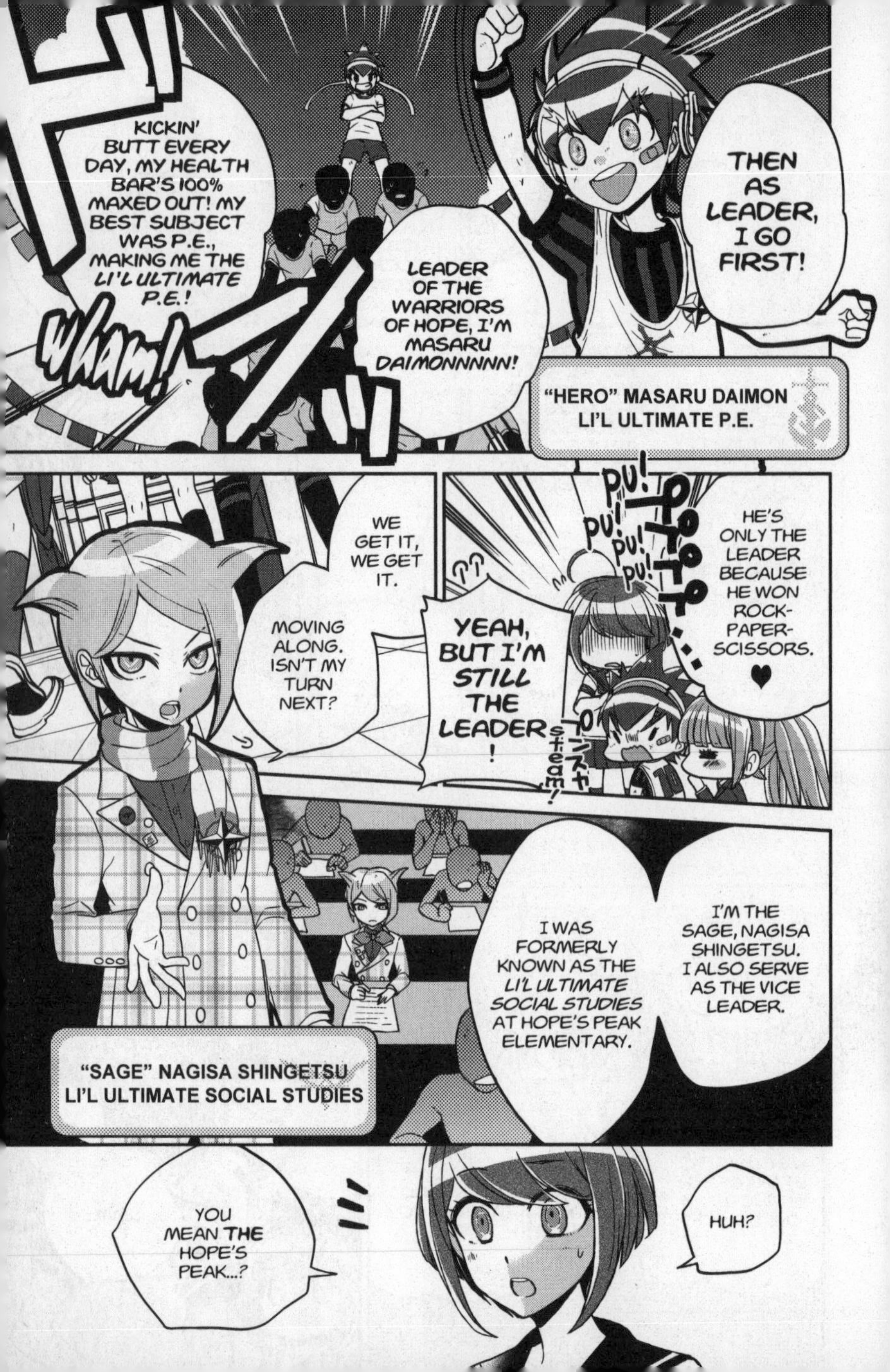
THEN AS LEADER, I GO FIRST!
LEADER OF THE WARRIORS OF HOPE, I'M MASARU DAIMONNNNN!
KICKIN' BUTT EVERY DAY, MY HEALTH BAR'S 100% MAXED OUT! MY BEST SUBJECT WAS P.E., MAKING ME THE *LI'L ULTIMATE P.E.*!
WHAM!
"HERO" MASARU DAIMON
LI'L ULTIMATE P.E.
PU! PU! PU! PU!
HE'S ONLY THE LEADER BECAUSE HE WON ROCK-PAPER-SCISSORS. ♥
YEAH, BUT I'M *STILL* THE LEADER!
steam!
WE GET IT, WE GET IT.
MOVING ALONG. ISN'T MY TURN NEXT?
I'M THE SAGE, NAGISA SHINGETSU. I ALSO SERVE AS THE VICE LEADER.
I WAS FORMERLY KNOWN AS THE *LI'L ULTIMATE SOCIAL STUDIES* AT HOPE'S PEAK ELEMENTARY.
"SAGE" NAGISA SHINGETSU
LI'L ULTIMATE SOCIAL STUDIES
HUH?
YOU MEAN THE HOPE'S PEAK...?

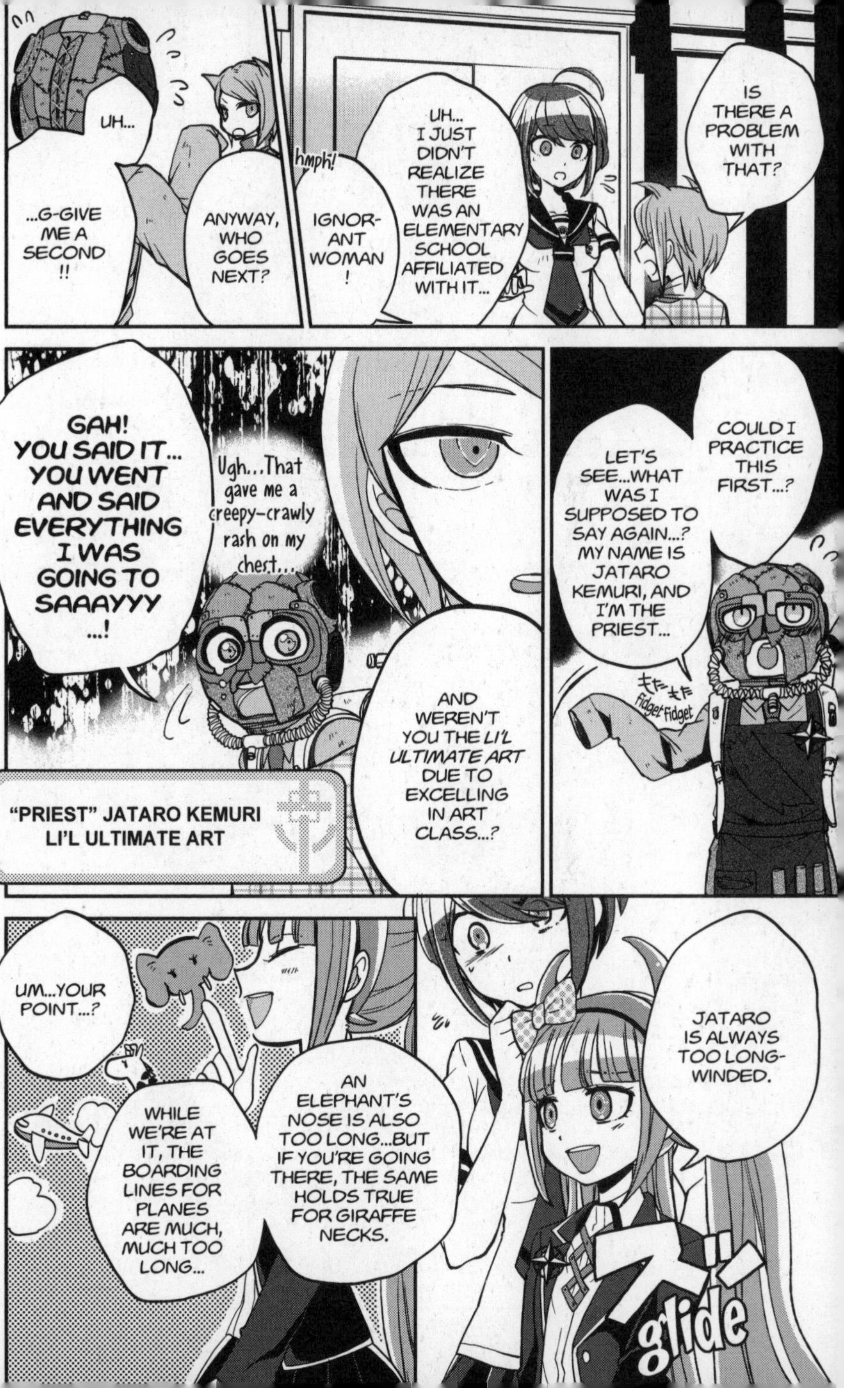

IS THERE A PROBLEM WITH THAT?
UH... I JUST DIDN'T REALIZE THERE WAS AN ELEMENTARY SCHOOL AFFILIATED WITH IT...
hmph!
IGNOR-ANT WOMAN!
ANYWAY, WHO GOES NEXT?
UH...
...G-GIVE ME A SECOND!!
COULD I PRACTICE THIS FIRST...?
LET'S SEE...WHAT WAS I SUPPOSED TO SAY AGAIN...? MY NAME IS JATARO KEMURI, AND I'M THE PRIEST...
Fidget Fidget
AND WEREN'T YOU THE LI'L ULTIMATE ART DUE TO EXCELLING IN ART CLASS...?
Ugh...That gave me a creepy-crawly rash on my chest...
GAH! YOU SAID IT... YOU WENT AND SAID EVERYTHING I WAS GOING TO SAAAYYY...!
"PRIEST" JATARO KEMURI
LI'L ULTIMATE ART
JATARO IS ALWAYS TOO LONG-WINDED.
glide
AN ELEPHANT'S NOSE IS ALSO TOO LONG...BUT IF YOU'RE GOING THERE, THE SAME HOLDS TRUE FOR GIRAFFE NECKS.
WHILE WE'RE AT IT, THE BOARDING LINES FOR PLANES ARE MUCH, MUCH TOO LONG...
UM...YOUR POINT...?

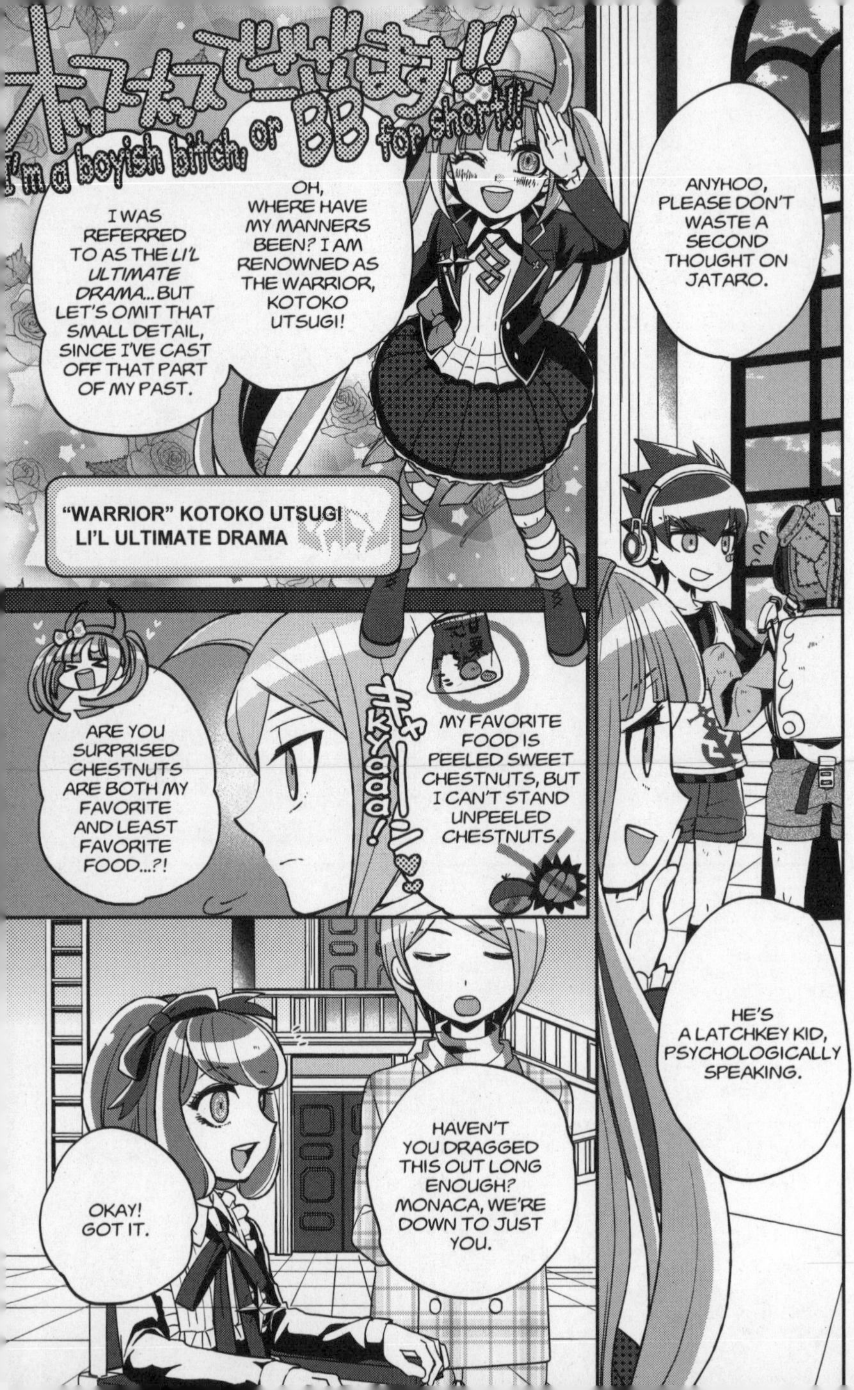
ANYHOO, PLEASE DON'T WASTE A SECOND THOUGHT ON JATARO.
HE'S A LATCHKEY KID, PSYCHOLOGICALLY SPEAKING.
I'm a boyish bitch, or BB for short!!
OH, WHERE HAVE MY MANNERS BEEN? I AM RENOWNED AS THE WARRIOR, KOTOKO UTSUGI!
I WAS REFERRED TO AS THE *LI'L ULTIMATE DRAMA*... BUT LET'S OMIT THAT SMALL DETAIL, SINCE I'VE CAST OFF THAT PART OF MY PAST.
"WARRIOR" KOTOKO UTSUGI LI'L ULTIMATE DRAMA
MY FAVORITE FOOD IS PEELED SWEET CHESTNUTS, BUT I CAN'T STAND UNPEELED CHESTNUTS.
ARE YOU SURPRISED CHESTNUTS ARE BOTH MY FAVORITE AND LEAST FAVORITE FOOD...?!
HAVEN'T YOU DRAGGED THIS OUT LONG ENOUGH? MONACA, WE'RE DOWN TO JUST YOU.
OKAY! GOT IT.

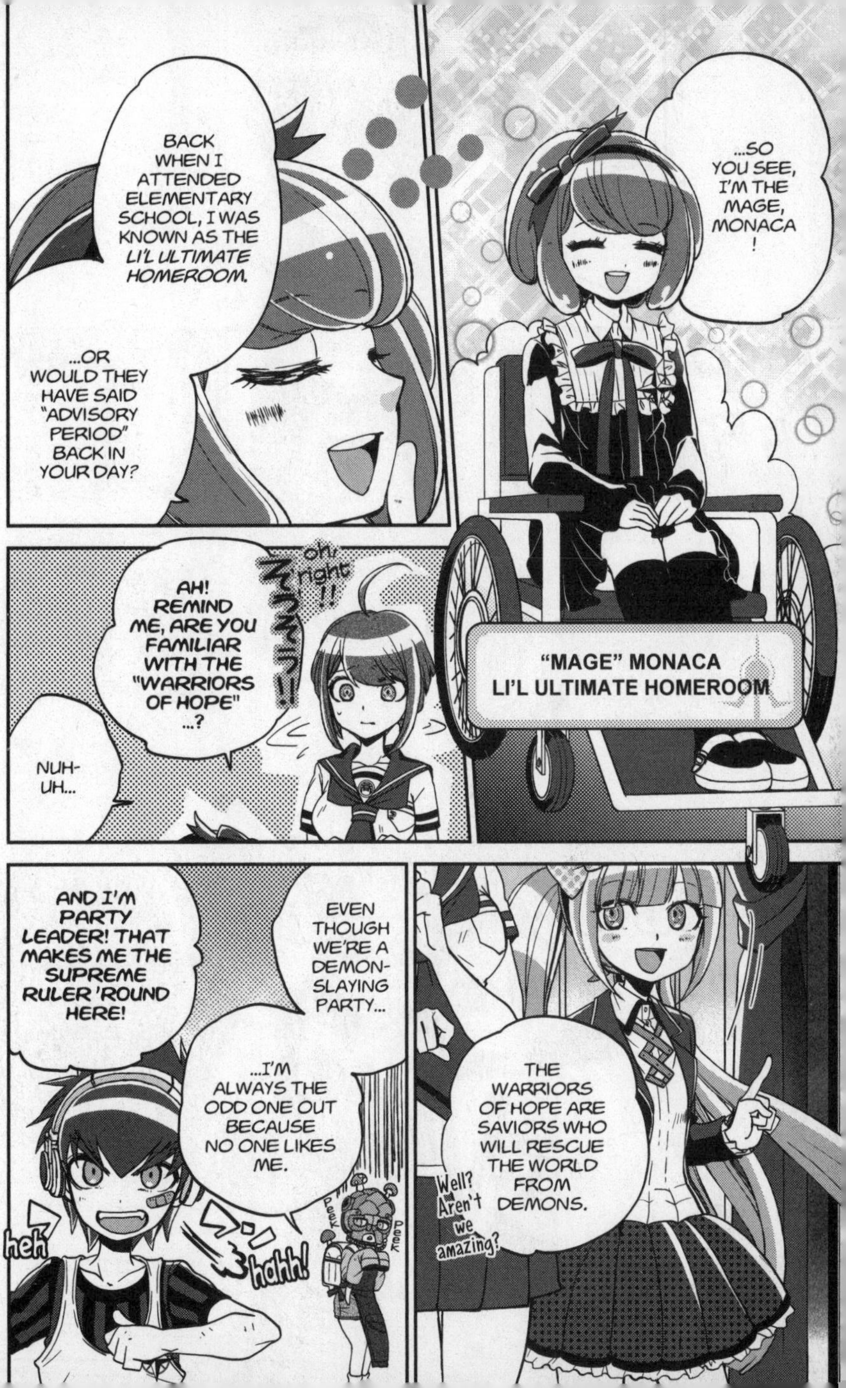
...SO YOU SEE, I'M THE MAGE, MONACA!
"MAGE" MONACA
LI'L ULTIMATE HOMEROOM
BACK WHEN I ATTENDED ELEMENTARY SCHOOL, I WAS KNOWN AS THE LI'L ULTIMATE HOMEROOM.
...OR WOULD THEY HAVE SAID "ADVISORY PERIOD" BACK IN YOUR DAY?
oh, right!!
AH! REMIND ME, ARE YOU FAMILIAR WITH THE "WARRIORS OF HOPE" ...?
NUH-UH...
THE WARRIORS OF HOPE ARE SAVIORS WHO WILL RESCUE THE WORLD FROM DEMONS.
Well? Aren't we amazing?
EVEN THOUGH WE'RE A DEMON-SLAYING PARTY...
AND I'M PARTY LEADER! THAT MAKES ME THE SUPREME RULER 'ROUND HERE!
...I'M ALWAYS THE ODD ONE OUT BECAUSE NO ONE LIKES ME.
PEEK
PEEK
heh
hahh!

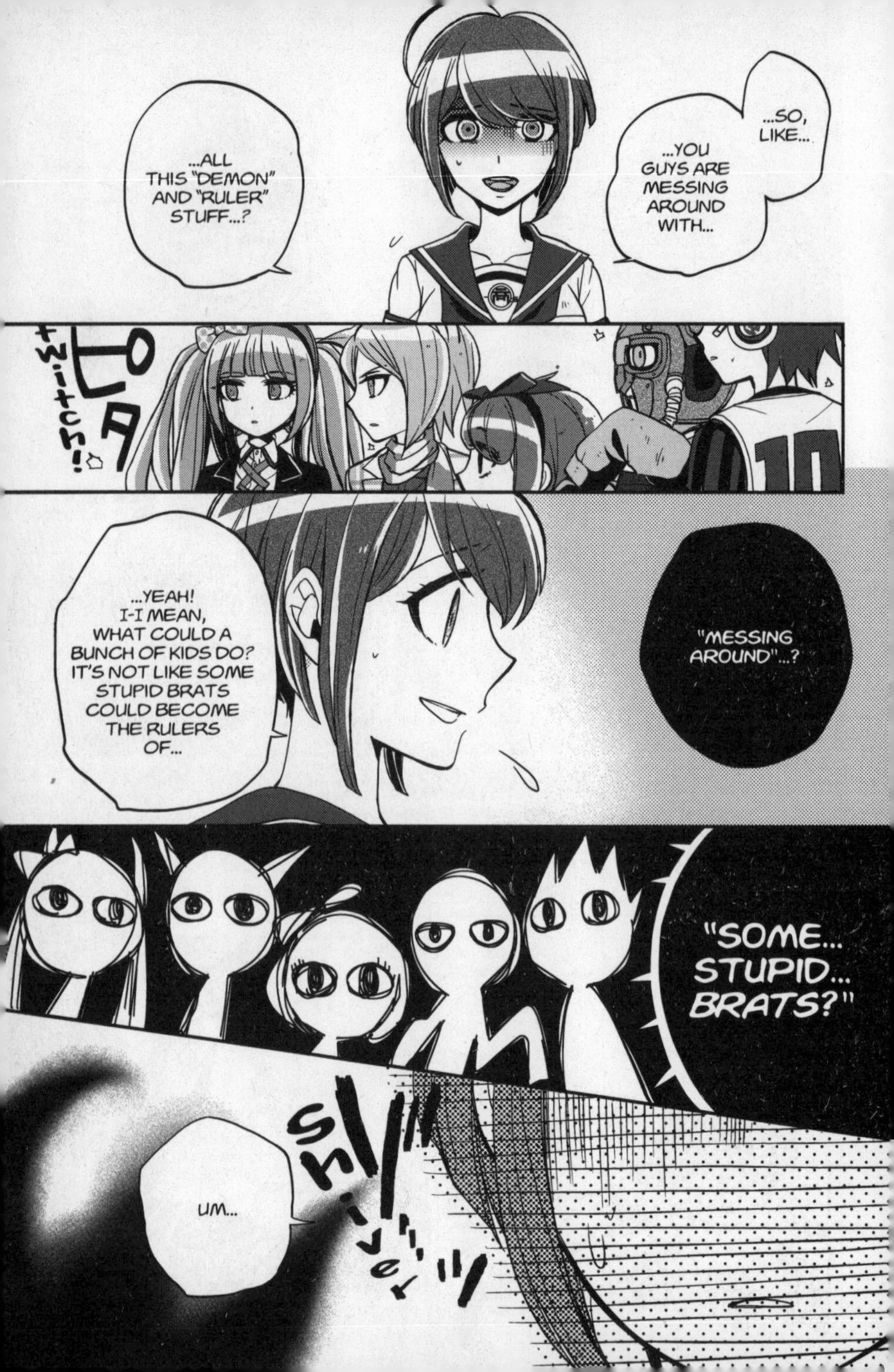
...SO, LIKE...
...YOU GUYS ARE MESSING AROUND WITH...
...ALL THIS "DEMON" AND "RULER" STUFF...?
ピク
twitch!
"MESSING AROUND"...?
...YEAH! I-I MEAN, WHAT COULD A BUNCH OF KIDS DO? IT'S NOT LIKE SOME STUPID BRATS COULD BECOME THE RULERS OF...
"SOME... STUPID... BRATS?"
shiver
UM...

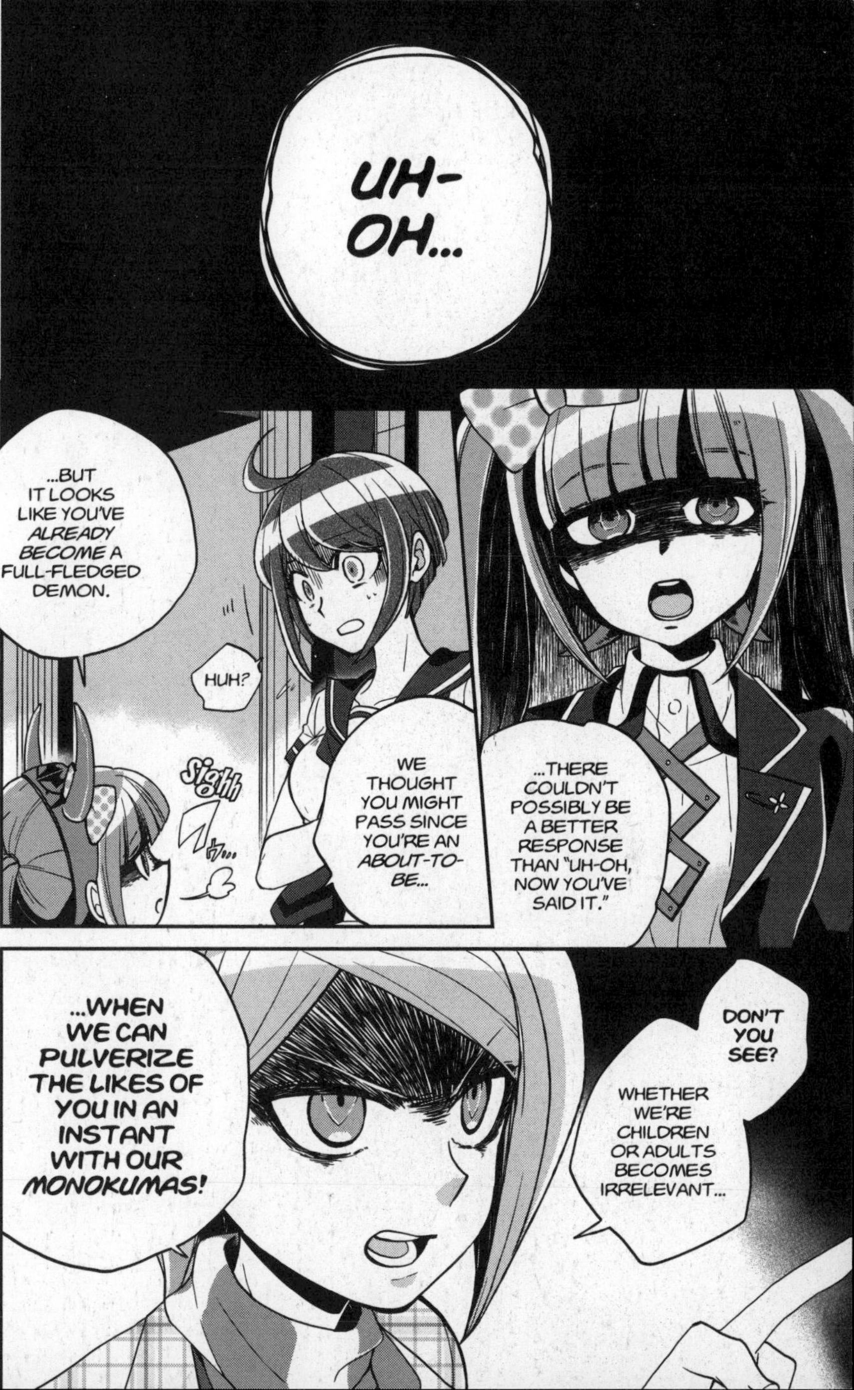
UH-OH...
...THERE COULDN'T POSSIBLY BE A BETTER RESPONSE THAN "UH-OH, NOW YOU'VE SAID IT."
WE THOUGHT YOU MIGHT PASS SINCE YOU'RE AN ABOUT-TO-BE...
...BUT IT LOOKS LIKE YOU'VE ALREADY BECOME A FULL-FLEDGED DEMON.
HUH?
Sighhh
DON'T YOU SEE?
WHETHER WE'RE CHILDREN OR ADULTS BECOMES IRRELEVANT...
...WHEN WE CAN PULVERIZE THE LIKES OF YOU IN AN INSTANT WITH OUR MONOKUMAS!

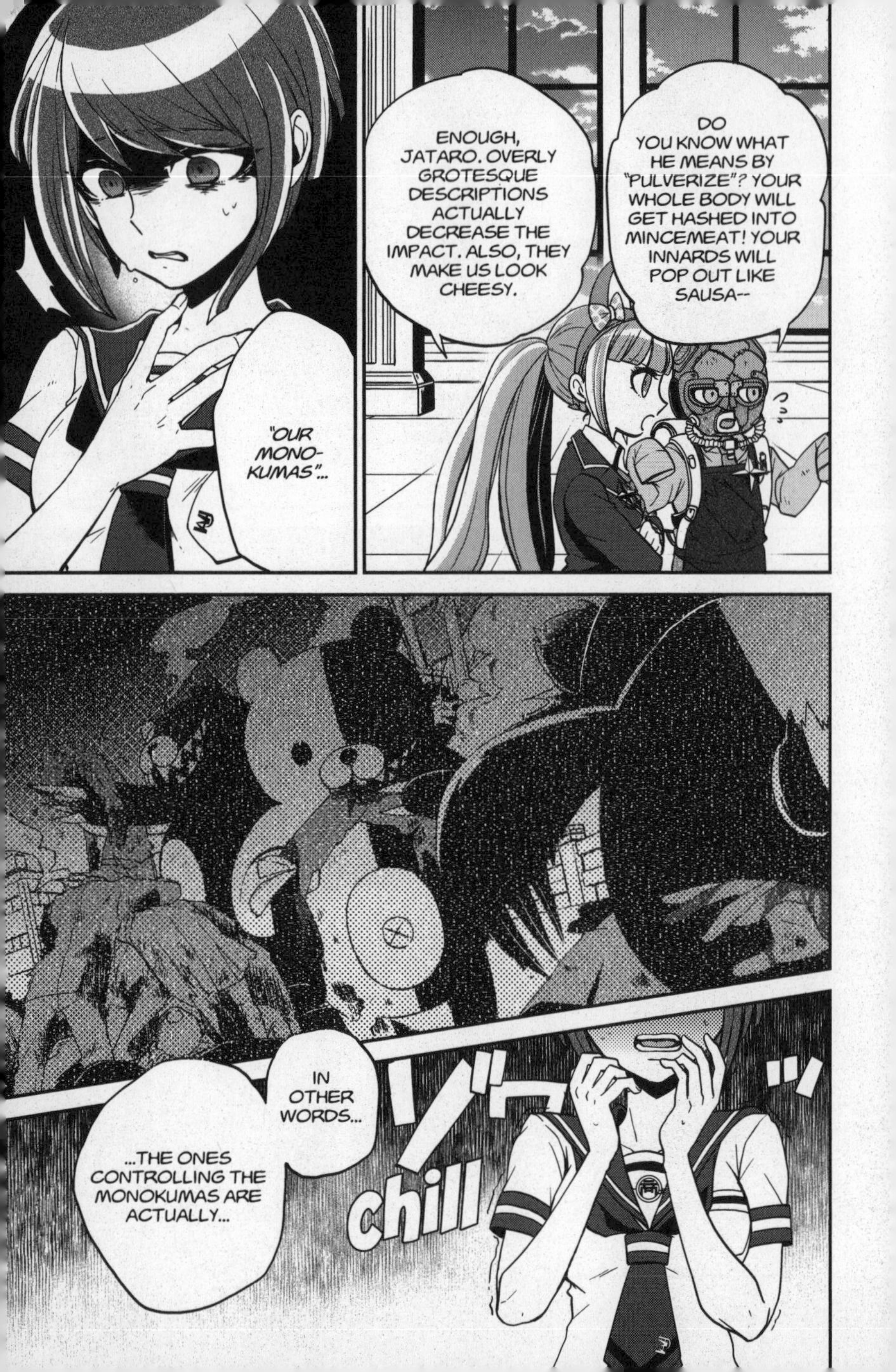
DO YOU KNOW WHAT HE MEANS BY "PULVERIZE"? YOUR WHOLE BODY WILL GET HASHED INTO MINCEMEAT! YOUR INNARDS WILL POP OUT LIKE SAUSA--
ENOUGH, JATARO. OVERLY GROTESQUE DESCRIPTIONS ACTUALLY DECREASE THE IMPACT. ALSO, THEY MAKE US LOOK CHEESY.
"OUR MONO-KUMAS"...
IN OTHER WORDS...
...THE ONES CONTROLLING THE MONOKUMAS ARE ACTUALLY...
Chill

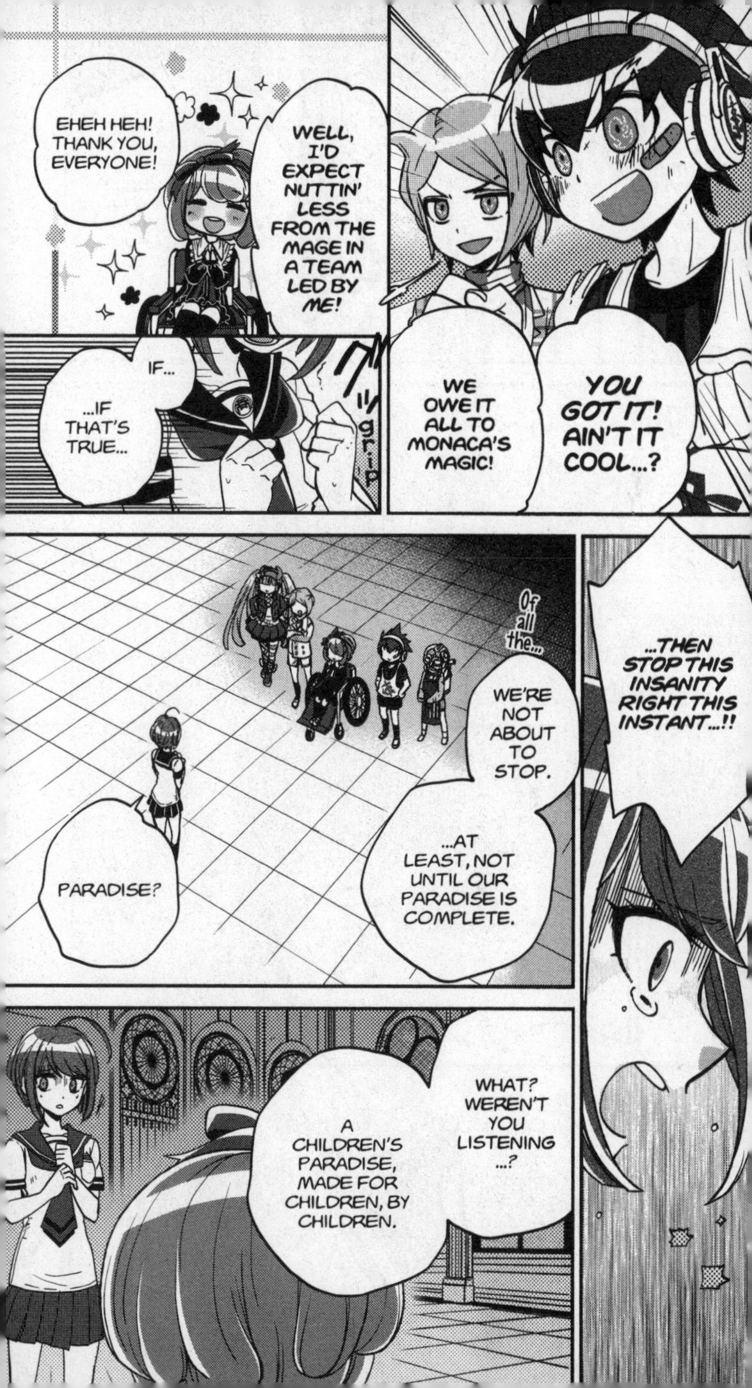
YOU GOT IT! AIN'T IT COOL...?
WE OWE IT ALL TO MONACA'S MAGIC!
WELL, I'D EXPECT NUTTIN' LESS FROM THE MAGE IN A TEAM LED BY ME!
EHEH HEH! THANK YOU, EVERYONE!
grip
IF...
...IF THAT'S TRUE...
...THEN STOP THIS INSANITY RIGHT THIS INSTANT...!!
Of all the...
WE'RE NOT ABOUT TO STOP.
...AT LEAST, NOT UNTIL OUR PARADISE IS COMPLETE.
PARADISE?
WHAT? WEREN'T YOU LISTENING...?
A CHILDREN'S PARADISE, MADE FOR CHILDREN, BY CHILDREN.

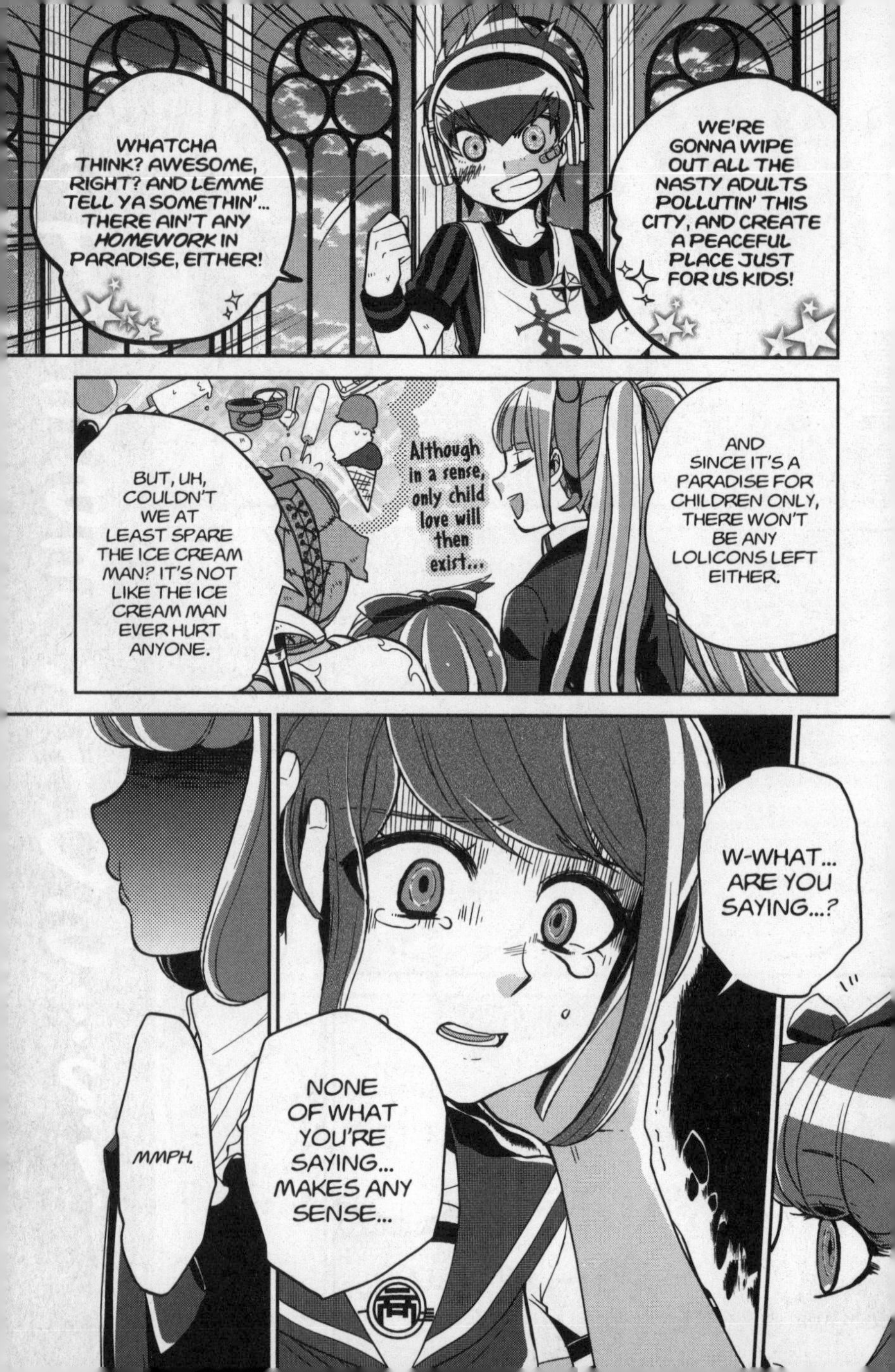
WE'RE GONNA WIPE OUT ALL THE NASTY ADULTS POLLUTIN' THIS CITY, AND CREATE A PEACEFUL PLACE JUST FOR US KIDS!
WHATCHA THINK? AWESOME, RIGHT? AND LEMME TELL YA SOMETHIN'... THERE AIN'T ANY *HOMEWORK* IN PARADISE, EITHER!
AND SINCE IT'S A PARADISE FOR CHILDREN ONLY, THERE WON'T BE ANY LOLICONS LEFT EITHER.
Although in a sense, only child love will then exist...
BUT, UH, COULDN'T WE AT LEAST SPARE THE ICE CREAM MAN? IT'S NOT LIKE THE ICE CREAM MAN EVER HURT ANYONE.
W-WHAT... ARE YOU SAYING...?
NONE OF WHAT YOU'RE SAYING... MAKES ANY SENSE...
MMPH.

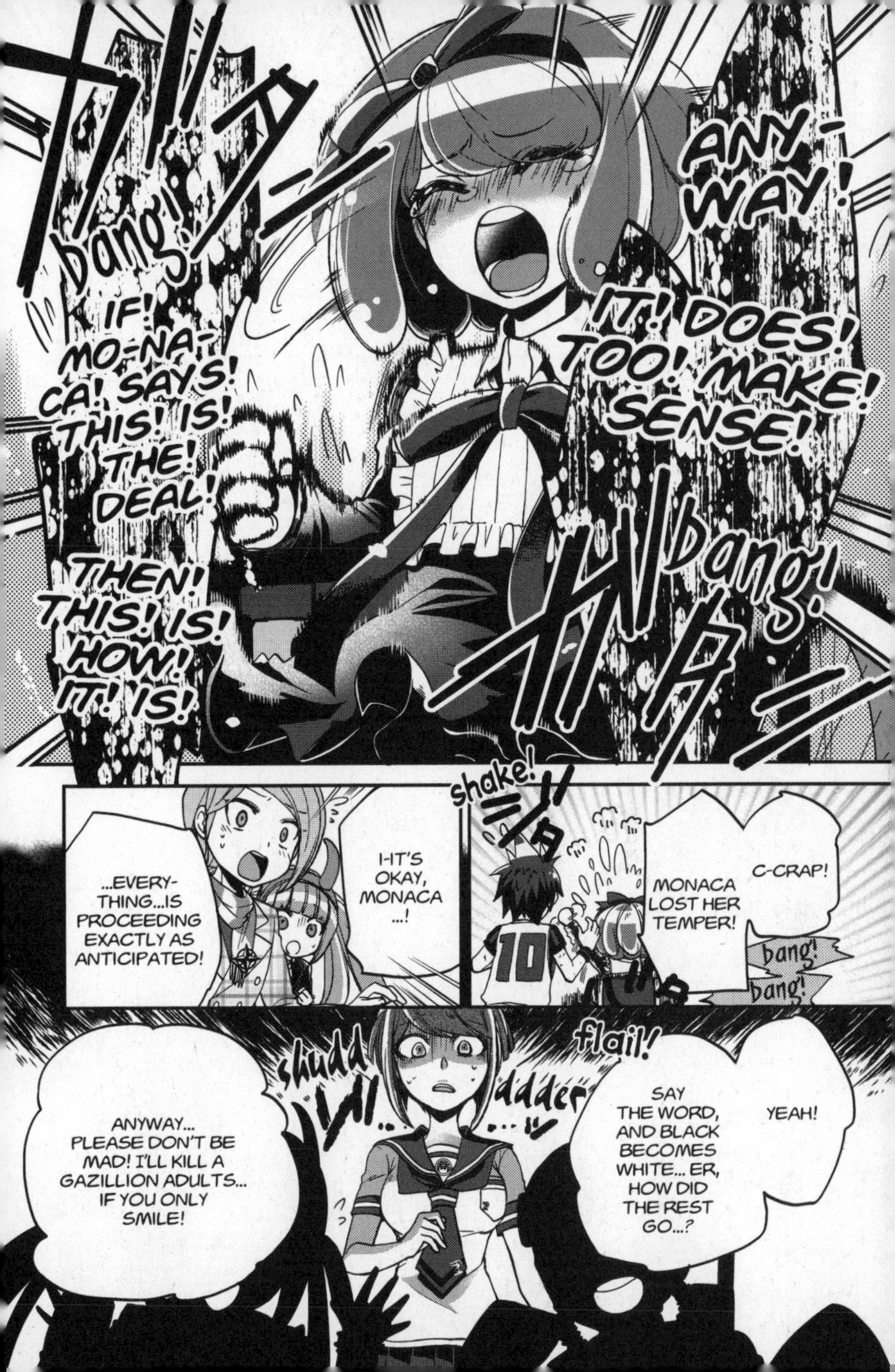
ANY-WAY!
IT! DOES! TOO! MAKE! SENSE!
bang!
IF! MO-NA-CA! SAYS! THIS! IS! THE! DEAL!
THEN! THIS! IS! HOW! IT! IS!
bang!
shake!
C-CRAP!
MONACA LOST HER TEMPER!
bang!
bang!
I-IT'S OKAY, MONACA ...!
...EVERY-THING...IS PROCEEDING EXACTLY AS ANTICIPATED!
flail!
YEAH!
SAY THE WORD, AND BLACK BECOMES WHITE... ER, HOW DID THE REST GO...?
shudd
adder
ANYWAY... PLEASE DON'T BE MAD! I'LL KILL A GAZILLION ADULTS... IF YOU ONLY SMILE!

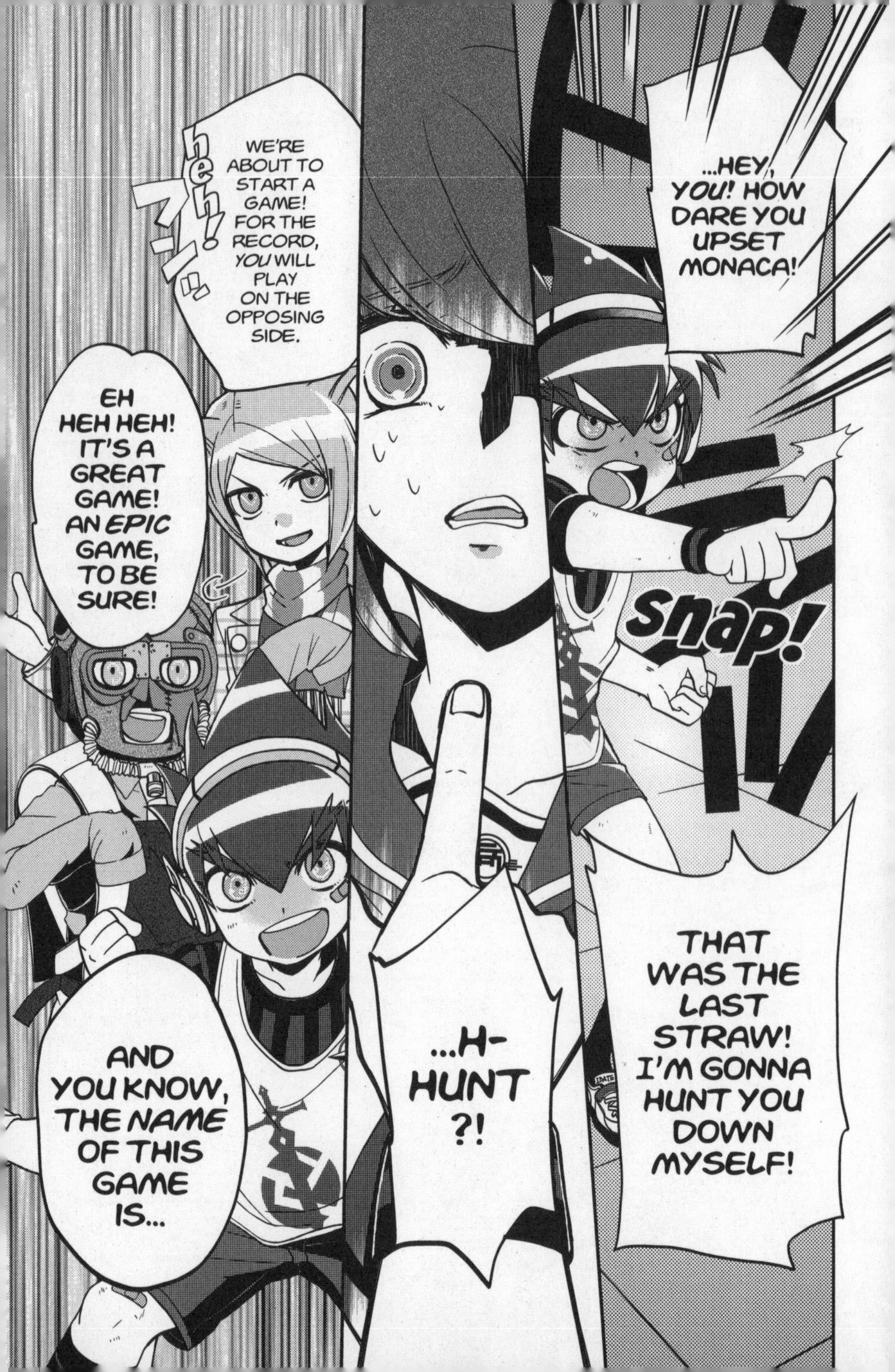
...HEY, YOU! HOW DARE YOU UPSET MONACA!
Snap!
THAT WAS THE LAST STRAW! I'M GONNA HUNT YOU DOWN MYSELF!
...H- HUNT?!
heh!
WE'RE ABOUT TO START A GAME! FOR THE RECORD, *YOU* WILL PLAY ON THE OPPOSING SIDE.
EH HEH HEH! IT'S A GREAT GAME! AN *EPIC* GAME, TO BE SURE!
AND YOU KNOW, THE *NAME* OF THIS GAME IS...

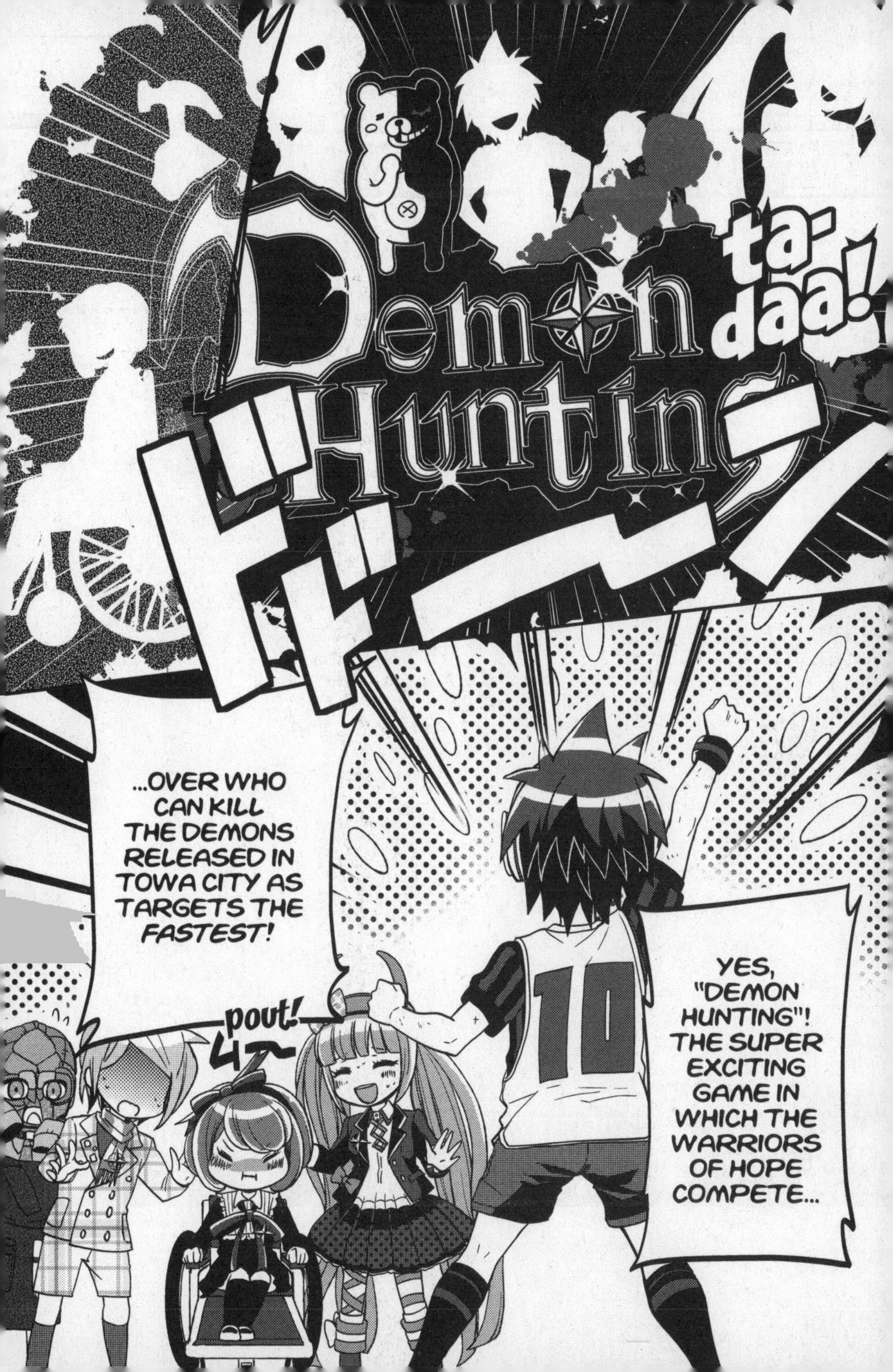
Demon Hunting
ta-daa!
ドドーン
YES, "DEMON HUNTING"! THE SUPER EXCITING GAME IN WHICH THE WARRIORS OF HOPE COMPETE...
...OVER WHO CAN KILL THE DEMONS RELEASED IN TOWA CITY AS TARGETS THE FASTEST!
pout!
ム~

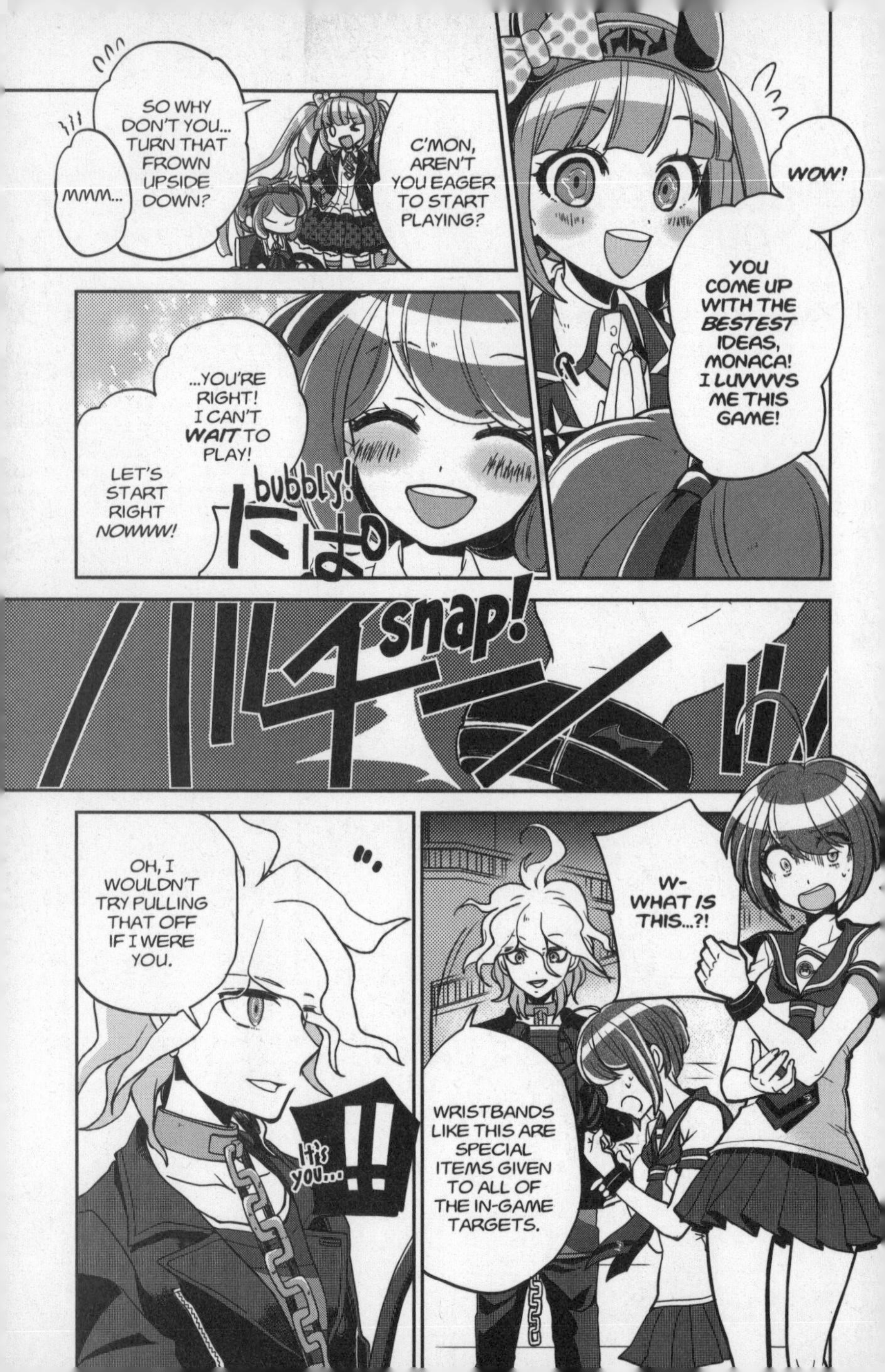
WOW!
YOU COME UP WITH THE BESTEST IDEAS, MONACA! I LUVVVVS ME THIS GAME!
C'MON, AREN'T YOU EAGER TO START PLAYING?
SO WHY DON'T YOU... TURN THAT FROWN UPSIDE DOWN?
MMM...
...YOU'RE RIGHT! I CAN'T WAIT TO PLAY!
LET'S START RIGHT NOWWW!
bubbly!
snap!
W- WHAT IS THIS...?!
WRISTBANDS LIKE THIS ARE SPECIAL ITEMS GIVEN TO ALL OF THE IN-GAME TARGETS.
OH, I WOULDN'T TRY PULLING THAT OFF IF I WERE YOU.
It's you...!!

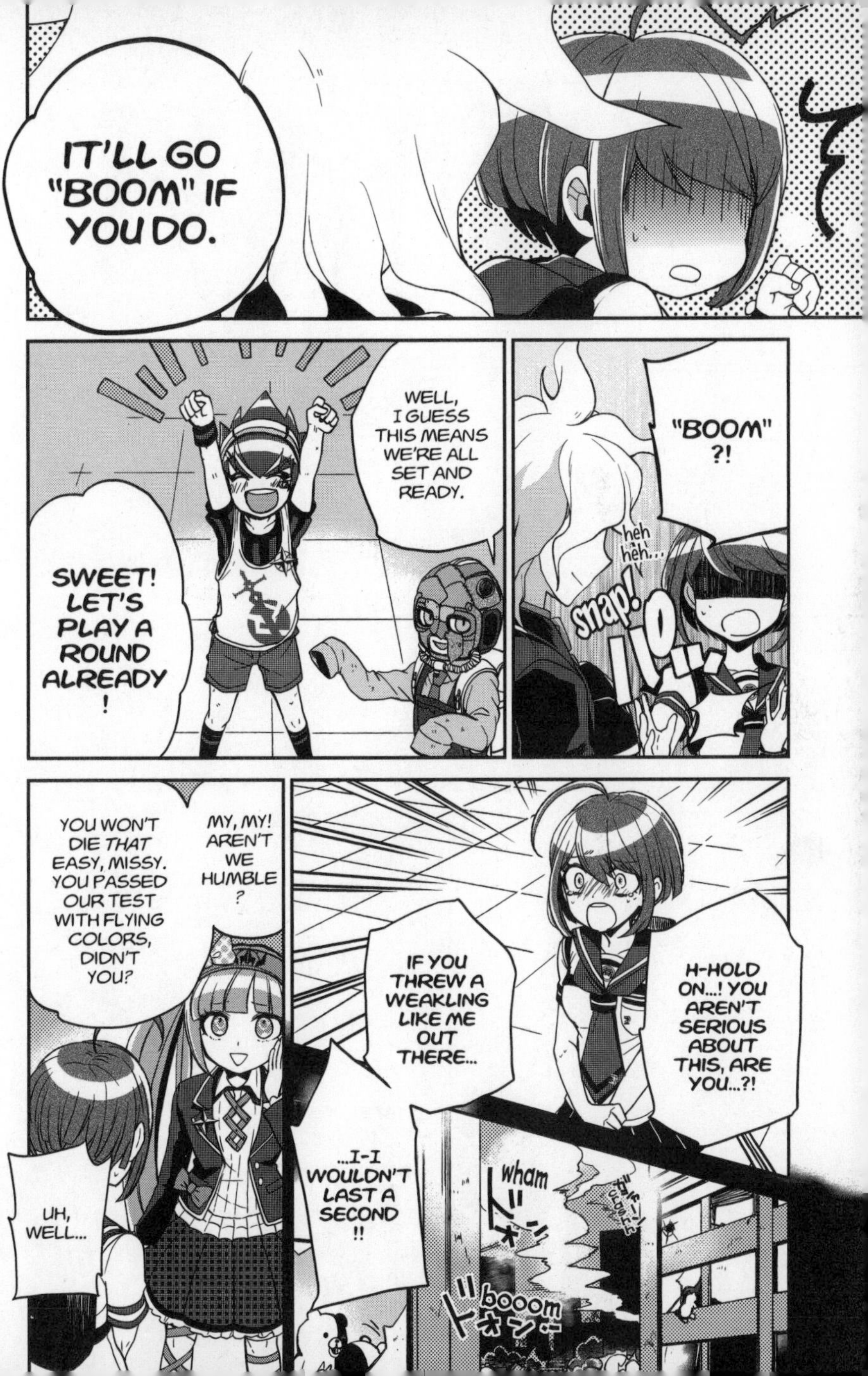
IT'LL GO "BOOM" IF YOU DO.
"BOOM"?!
heh heh...
snap!
WELL, I GUESS THIS MEANS WE'RE ALL SET AND READY.
SWEET! LET'S PLAY A ROUND ALREADY!
H-HOLD ON...! YOU AREN'T SERIOUS ABOUT THIS, ARE YOU...?!
IF YOU THREW A WEAKLING LIKE ME OUT THERE...
...I-I WOULDN'T LAST A SECOND!!
wham
crash
booom
MY, MY! AREN'T WE HUMBLE?
YOU WON'T DIE THAT EASY, MISSY. YOU PASSED OUR TEST WITH FLYING COLORS, DIDN'T YOU?
UH, WELL...

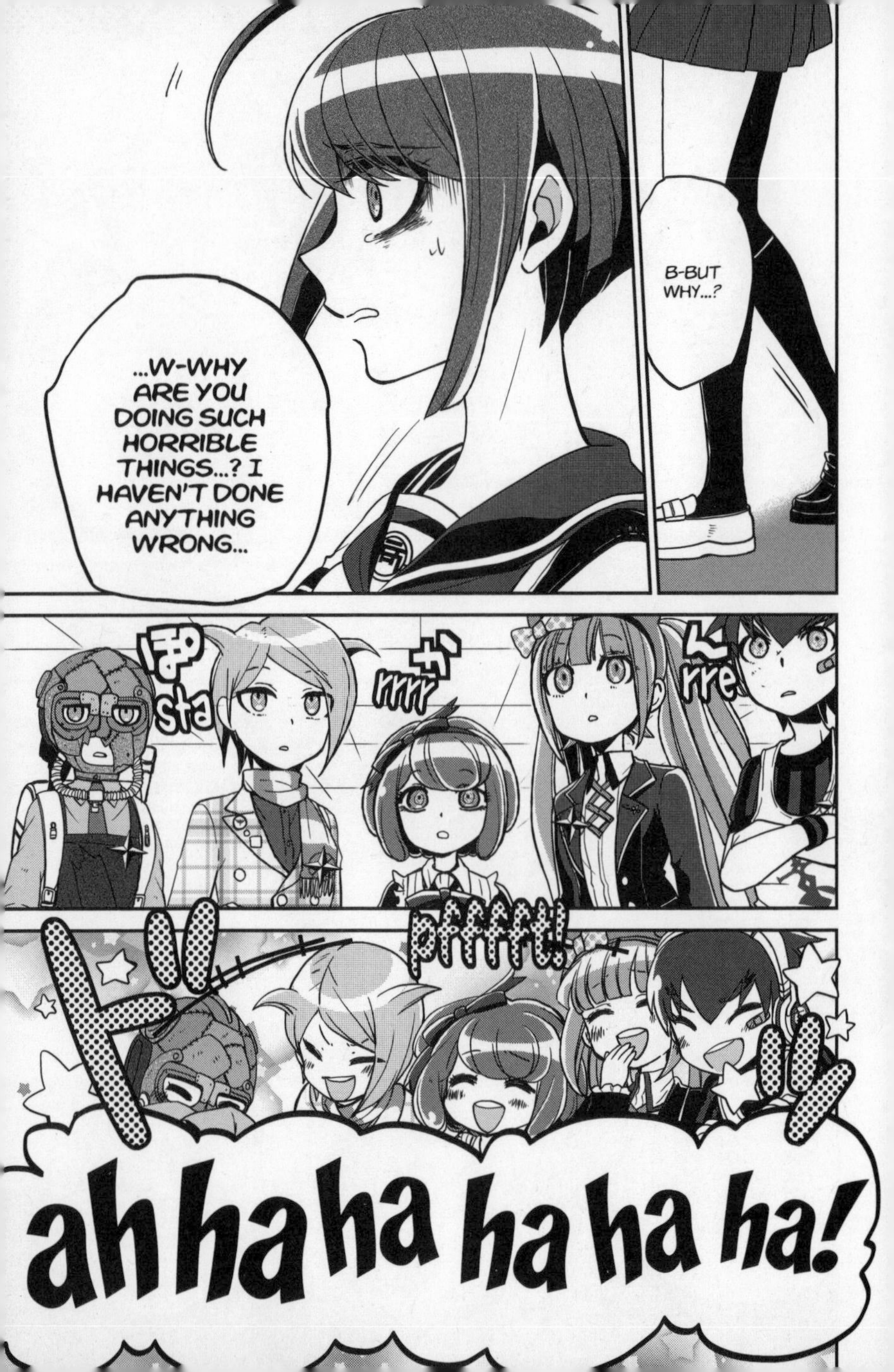
B-BUT WHY...?
...W-WHY ARE YOU DOING SUCH HORRIBLE THINGS...? I HAVEN'T DONE ANYTHING WRONG...
ぽ sta
が rrrr
ん rre
ドッ
pffft!
ah ha ha ha ha ha ha!

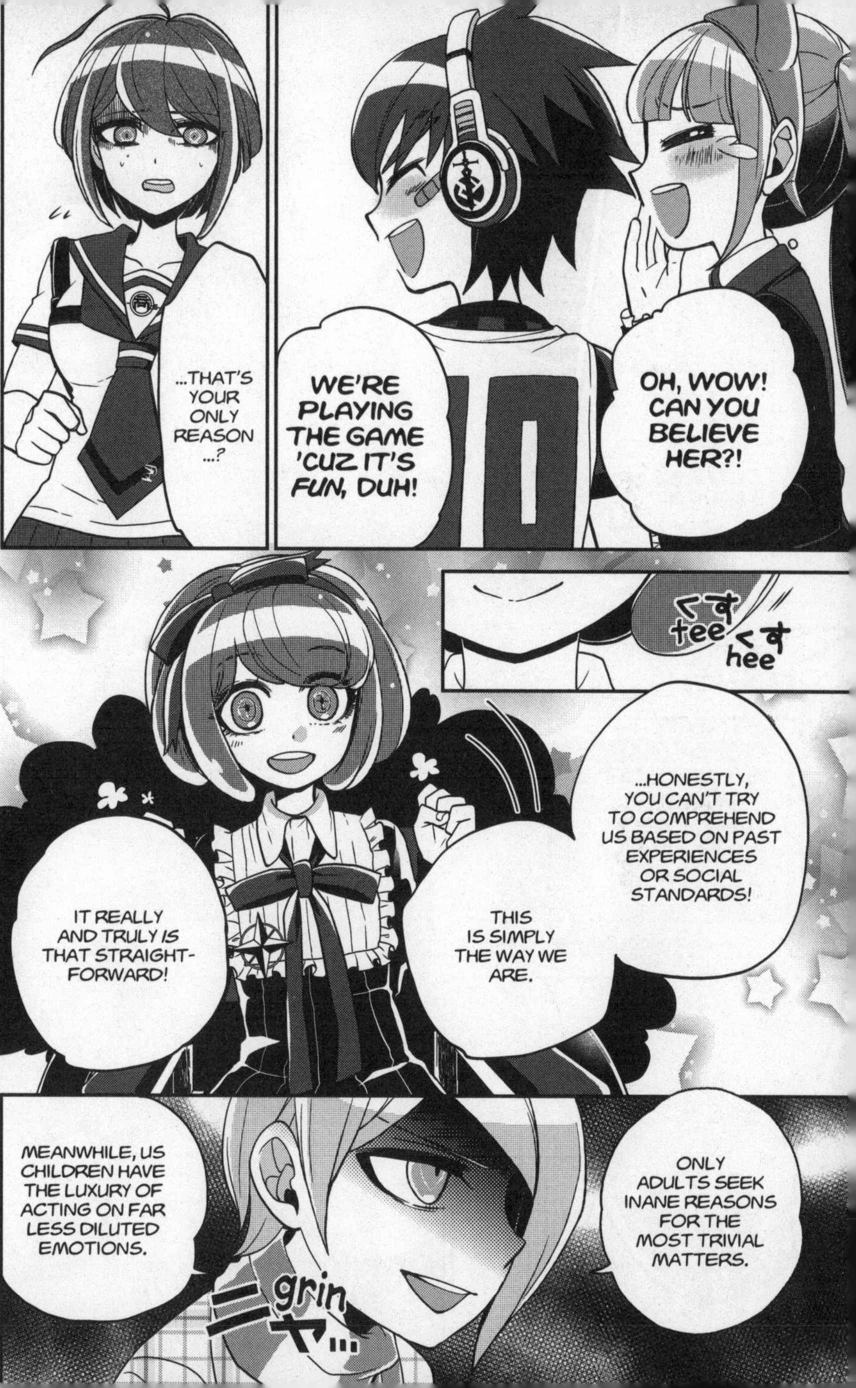
OH, WOW! CAN YOU BELIEVE HER?!
WE'RE PLAYING THE GAME 'CUZ IT'S FUN, DUH!
...THAT'S YOUR ONLY REASON ...?
くす tee くす hee
...HONESTLY, YOU CAN'T TRY TO COMPREHEND US BASED ON PAST EXPERIENCES OR SOCIAL STANDARDS!
THIS IS SIMPLY THE WAY WE ARE.
IT REALLY AND TRULY IS THAT STRAIGHT-FORWARD!
ONLY ADULTS SEEK INANE REASONS FOR THE MOST TRIVIAL MATTERS.
MEANWHILE, US CHILDREN HAVE THE LUXURY OF ACTING ON FAR LESS DILUTED EMOTIONS.
ニヤ... grin

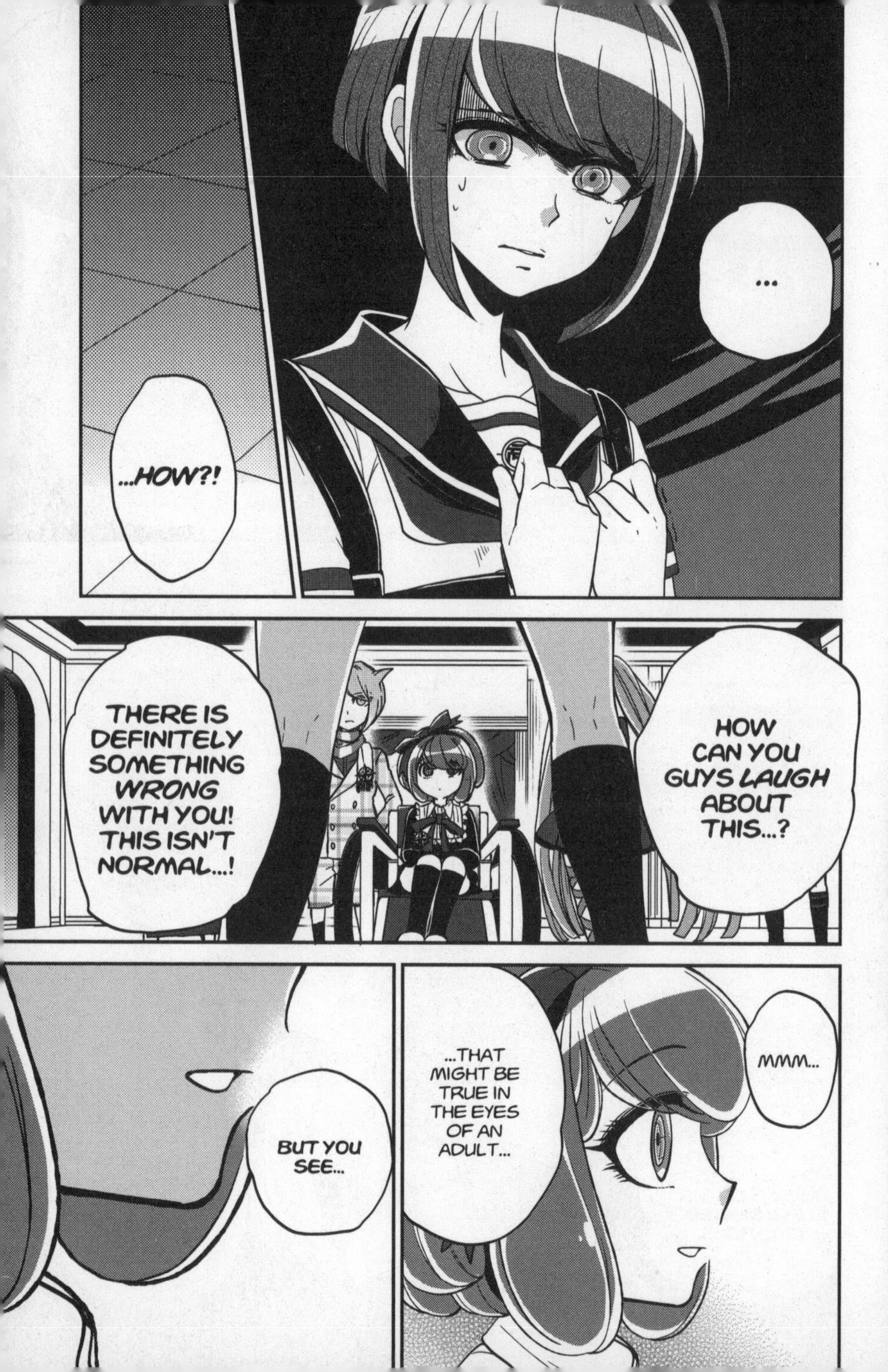
...
...HOW?!
HOW CAN YOU GUYS LAUGH ABOUT THIS...?
THERE IS DEFINITELY SOMETHING WRONG WITH YOU! THIS ISN'T NORMAL...!
MMM...
...THAT MIGHT BE TRUE IN THE EYES OF AN ADULT...
BUT YOU SEE...

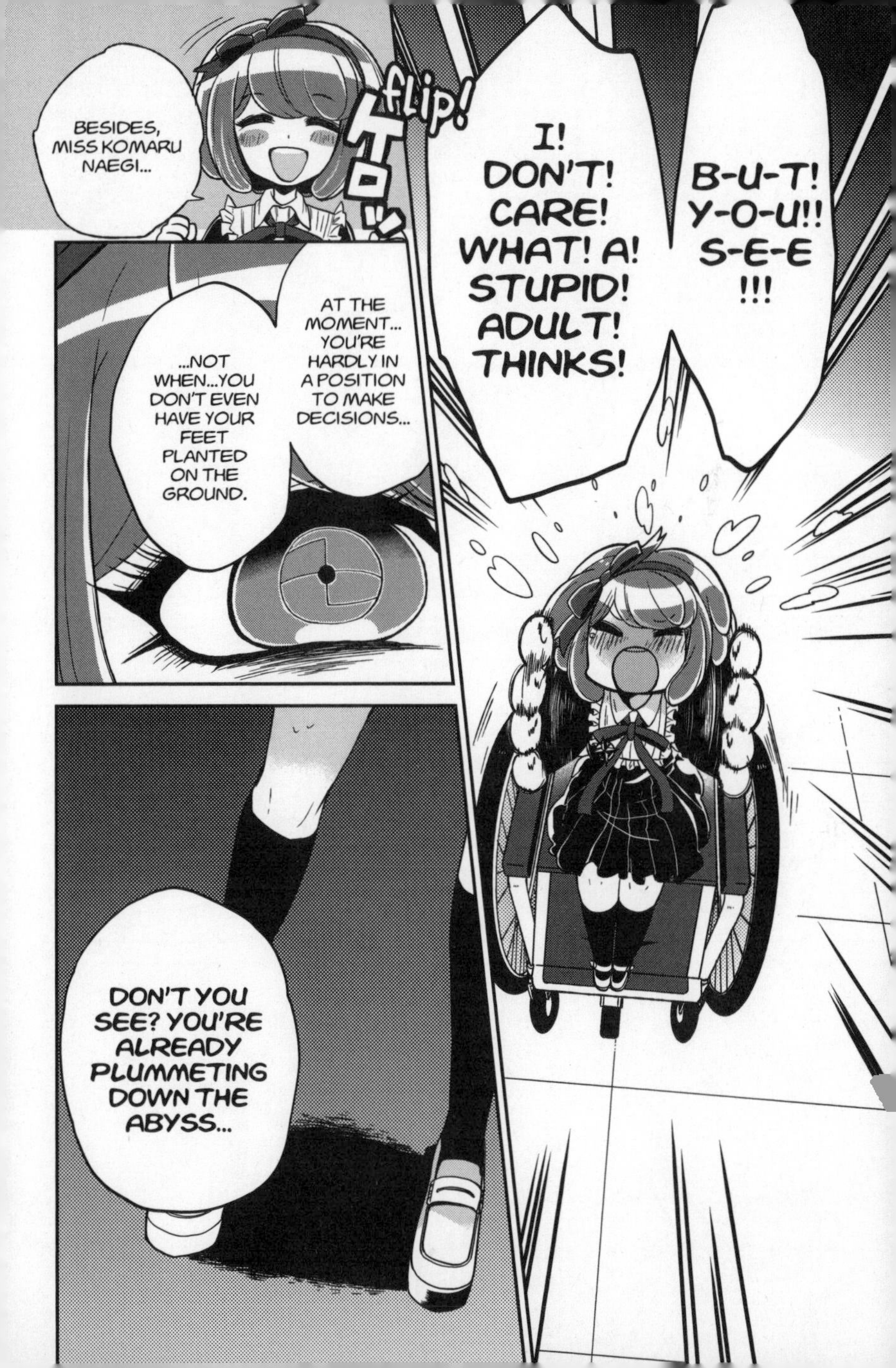

B-U-T! Y-O-U!! S-E-E !!!
I! DON'T! CARE! WHAT! A! STUPID! ADULT! THINKS!
BESIDES, MISS KOMARU NAEGI...
FLIP!
AT THE MOMENT... YOU'RE HARDLY IN A POSITION TO MAKE DECISIONS...
...NOT WHEN...YOU DON'T EVEN HAVE YOUR FEET PLANTED ON THE GROUND.
DON'T YOU SEE? YOU'RE ALREADY PLUMMETING DOWN THE ABYSS...

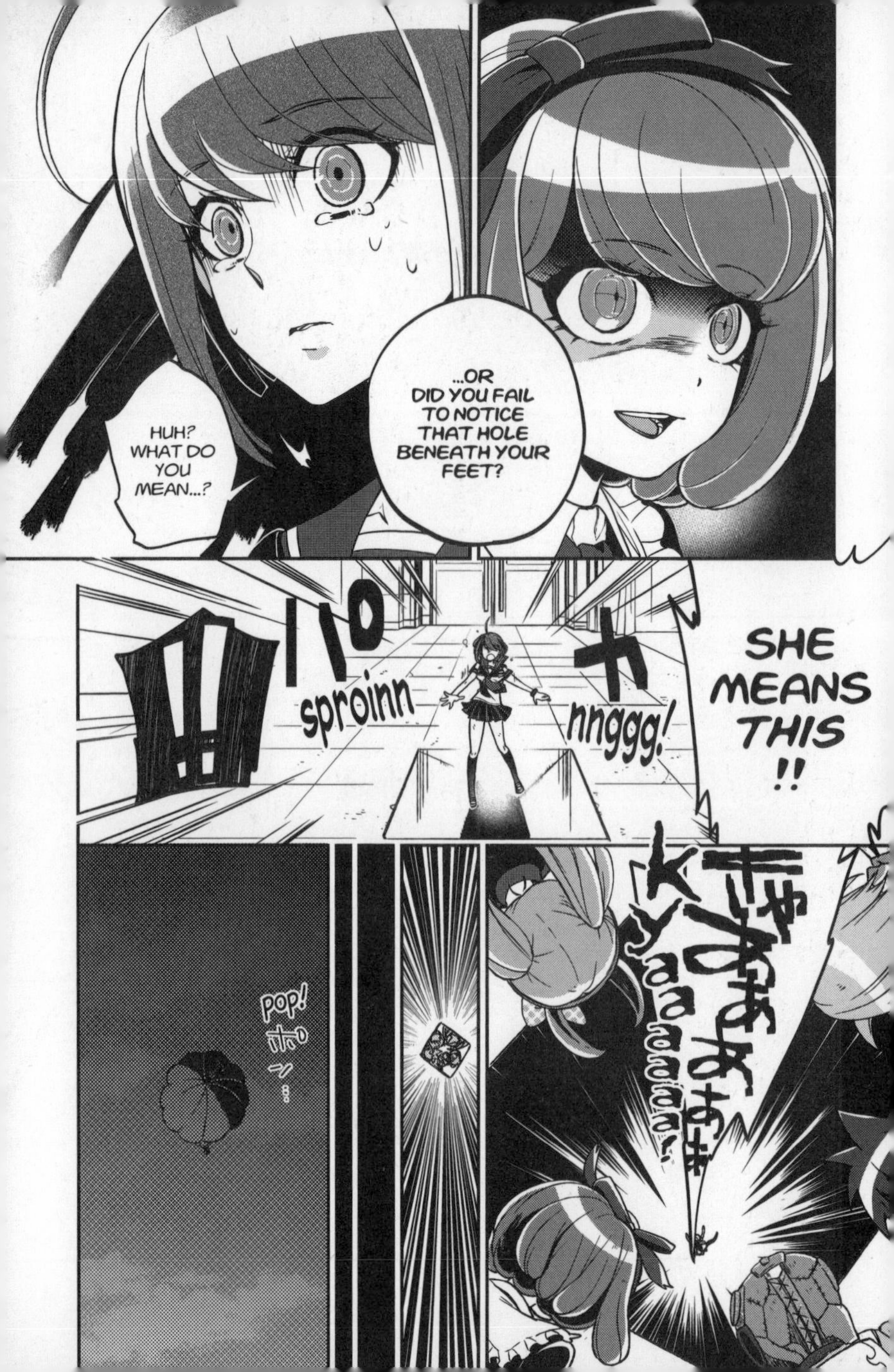
...OR DID YOU FAIL TO NOTICE THAT HOLE BENEATH YOUR FEET?
HUH? WHAT DO YOU MEAN...?
SHE MEANS THIS!!
nnggg!
sproinn
!!
Kyaaaaaaaaa!
pop!

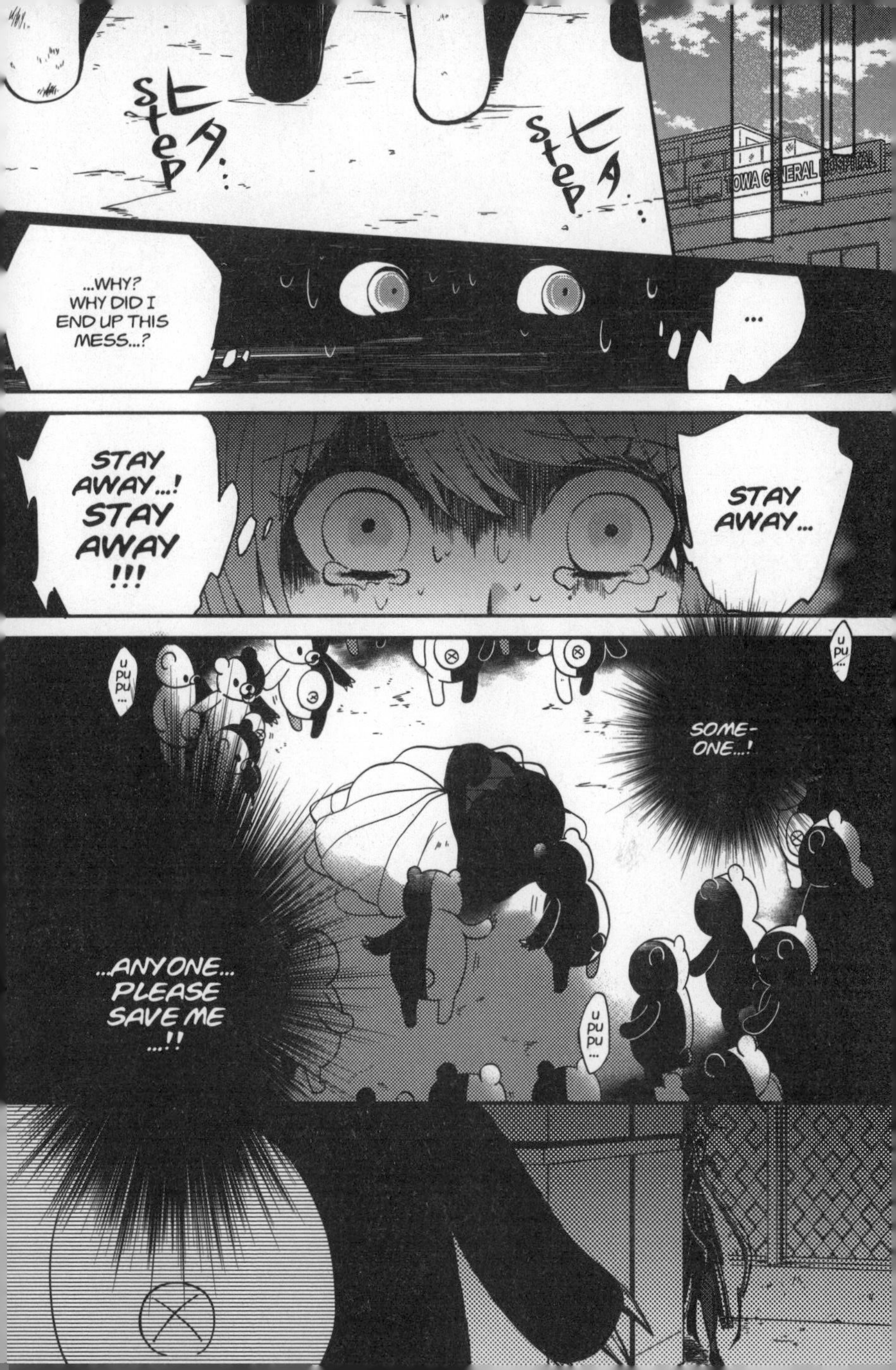

ヒタ step
TOWA GENERAL HOSPITAL
ヒタ step
...
...WHY? WHY DID I END UP THIS MESS...?
STAY AWAY...
STAY AWAY...! STAY AWAY!!!
u pu ...
SOME-ONE...!
u pu pu ...
u pu pu ...
...ANYONE... PLEASE SAVE ME ...!!

Danganronpa Another Episode:
Ultra Despair Girls

WARRIOR OF HOPE:
MASARU DAIMON'S FEAR

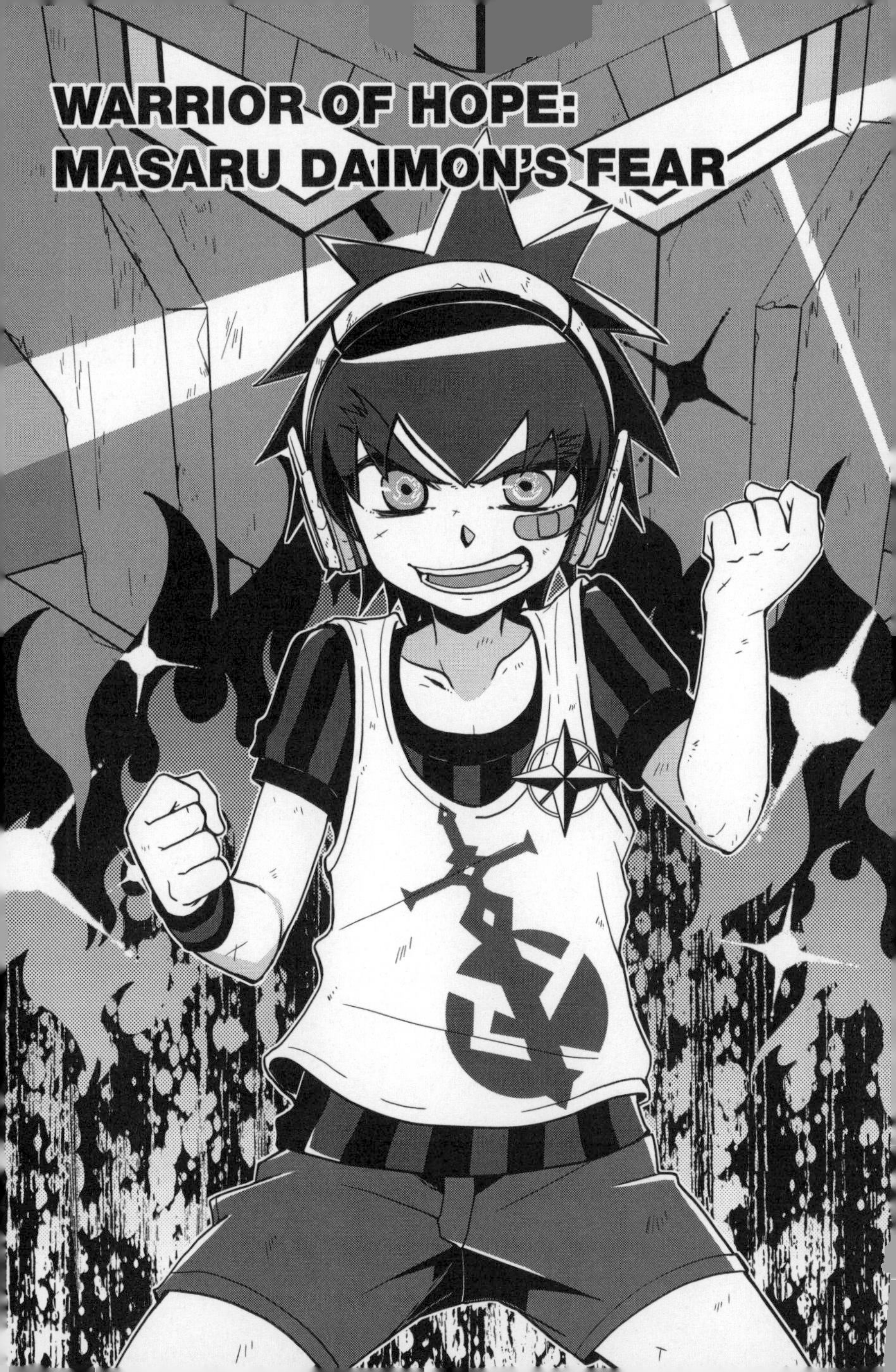

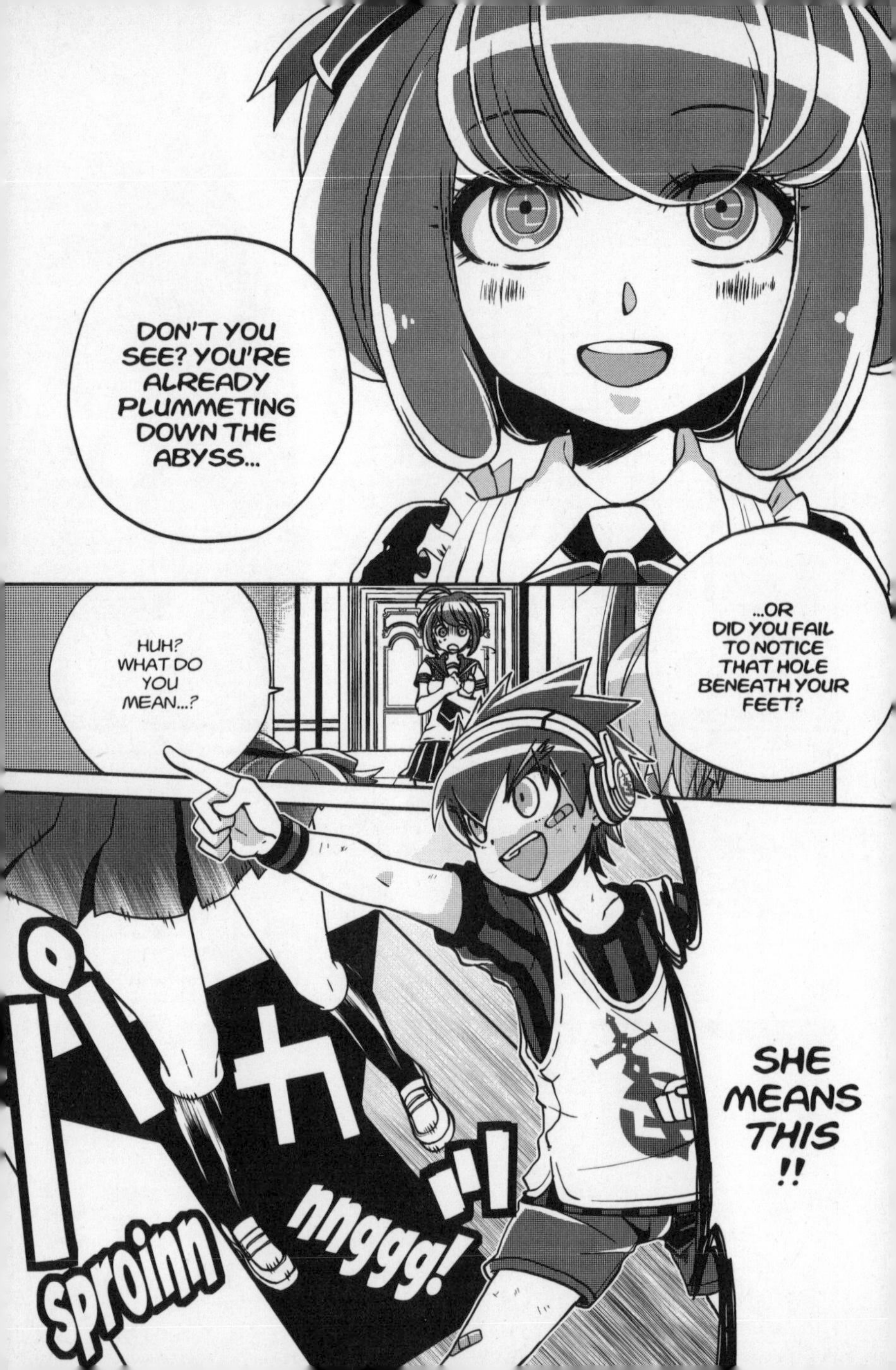
DON'T YOU SEE? YOU'RE ALREADY PLUMMETING DOWN THE ABYSS...
...OR DID YOU FAIL TO NOTICE THAT HOLE BENEATH YOUR FEET?
HUH? WHAT DO YOU MEAN...?
SHE MEANS THIS!!
sproinnnggg!

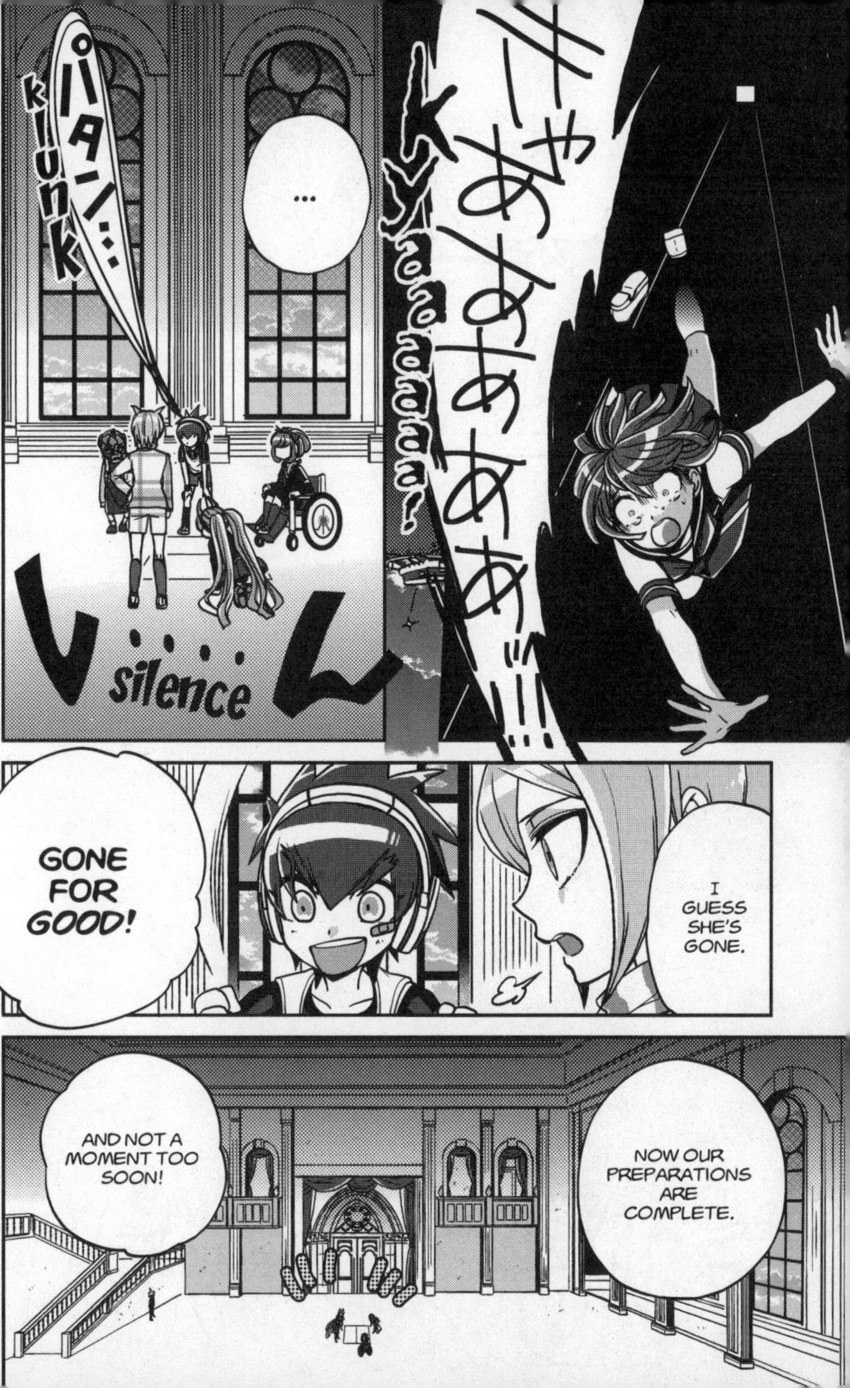

ぎゃあああああ゛!!
Kyaaaaaaaaa!
…
ぴゅーん…
Kiiunk
し…ん
silence
I GUESS SHE'S GONE.
GONE FOR GOOD!
NOW OUR PREPARATIONS ARE COMPLETE.
AND NOT A MOMENT TOO SOON!

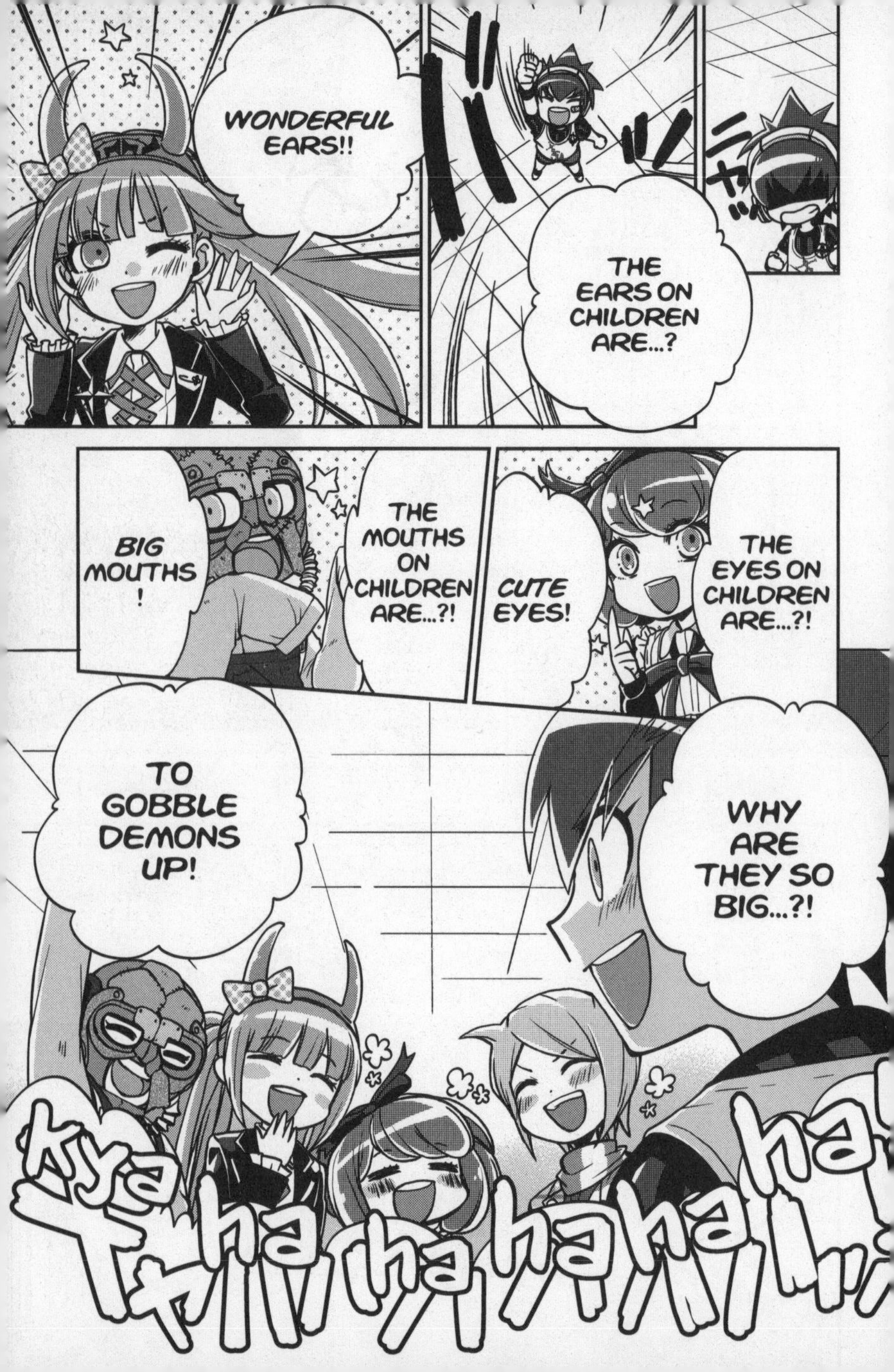

ニヤッ
THE EARS ON CHILDREN ARE...?
WONDERFUL EARS!!
THE EYES ON CHILDREN ARE...?!
CUTE EYES!
THE MOUTHS ON CHILDREN ARE...?!
BIG MOUTHS!
WHY ARE THEY SO BIG...?!
TO GOBBLE DEMONS UP!
Kya ha ha ha ha ha ha!

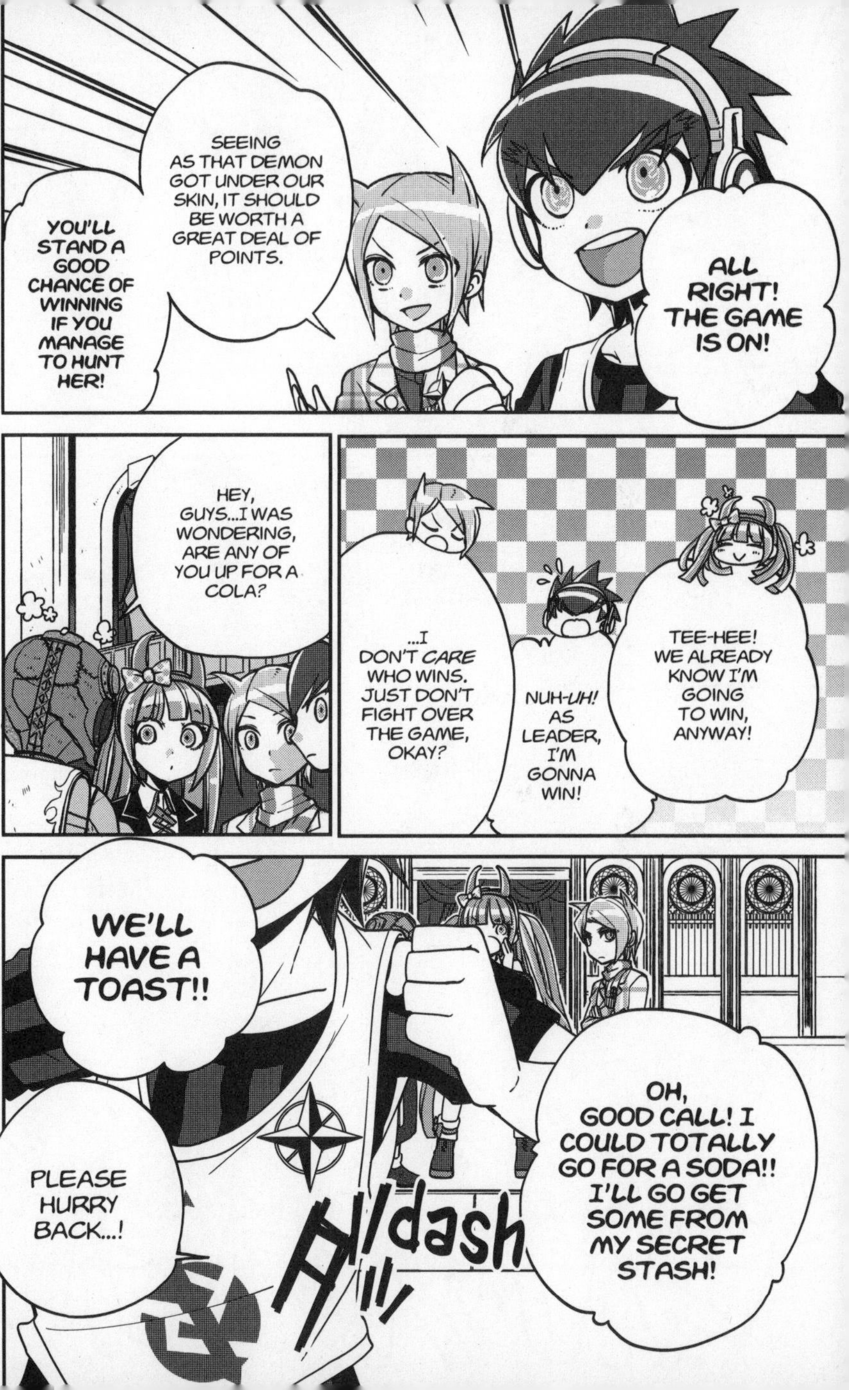
ALL RIGHT! THE GAME IS ON!
SEEING AS THAT DEMON GOT UNDER OUR SKIN, IT SHOULD BE WORTH A GREAT DEAL OF POINTS.
YOU'LL STAND A GOOD CHANCE OF WINNING IF YOU MANAGE TO HUNT HER!
TEE-HEE! WE ALREADY KNOW I'M GOING TO WIN, ANYWAY!
NUH-*UH*! AS LEADER, I'M GONNA WIN!
...I DON'T *CARE* WHO WINS. JUST DON'T FIGHT OVER THE GAME, OKAY?
HEY, GUYS...I WAS WONDERING, ARE ANY OF YOU UP FOR A COLA?
WE'LL HAVE A TOAST!!
OH, GOOD CALL! I COULD TOTALLY GO FOR A SODA!! I'LL GO GET SOME FROM MY SECRET STASH!
dash
PLEASE HURRY BACK...!

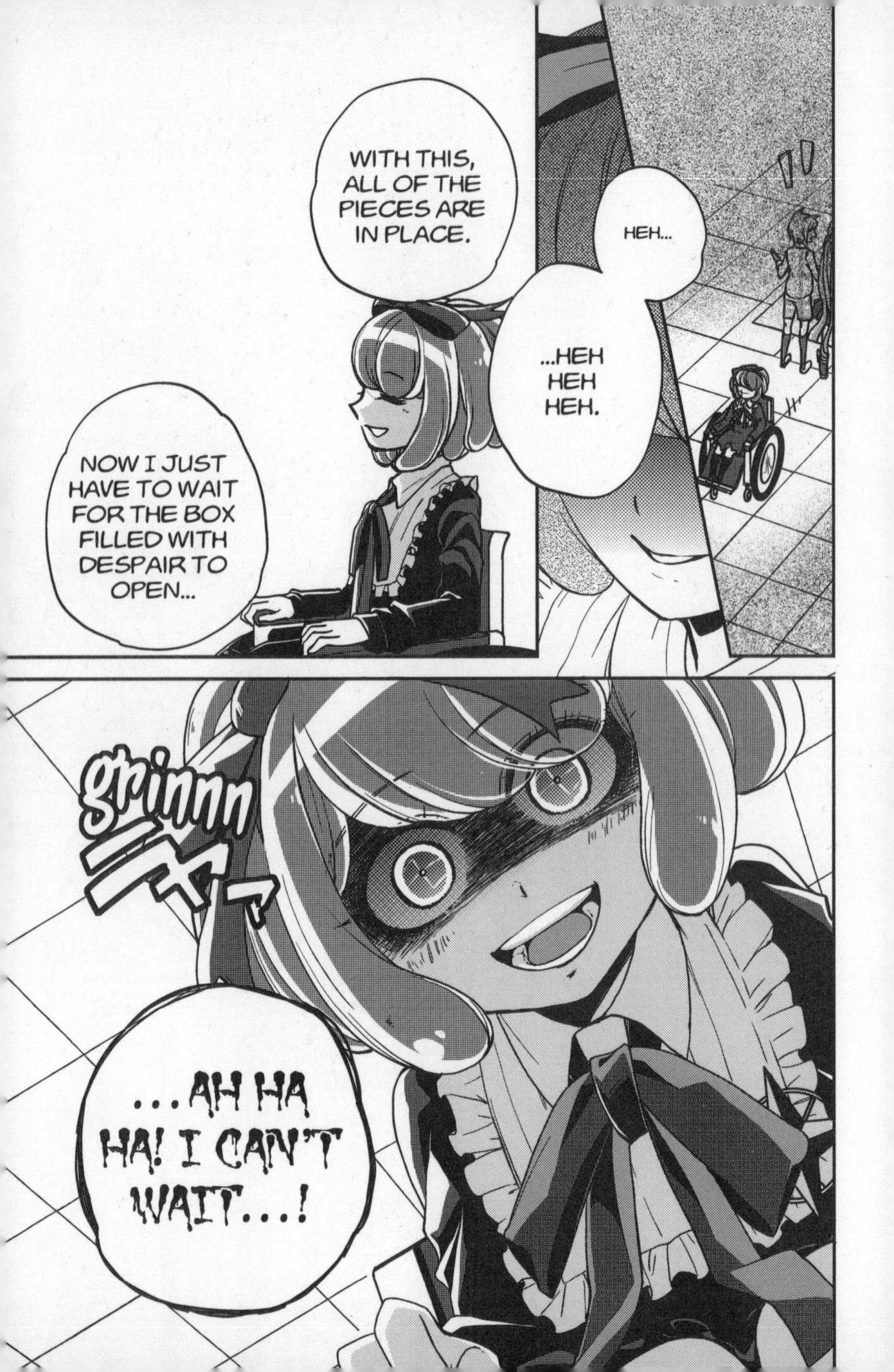
HEH...
...HEH HEH HEH.
WITH THIS, ALL OF THE PIECES ARE IN PLACE.
NOW I JUST HAVE TO WAIT FOR THE BOX FILLED WITH DESPAIR TO OPEN...
grinnn
...AH HA HA! I CAN'T WAIT...!

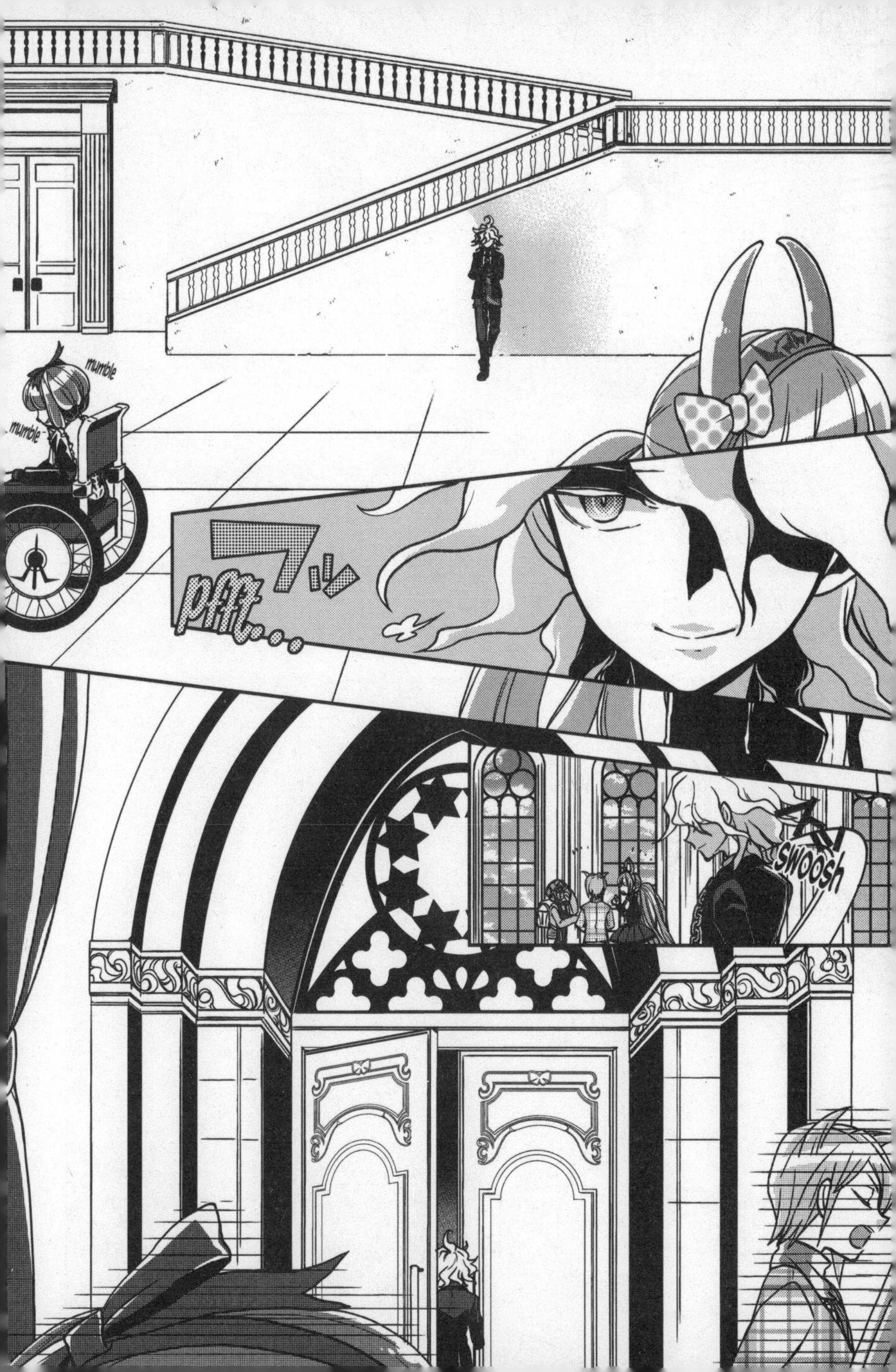

mumble
mumble
pfft...
SWOOSH

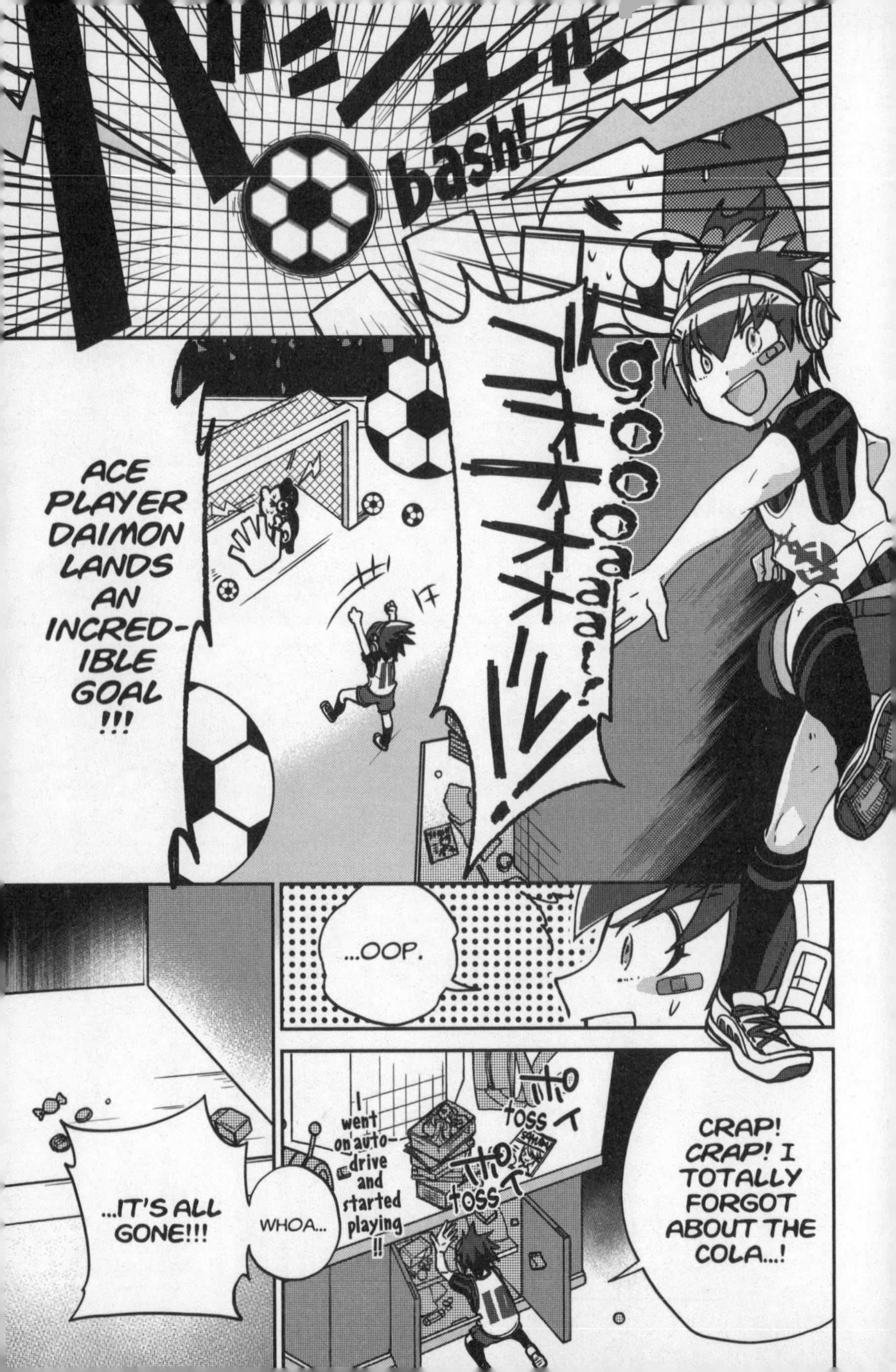
bash!
goooaaa~!
ACE PLAYER DAIMON LANDS AN INCRED-IBLE GOAL!!!
...OOP.
CRAP! CRAP! I TOTALLY FORGOT ABOUT THE COLA...!
toss
toss
I went on auto-drive and started playing!!
WHOA...
...IT'S ALL GONE!!!

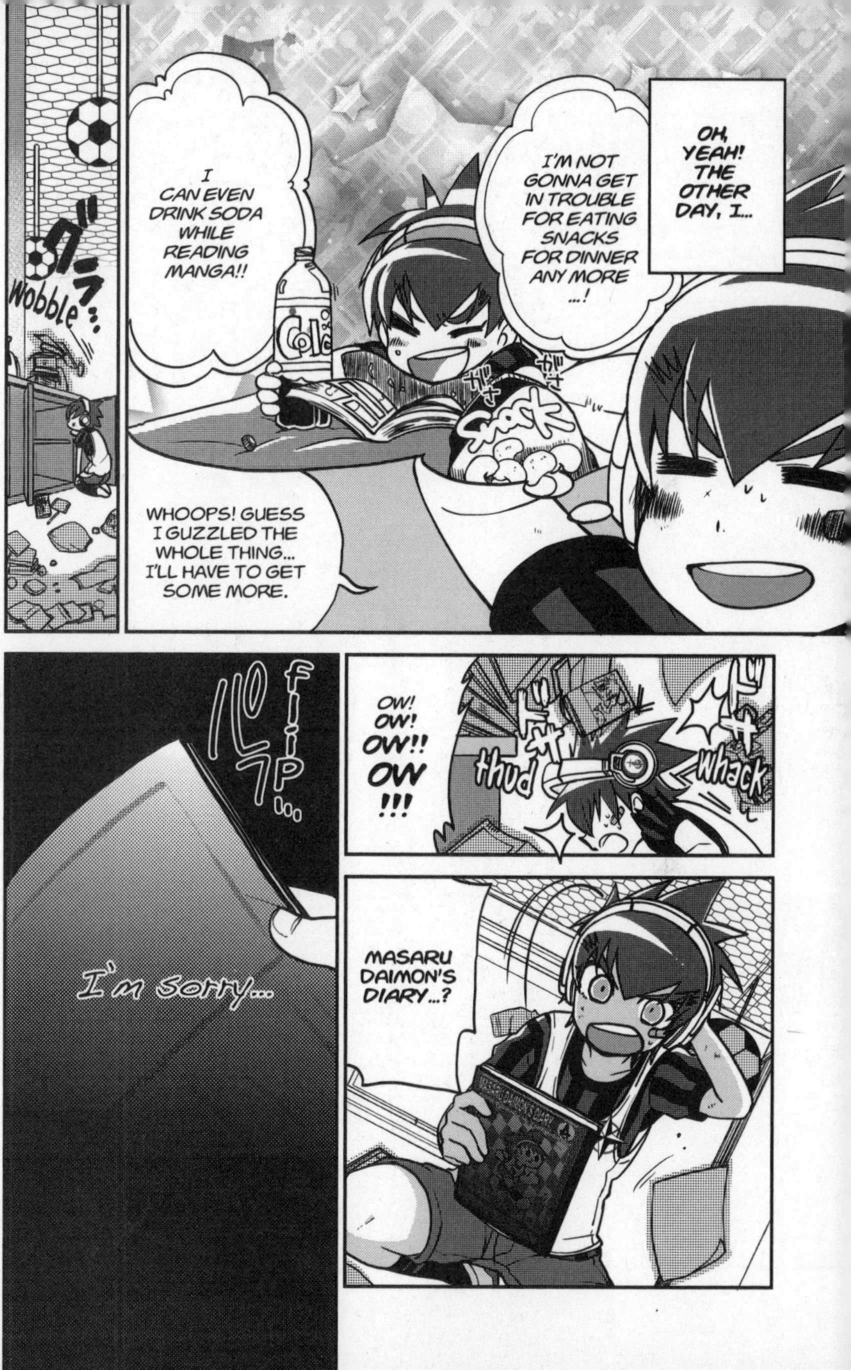
OH, YEAH! THE OTHER DAY, I...
I'M NOT GONNA GET IN TROUBLE FOR EATING SNACKS FOR DINNER ANY MORE ...!
I CAN EVEN DRINK SODA WHILE READING MANGA!!
Cola
Snack
WHOOPS! GUESS I GUZZLED THE WHOLE THING... I'LL HAVE TO GET SOME MORE.
Wobble
whack
thud
OW! OW! OW!! OW !!!
MASARU DAIMON'S DIARY...?
fliiP...
I'm sorry...

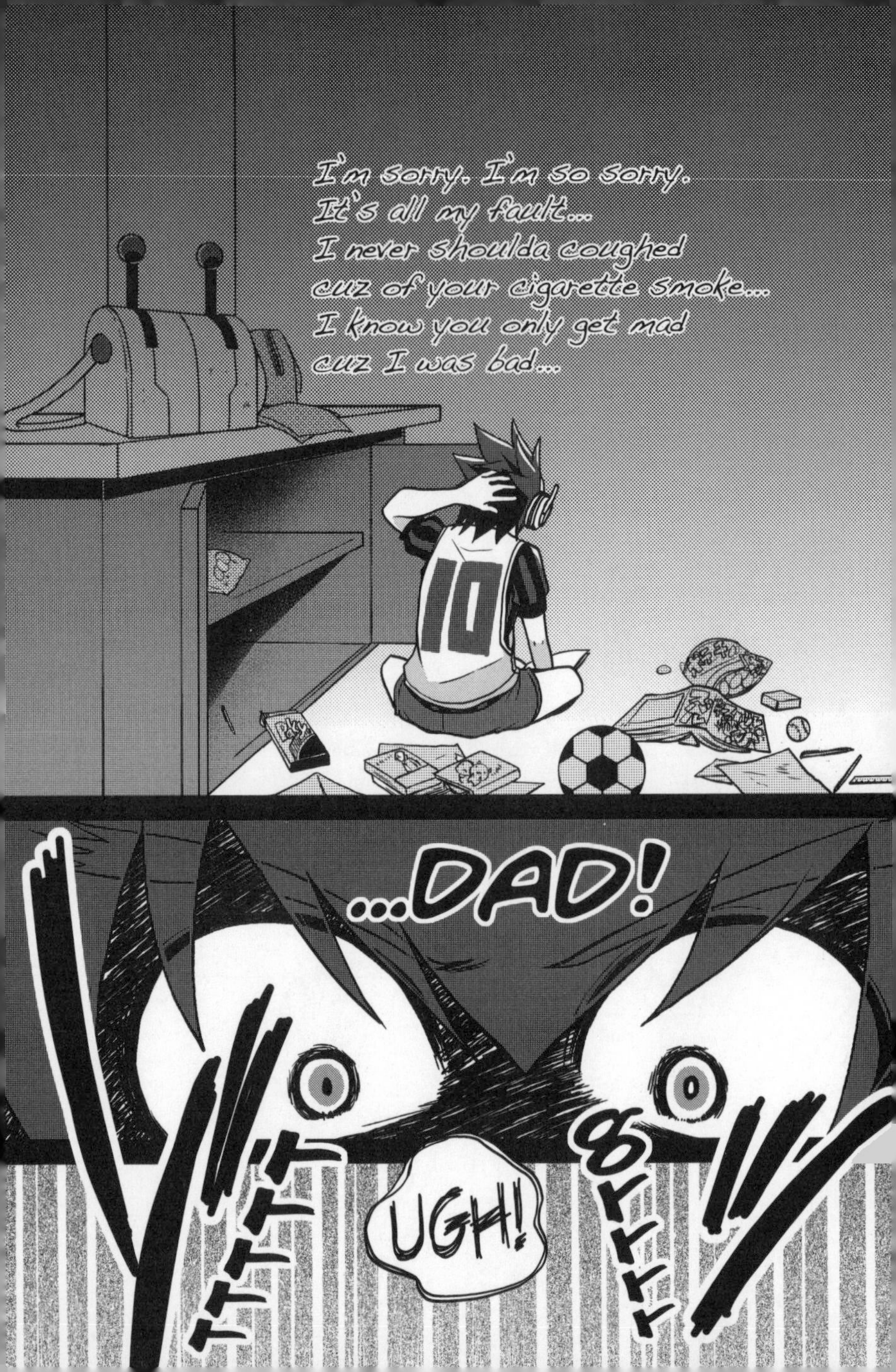
I'm sorry. I'm so sorry.
It's all my fault...
I never shoulda coughed
cuz of your cigarette smoke...
I know you only get mad
cuz I was bad...
...DAD!
UGH!

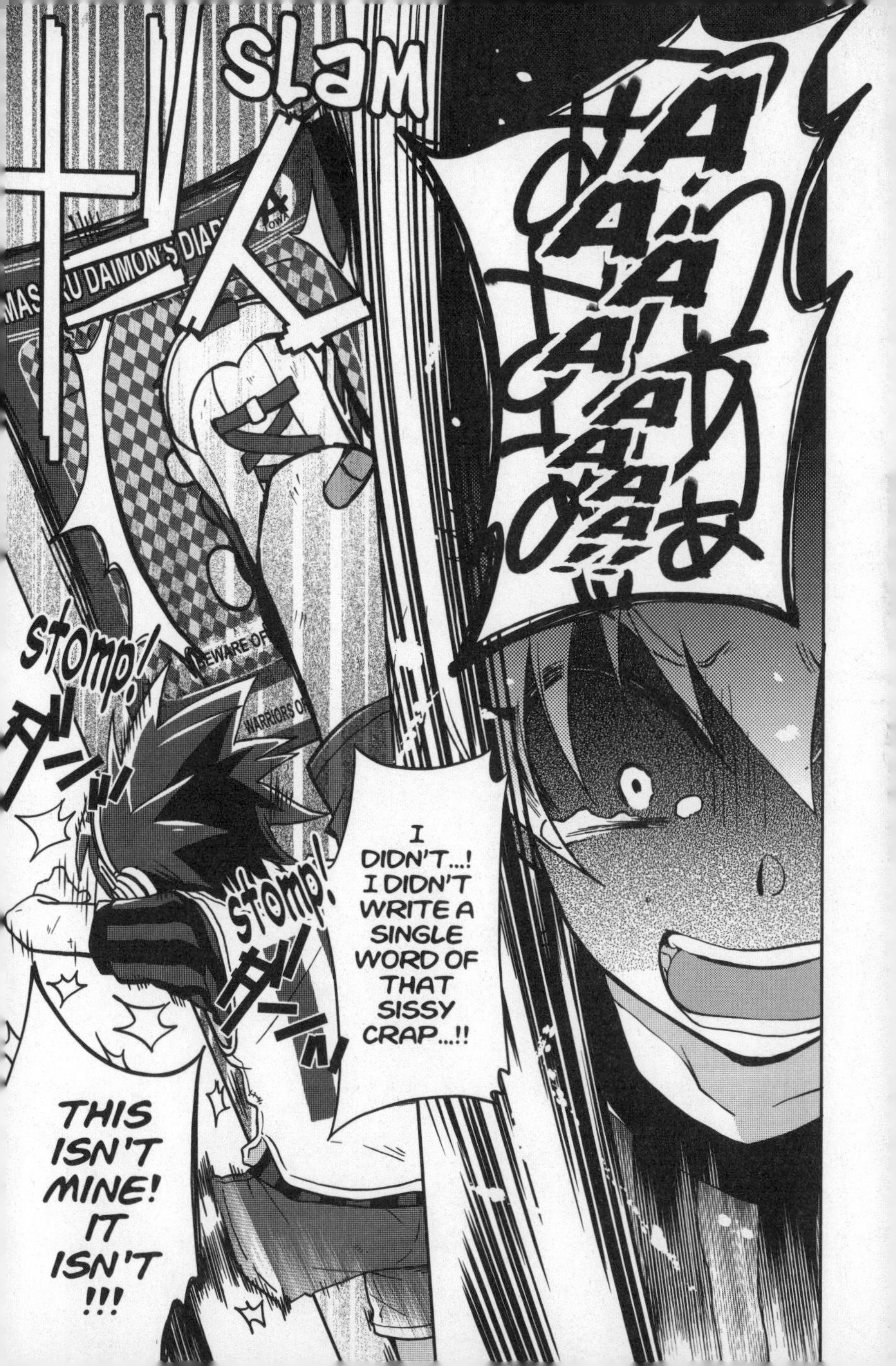
HAAAAAAAA...!!
SLAM
MASARU DAIMON'S DIARY
BEWARE OF
WARRIORS OF
I DIDN'T...! I DIDN'T WRITE A SINGLE WORD OF THAT SISSY CRAP...!!
stomp!
stomp!
THIS ISN'T MINE! IT ISN'T !!!

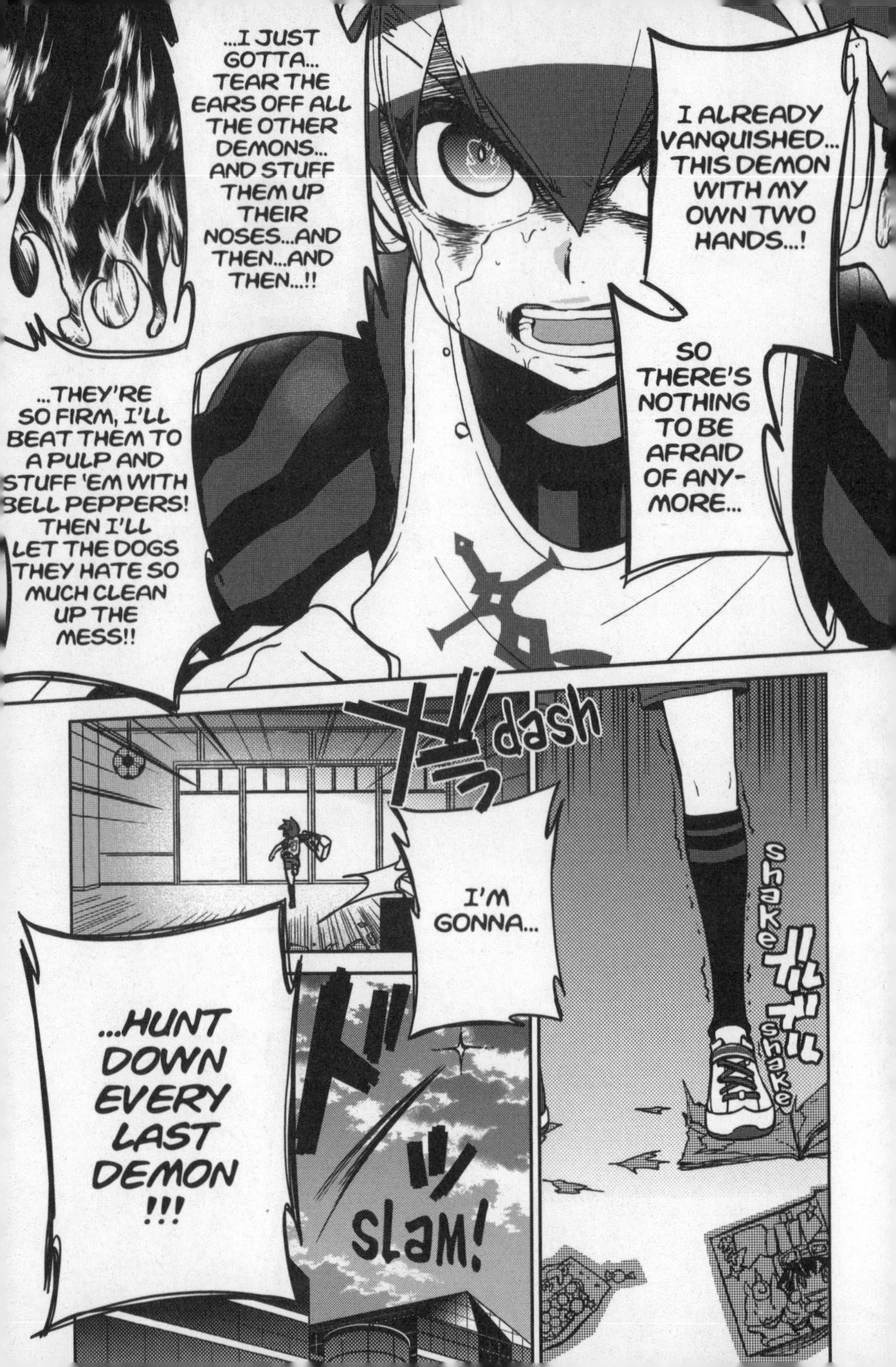
I ALREADY VANQUISHED... THIS DEMON WITH MY OWN TWO HANDS...!
SO THERE'S NOTHING TO BE AFRAID OF ANY-MORE...
...I JUST GOTTA... TEAR THE EARS OFF ALL THE OTHER DEMONS... AND STUFF THEM UP THEIR NOSES...AND THEN...AND THEN...!!
...THEY'RE SO FIRM, I'LL BEAT THEM TO A PULP AND STUFF 'EM WITH BELL PEPPERS! THEN I'LL LET THE DOGS THEY HATE SO MUCH CLEAN UP THE MESS!!
shake shake
dash
I'M GONNA...
...HUNT DOWN EVERY LAST DEMON!!!
SLAM!

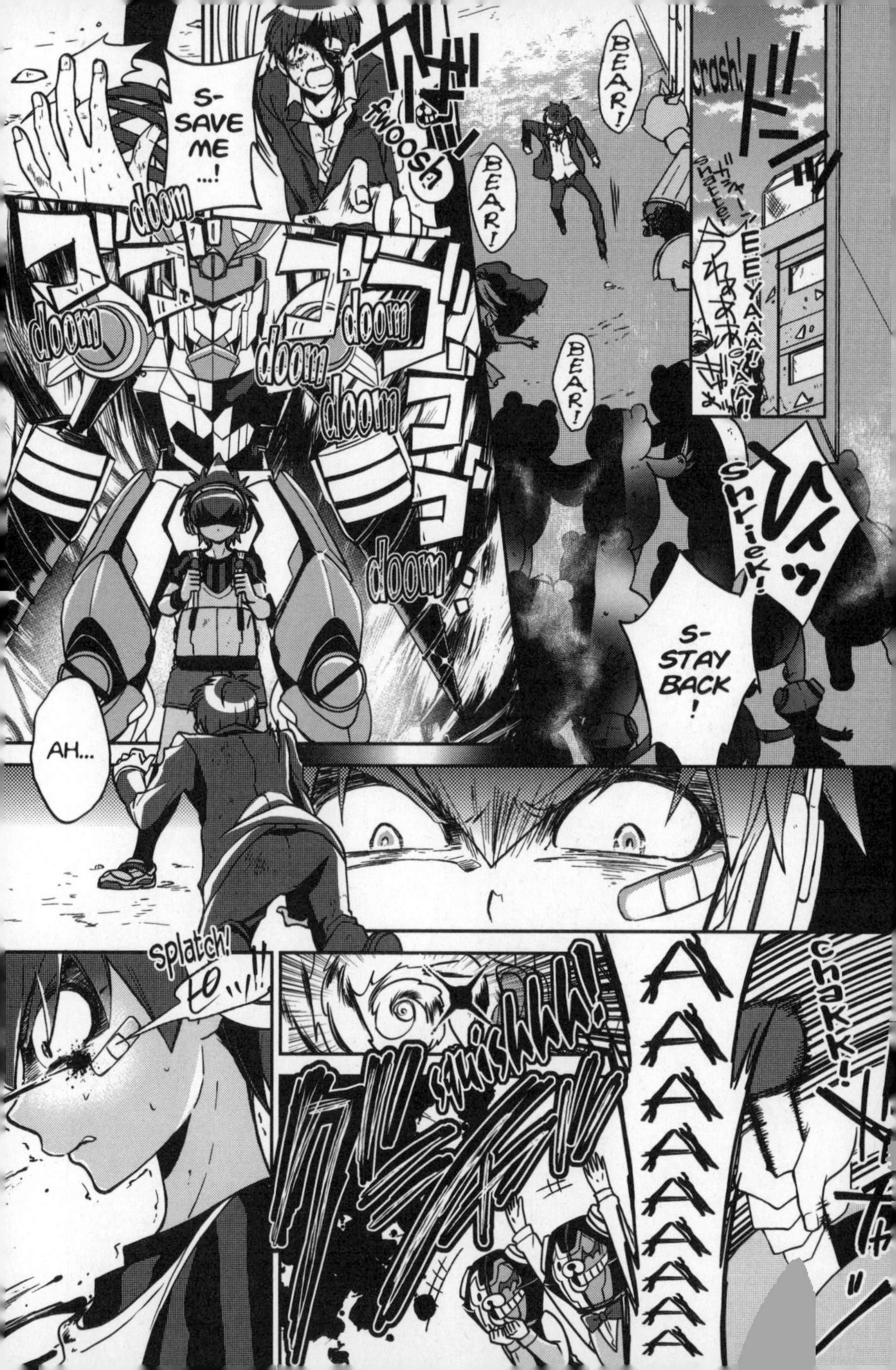
crash!
shatter!
EEEYAAAA!
NGYAAA!
shriek!
S-STAY BACK!
BEAR!
BEAR!
BEAR!
fwoosh
S-SAVE ME...!
doom
doom
doom
doom
doom
doom
AH...
chakk!
AAAAAAAAAA
squishhh!
splatch!

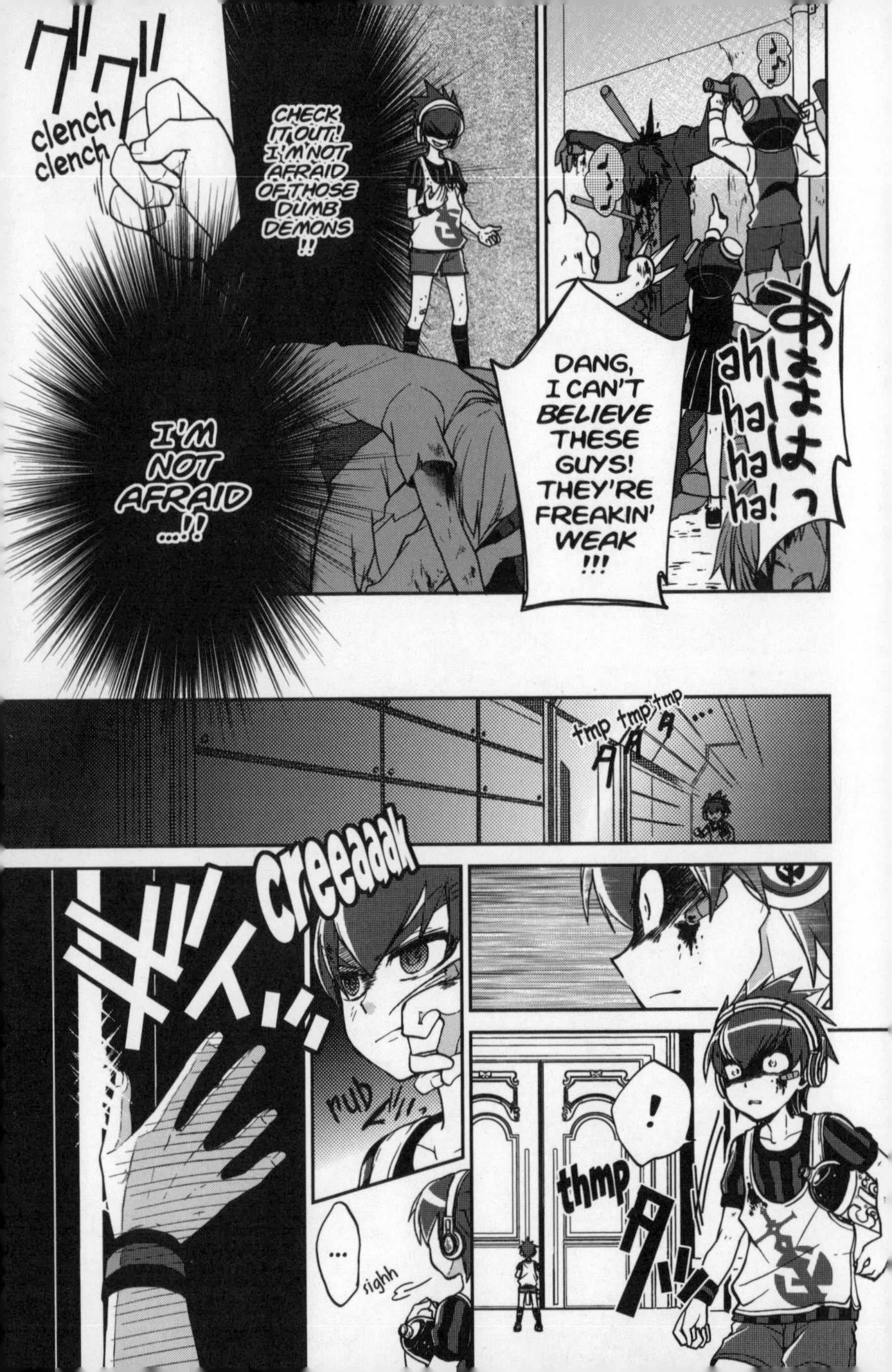
あははっ
ah ha ha ha!
DANG, I CAN'T BELIEVE THESE GUYS! THEY'RE FREAKIN' WEAK!!!
CHECK IT OUT! I'M NOT AFRAID OF THOSE DUMB DEMONS!!
I'M NOT AFRAID ...!!
clench clench
tmp tmp tmp
タタタ...
!
thmp
タッ
creeaaak
ギィ...
rub
...
sighh

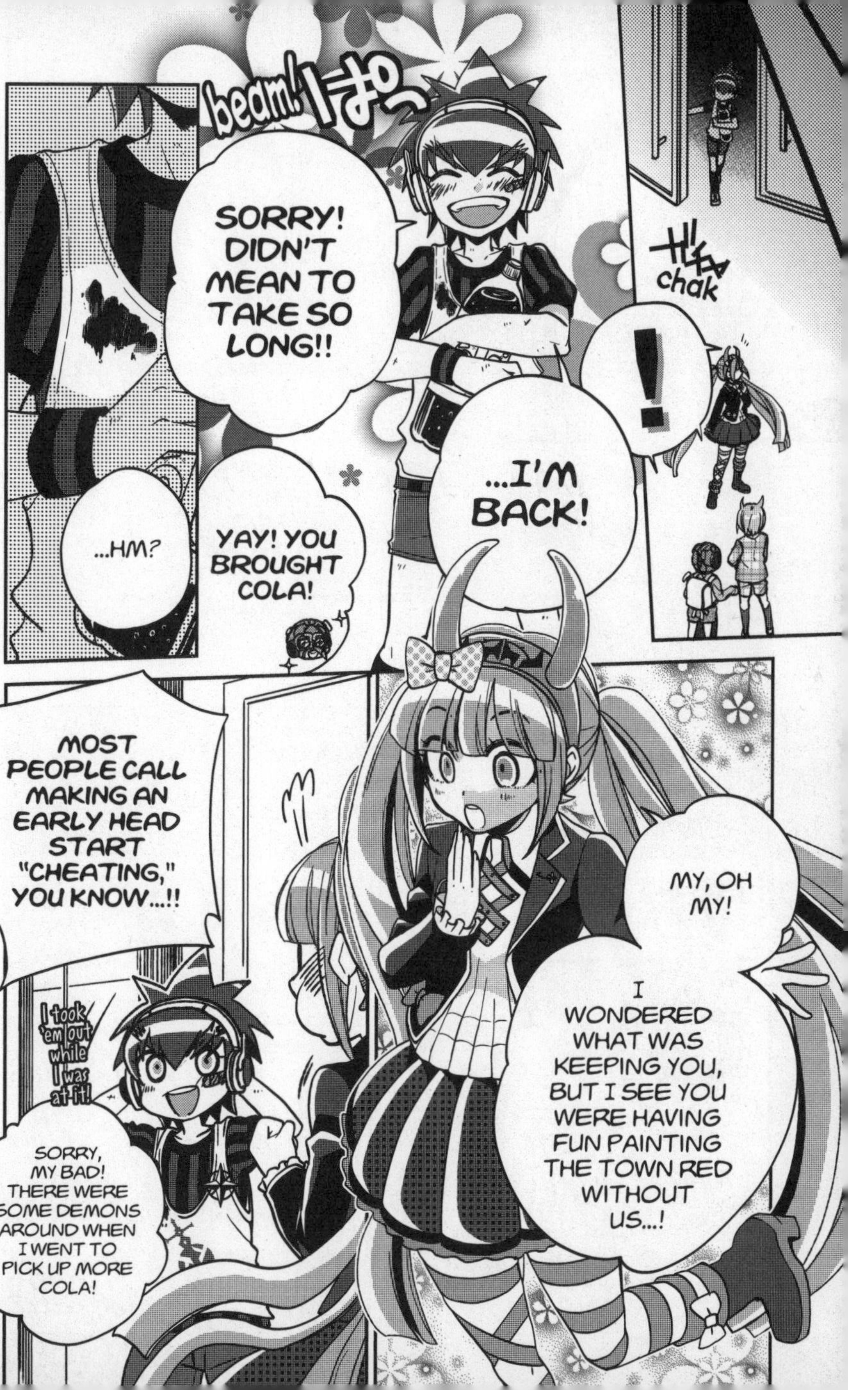
chak
!
...I'M BACK!
beam!
SORRY! DIDN'T MEAN TO TAKE SO LONG!!
YAY! YOU BROUGHT COLA!
...HM?
MY, OH MY!
I WONDERED WHAT WAS KEEPING YOU, BUT I SEE YOU WERE HAVING FUN PAINTING THE TOWN RED WITHOUT US...!
MOST PEOPLE CALL MAKING AN EARLY HEAD START "CHEATING," YOU KNOW...!!
I took 'em out while I was at it!
SORRY, MY BAD! THERE WERE SOME DEMONS AROUND WHEN I WENT TO PICK UP MORE COLA!

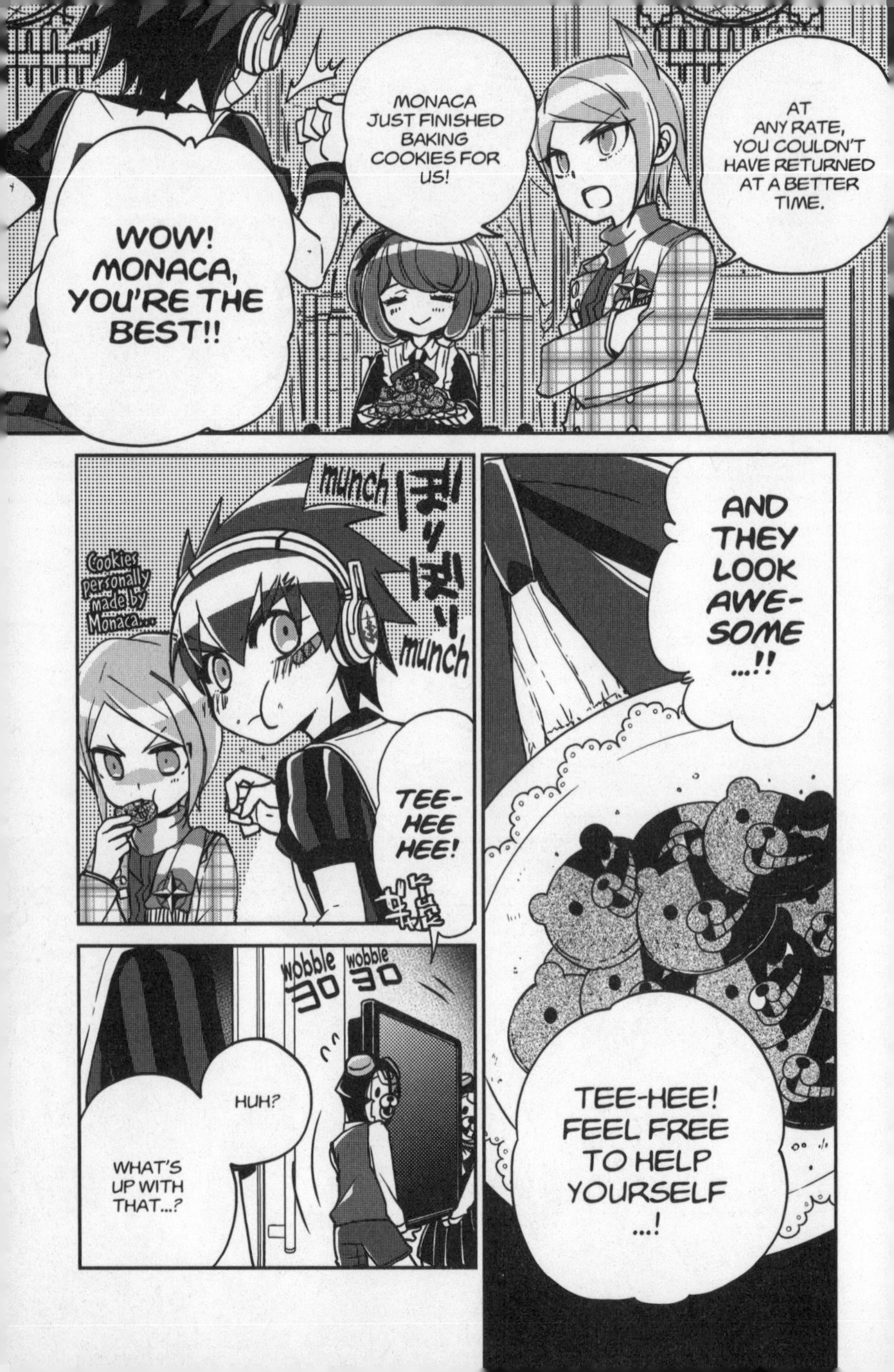
AT ANY RATE, YOU COULDN'T HAVE RETURNED AT A BETTER TIME.
MONACA JUST FINISHED BAKING COOKIES FOR US!
WOW! MONACA, YOU'RE THE BEST!!
AND THEY LOOK AWESOME ...!!
TEE-HEE! FEEL FREE TO HELP YOURSELF ...!
munch
munch
Cookies personally made by Monaca...
TEE-HEE HEE!
wobble
wobble
HUH?
WHAT'S UP WITH THAT...?

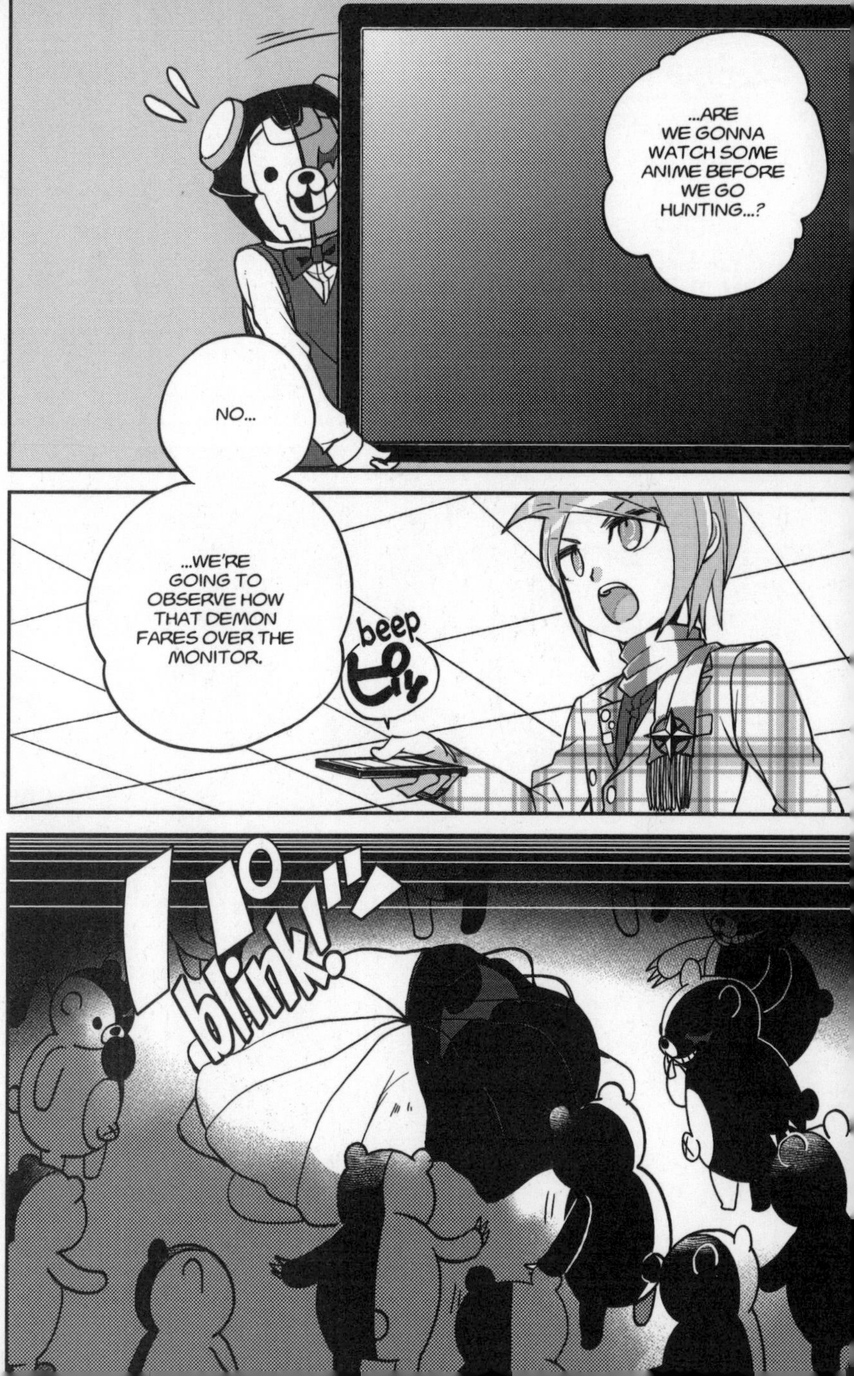
...ARE WE GONNA WATCH SOME ANIME BEFORE WE GO HUNTING...?
NO...
...WE'RE GOING TO OBSERVE HOW THAT DEMON FARES OVER THE MONITOR.
beep
blink!

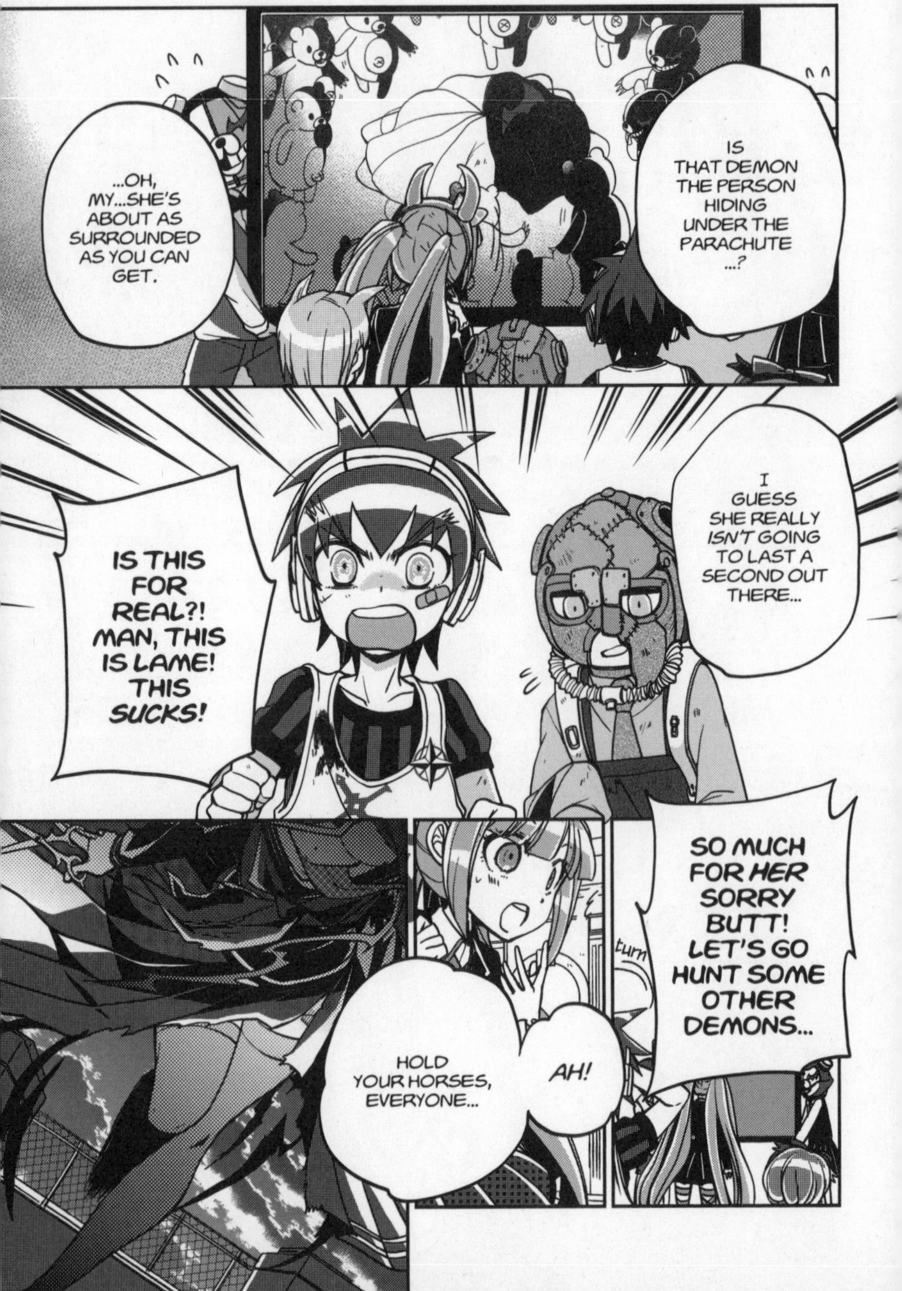
IS THAT DEMON THE PERSON HIDING UNDER THE PARACHUTE ...?
...OH, MY...SHE'S ABOUT AS SURROUNDED AS YOU CAN GET.
I GUESS SHE REALLY *ISN'T* GOING TO LAST A SECOND OUT THERE...
IS THIS FOR REAL?! MAN, THIS IS LAME! THIS *SUCKS!*
SO MUCH FOR *HER* SORRY BUTT! LET'S GO HUNT SOME OTHER DEMONS...
turn
AH!
HOLD YOUR HORSES, EVERYONE...

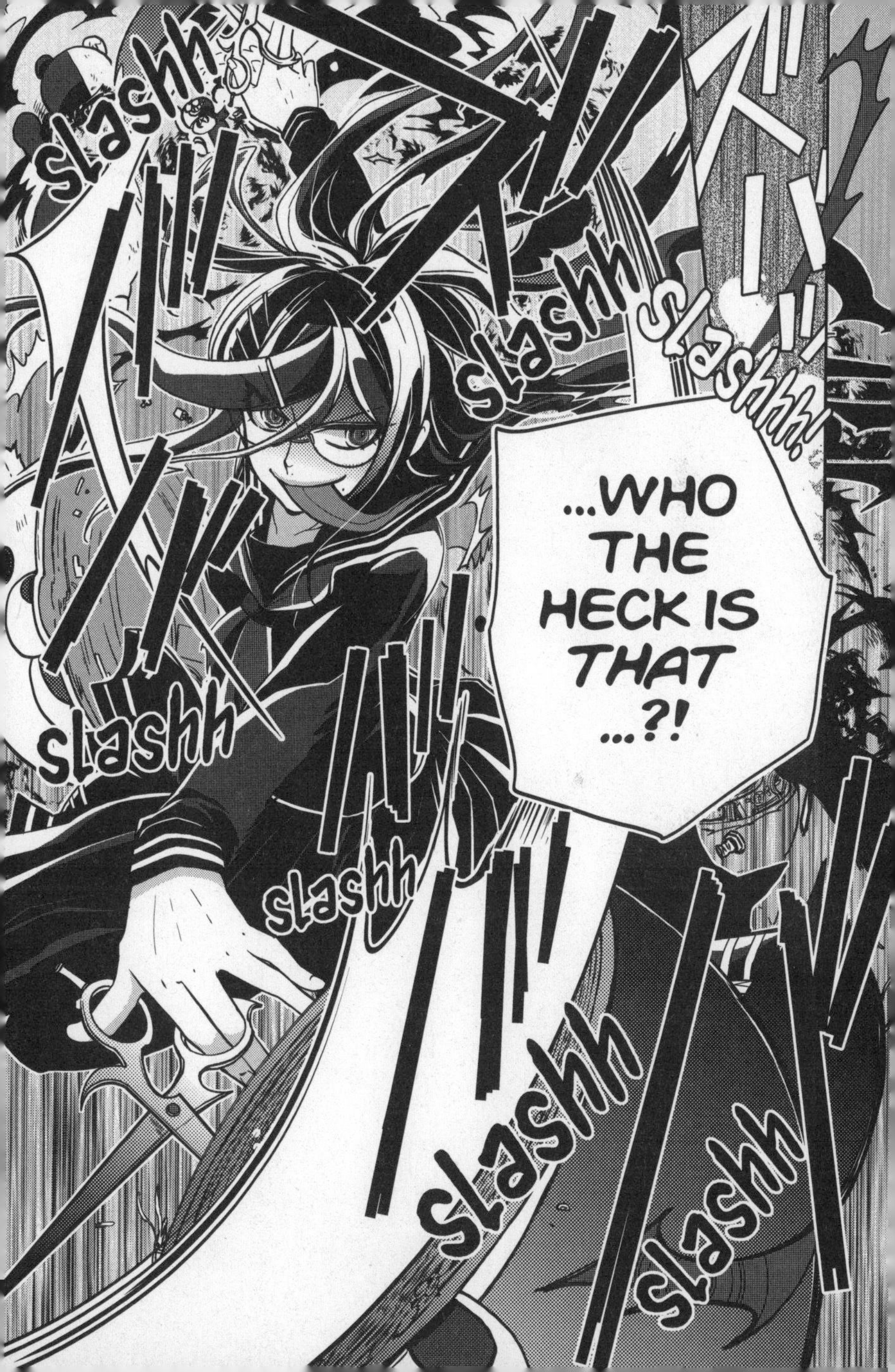
slashh!
slashh
slashh
slashh
...WHO THE HECK IS THAT ...?!
slashh
slashh
slashh
slashh

Danganronpa Another Episode:
Ultra Despair Girls

Danganronpa Another Episode:
Ultra Despair Girls

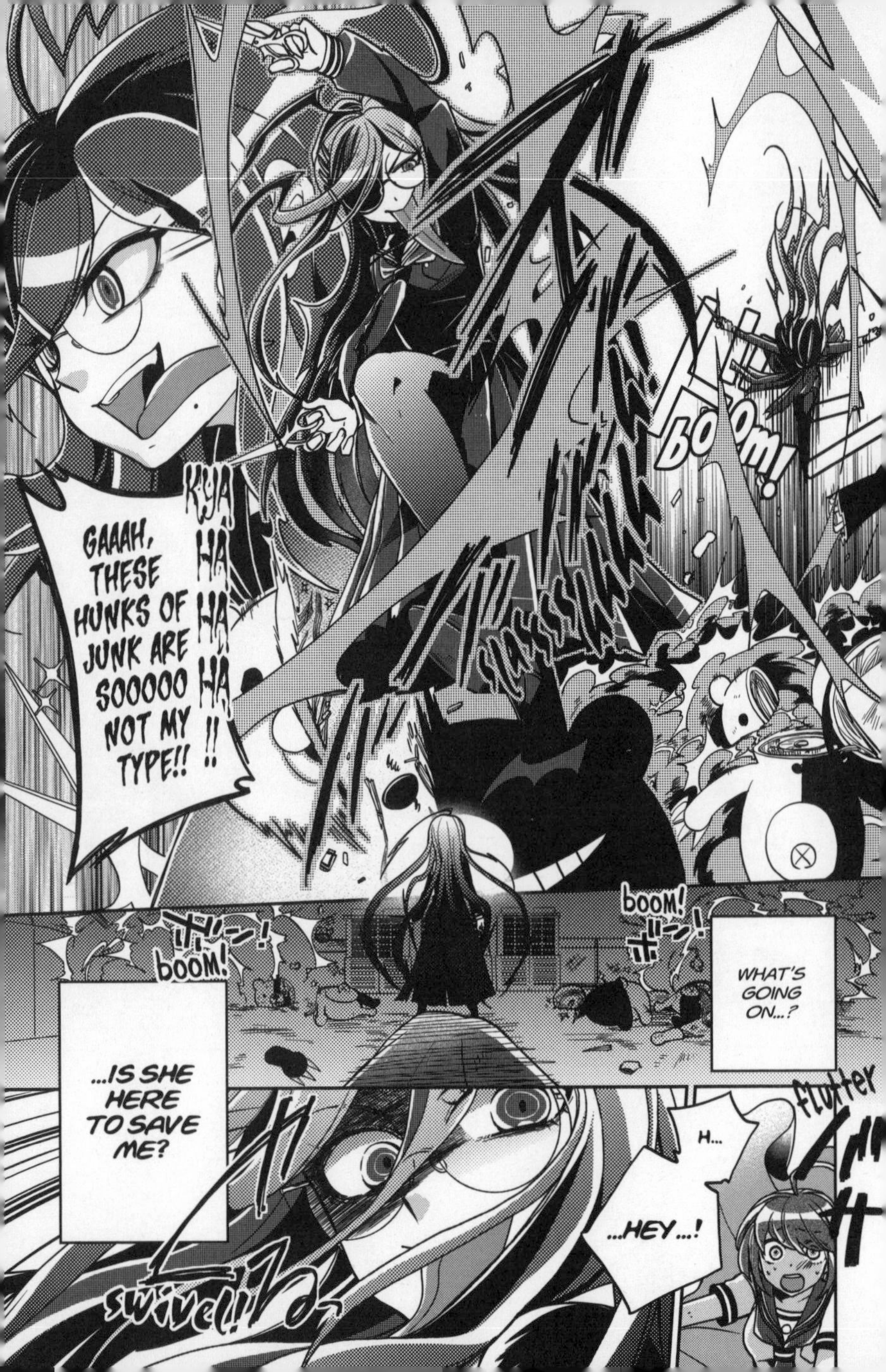
boom!
KYA HA HA HA !!
GAAAH, THESE HUNKS OF JUNK ARE SOOOOO NOT MY TYPE!!
boom!
WHAT'S GOING ON...?
boom!
...IS SHE HERE TO SAVE ME?
flutter
H...
...HEY...!
swivel

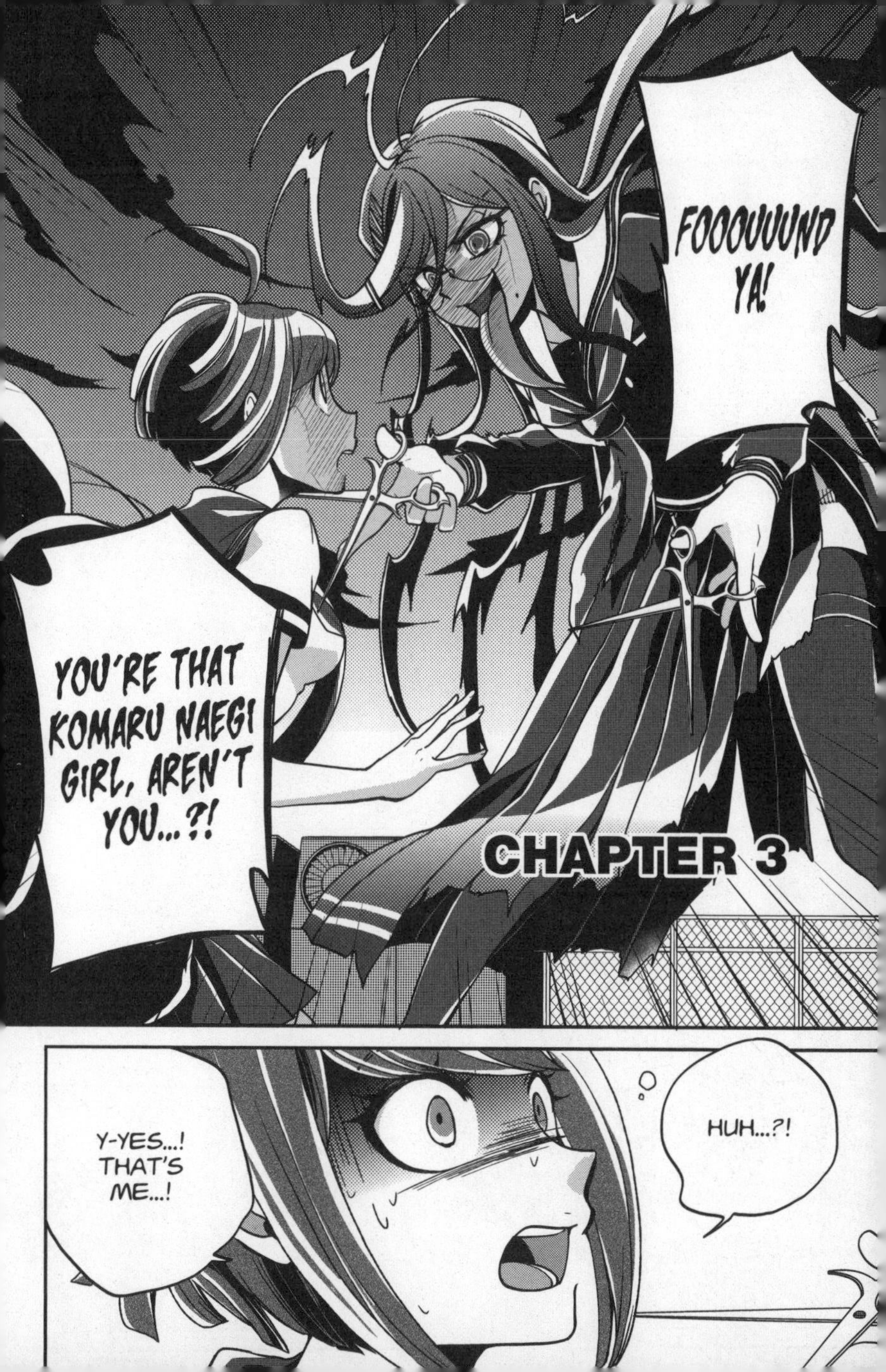
FOOOUUUND YA!
YOU'RE THAT KOMARU NAEGI GIRL, AREN'T YOU...?!
CHAPTER 3
HUH...?!
Y-YES...! THAT'S ME...!

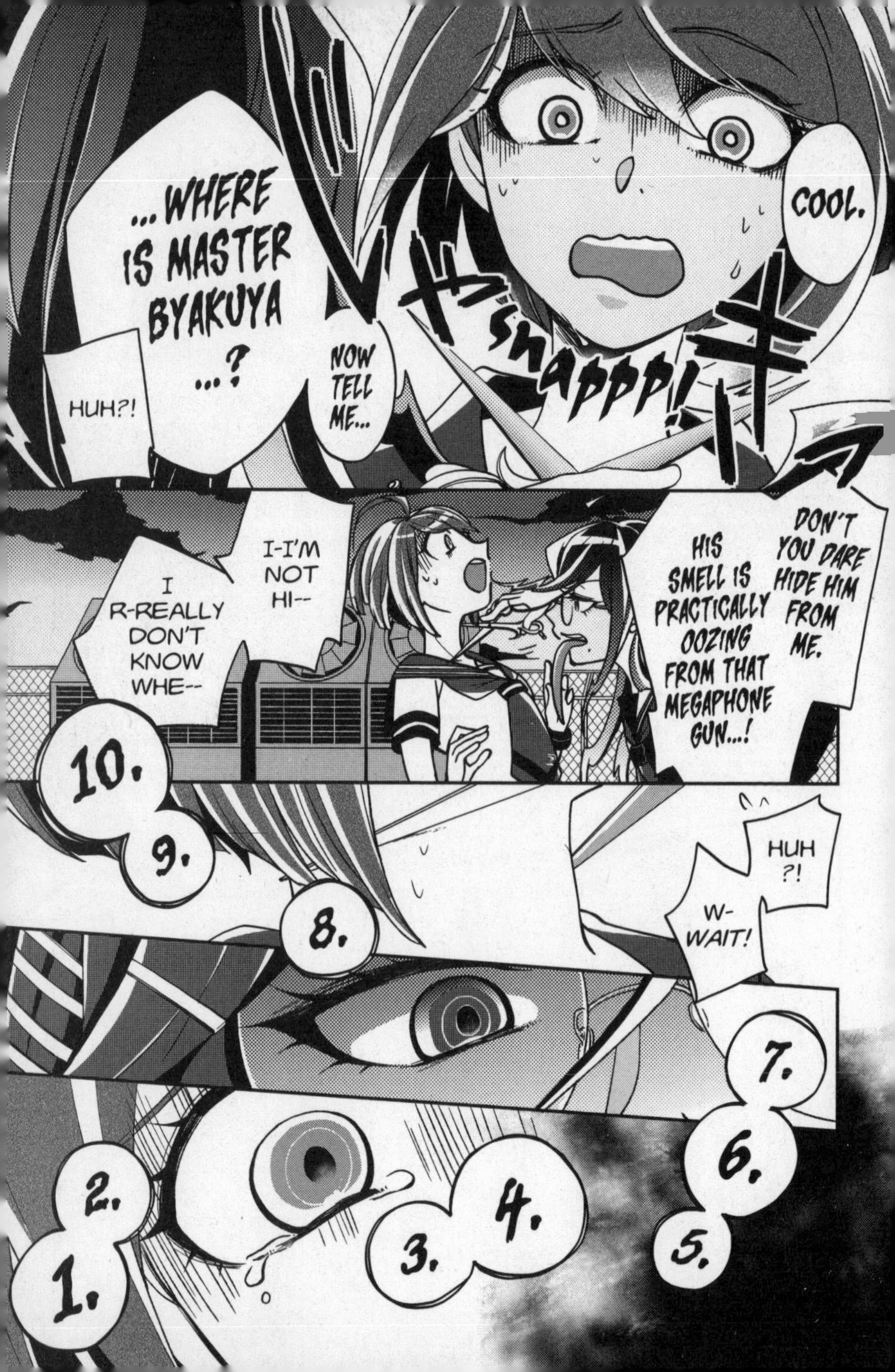
COOL.
SNAPPP!!
NOW TELL ME...
...WHERE IS MASTER BYAKUYA ...?
HUH?!
DON'T YOU DARE HIDE HIM FROM ME.
HIS SMELL IS PRACTICALLY OOZING FROM THAT MEGAPHONE GUN...!
I-I'M NOT HI--
I R-REALLY DON'T KNOW WHE--
10.
HUH ?!
W- WAIT!
9.
8.
7.
6.
5.
4.
3.
2.
1.

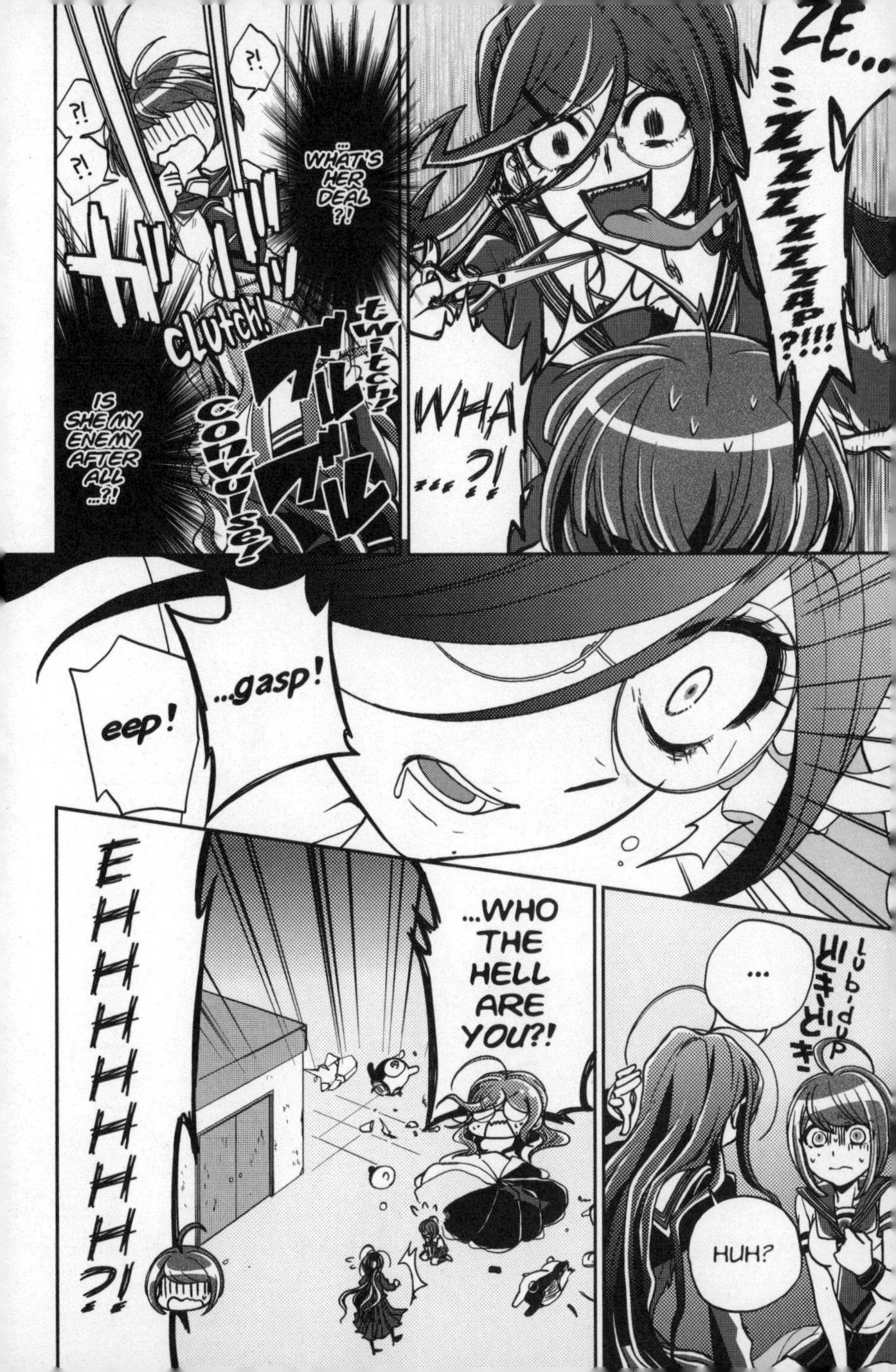
ZE...ZZZZZZZAP?!!!
WHA...?!
?!
?!
?!
?!
...WHAT'S HER DEAL?!
CLUTCH!
twitch!
CONVULSE!
IS SHE MY ENEMY AFTER ALL...?!
...gasp!
eep!
...
lub-dup
どきどき
HUH?
...WHO THE HELL ARE YOU?!
EHHHHHHHHHH?!

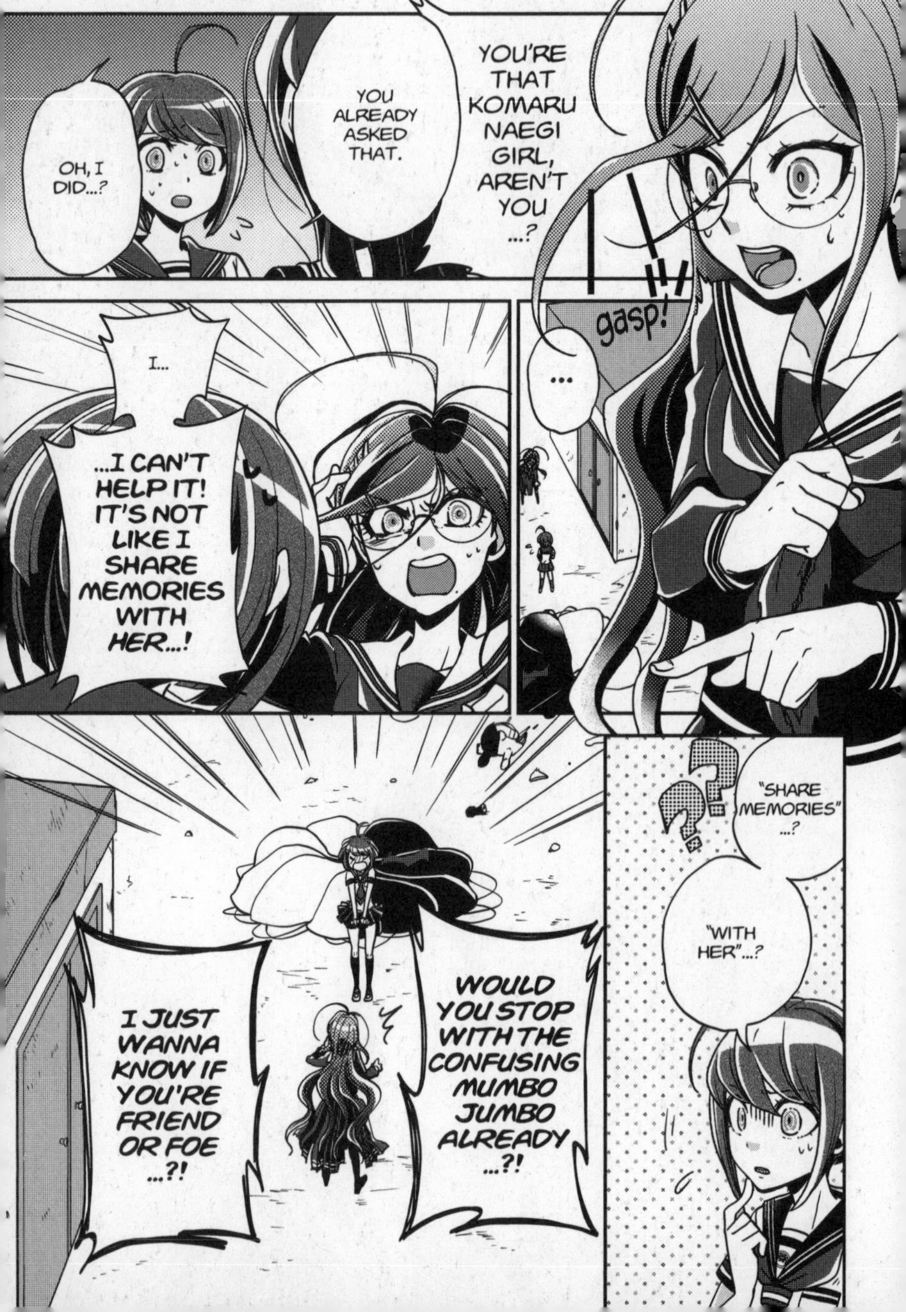
YOU'RE THAT KOMARU NAEGI GIRL, AREN'T YOU ...?
gasp!
YOU ALREADY ASKED THAT.
OH, I DID...?
...
I...
...I CAN'T HELP IT! IT'S NOT LIKE I SHARE MEMORIES WITH HER...!
"SHARE MEMORIES" ...?
"WITH HER"...?
WOULD YOU STOP WITH THE CONFUSING MUMBO JUMBO ALREADY ...?!
I JUST WANNA KNOW IF YOU'RE FRIEND OR FOE ...?!

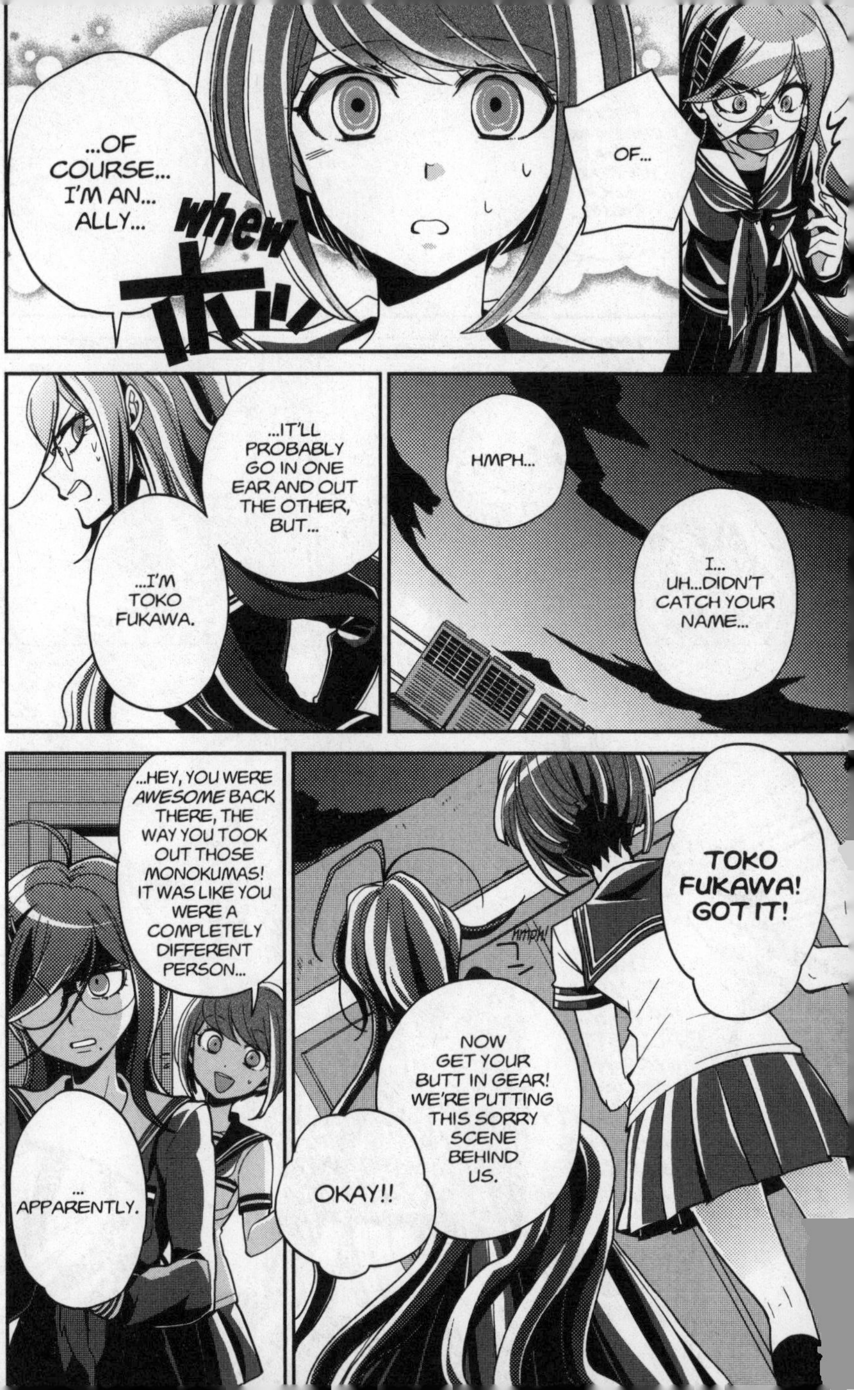
OF...
...OF COURSE... I'M AN... ALLY...
whew
ホッ
HMPH...
I... UH...DIDN'T CATCH YOUR NAME...
...IT'LL PROBABLY GO IN ONE EAR AND OUT THE OTHER, BUT...
...I'M TOKO FUKAWA.
TOKO FUKAWA! GOT IT!
hmph!
NOW GET YOUR BUTT IN GEAR! WE'RE PUTTING THIS SORRY SCENE BEHIND US.
OKAY!!
...HEY, YOU WERE *AWESOME* BACK THERE, THE WAY YOU TOOK OUT THOSE MONOKUMAS! IT WAS LIKE YOU WERE A COMPLETELY DIFFERENT PERSON...
... APPARENTLY.

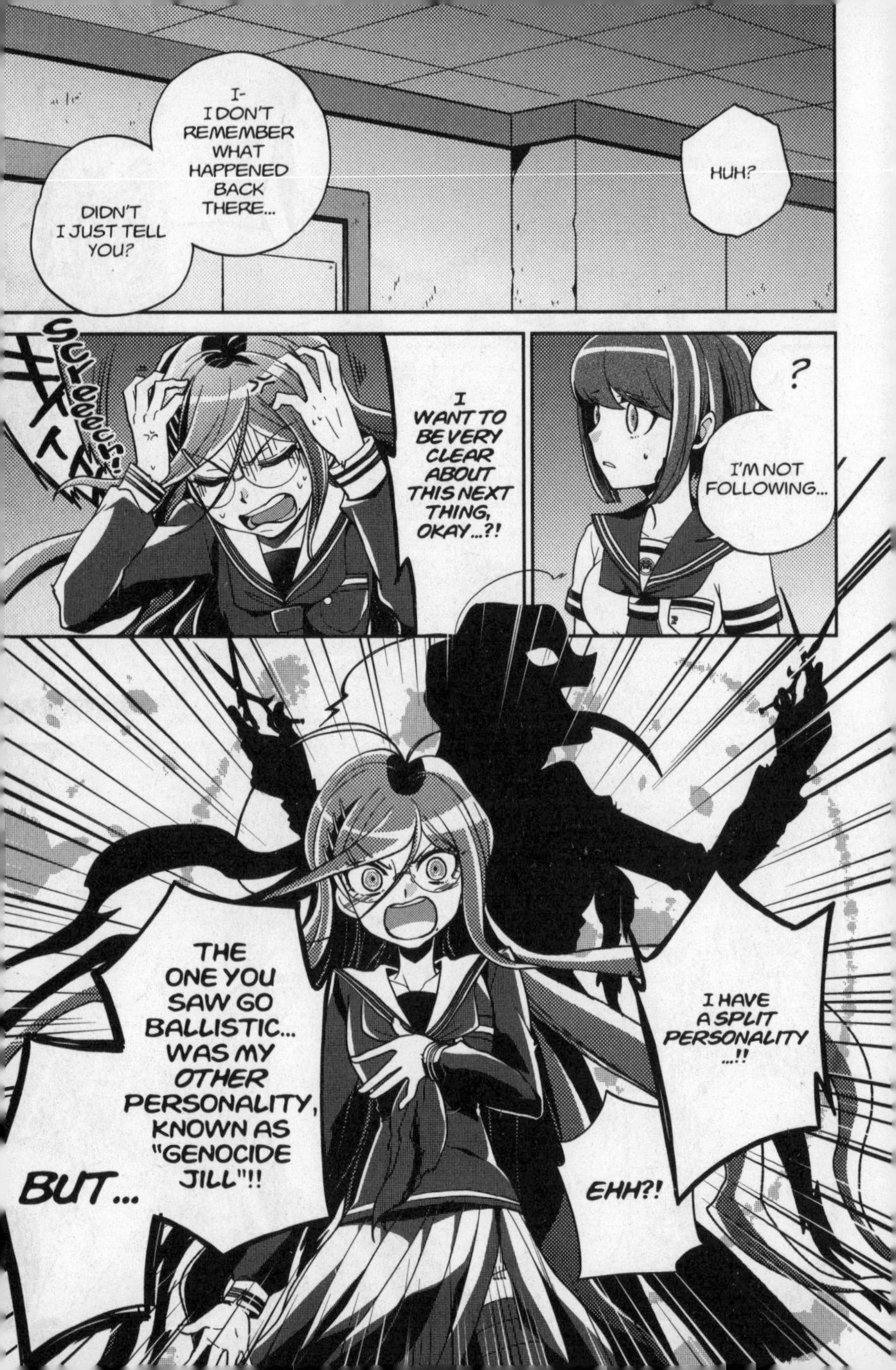
HUH?
I- I DON'T REMEMBER WHAT HAPPENED BACK THERE...
DIDN'T I JUST TELL YOU?
?
I'M NOT FOLLOWING...
I WANT TO BE VERY CLEAR ABOUT THIS NEXT THING, OKAY...?!
SCREEECH!!
I HAVE A SPLIT PERSONALITY ...!!
THE ONE YOU SAW GO BALLISTIC... WAS MY *OTHER* PERSONALITY, KNOWN AS "GENOCIDE JILL"!!
EHH?!
BUT...

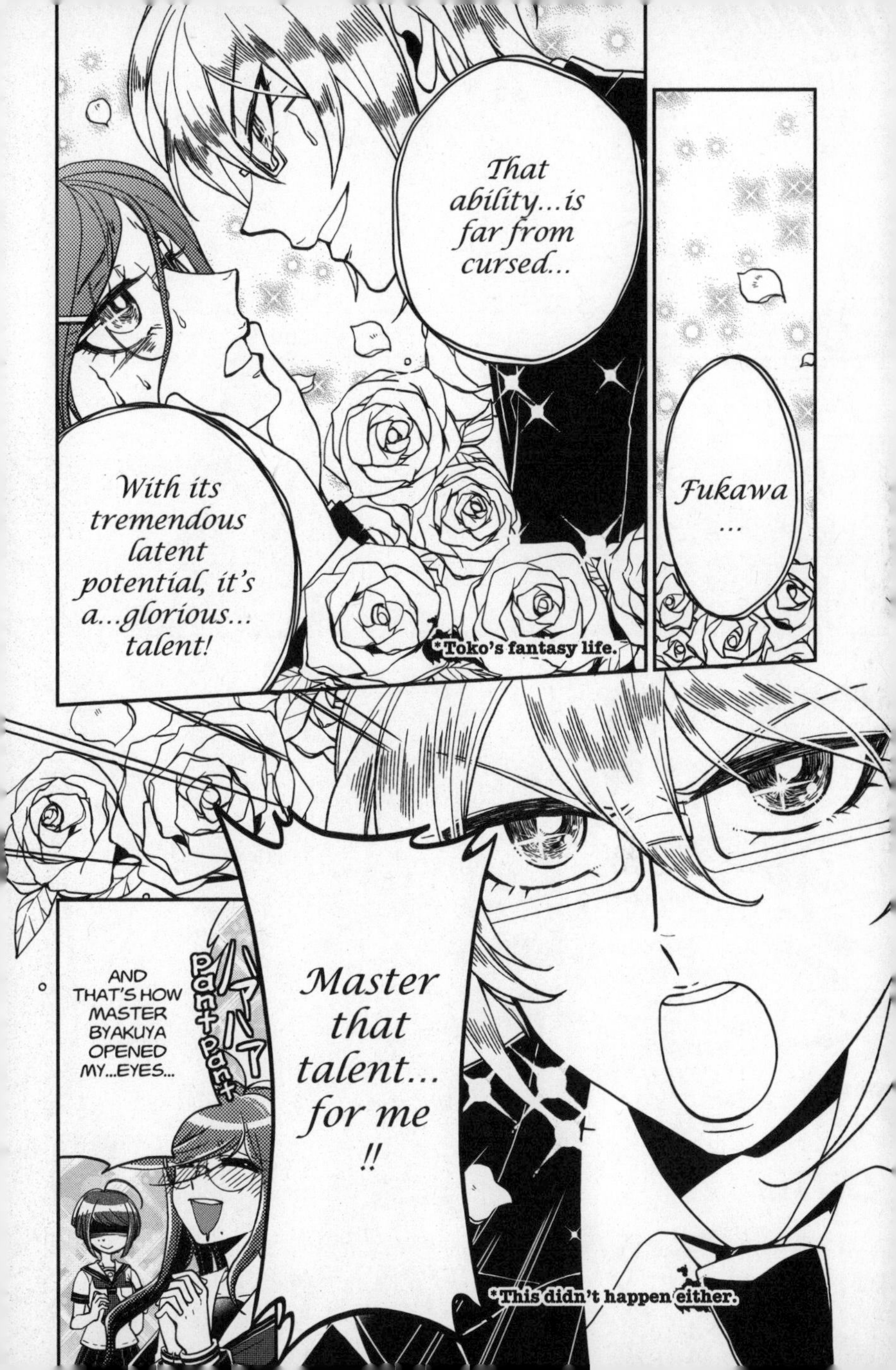

Fukawa …
That ability…is far from cursed…
With its tremendous latent potential, it's a…glorious… talent!
*Toko's fantasy life.
Master that talent… for me !!
*This didn't happen either.
ハァハァ
pant pant
AND THAT'S HOW MASTER BYAKUYA OPENED MY…EYES…

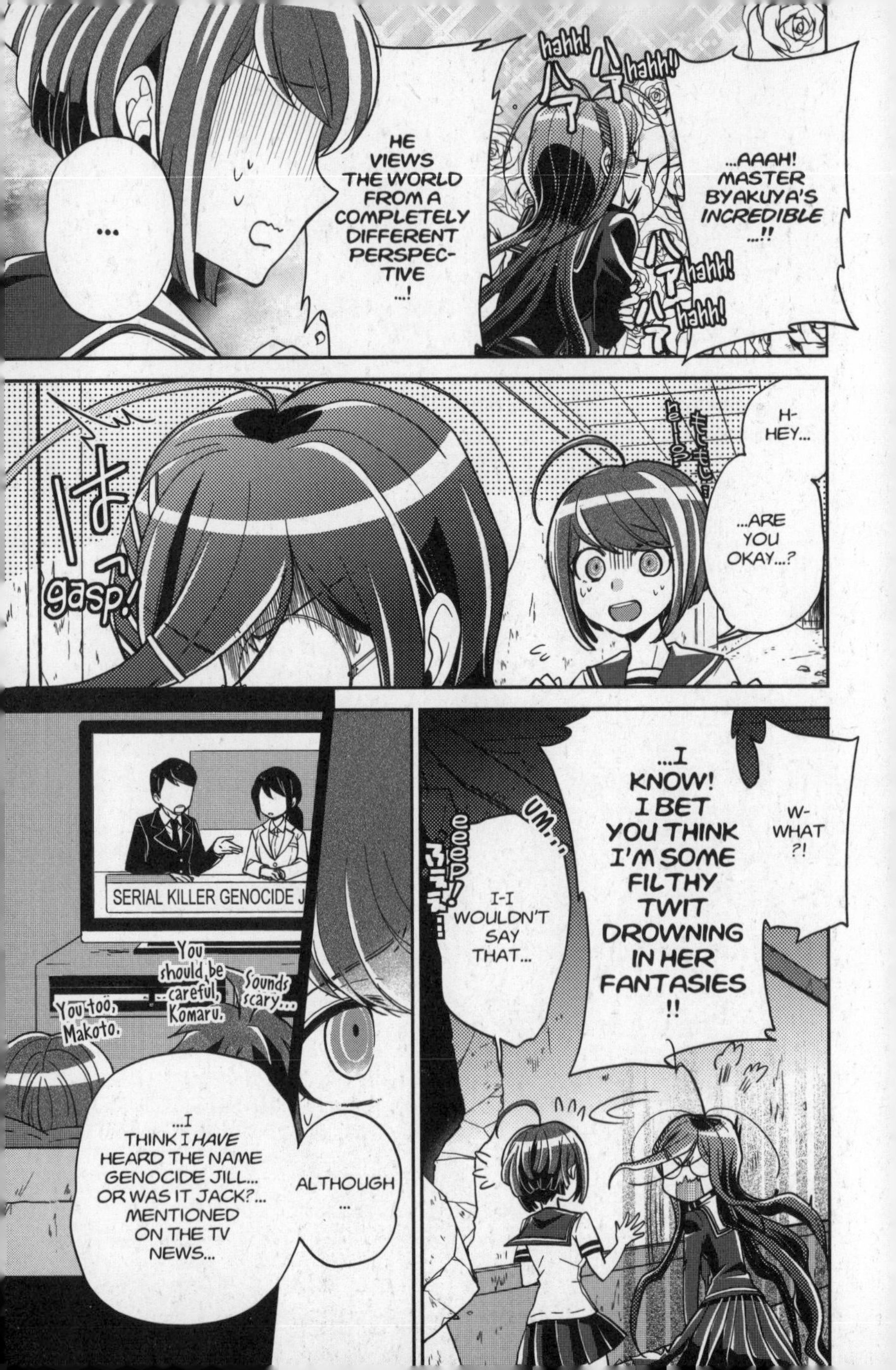

hahh! hahh!
...AAAH! MASTER BYAKUYA'S INCREDIBLE ...!!
hahh! hahh!
HE VIEWS THE WORLD FROM A COMPLETELY DIFFERENT PERSPEC-TIVE ...!
...
H-HEY...
...ARE YOU OKAY...?
gasp!
W-WHAT ?!
...I KNOW! I BET YOU THINK I'M SOME FILTHY TWIT DROWNING IN HER FANTASIES !!
UM...
eeep!
I-I WOULDN'T SAY THAT...
SERIAL KILLER GENOCIDE J
Sounds scary...
You should be careful, Komaru.
You too, Makoto.
ALTHOUGH ...
...I THINK I *HAVE* HEARD THE NAME GENOCIDE JILL... OR WAS IT JACK?... MENTIONED ON THE TV NEWS...

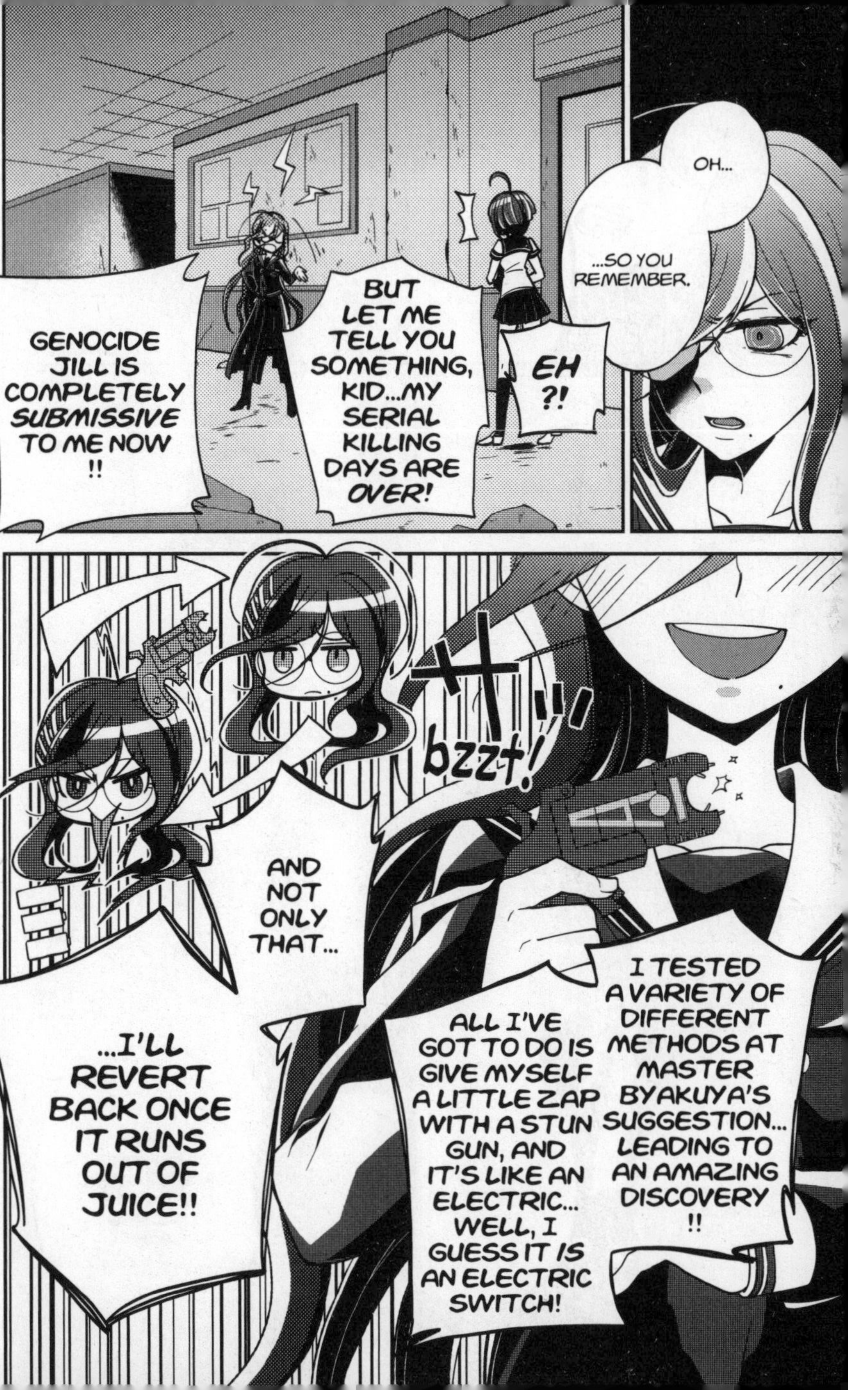
OH...
...SO YOU REMEMBER.
EH ?!
BUT LET ME TELL YOU SOMETHING, KID...MY SERIAL KILLING DAYS ARE OVER!
GENOCIDE JILL IS COMPLETELY SUBMISSIVE TO ME NOW !!
bzzt!
I TESTED A VARIETY OF DIFFERENT METHODS AT MASTER BYAKUYA'S SUGGESTION... LEADING TO AN AMAZING DISCOVERY !!
ALL I'VE GOT TO DO IS GIVE MYSELF A LITTLE ZAP WITH A STUN GUN, AND IT'S LIKE AN ELECTRIC... WELL, I GUESS IT IS AN ELECTRIC SWITCH!
AND NOT ONLY THAT...
...I'LL REVERT BACK ONCE IT RUNS OUT OF JUICE!!

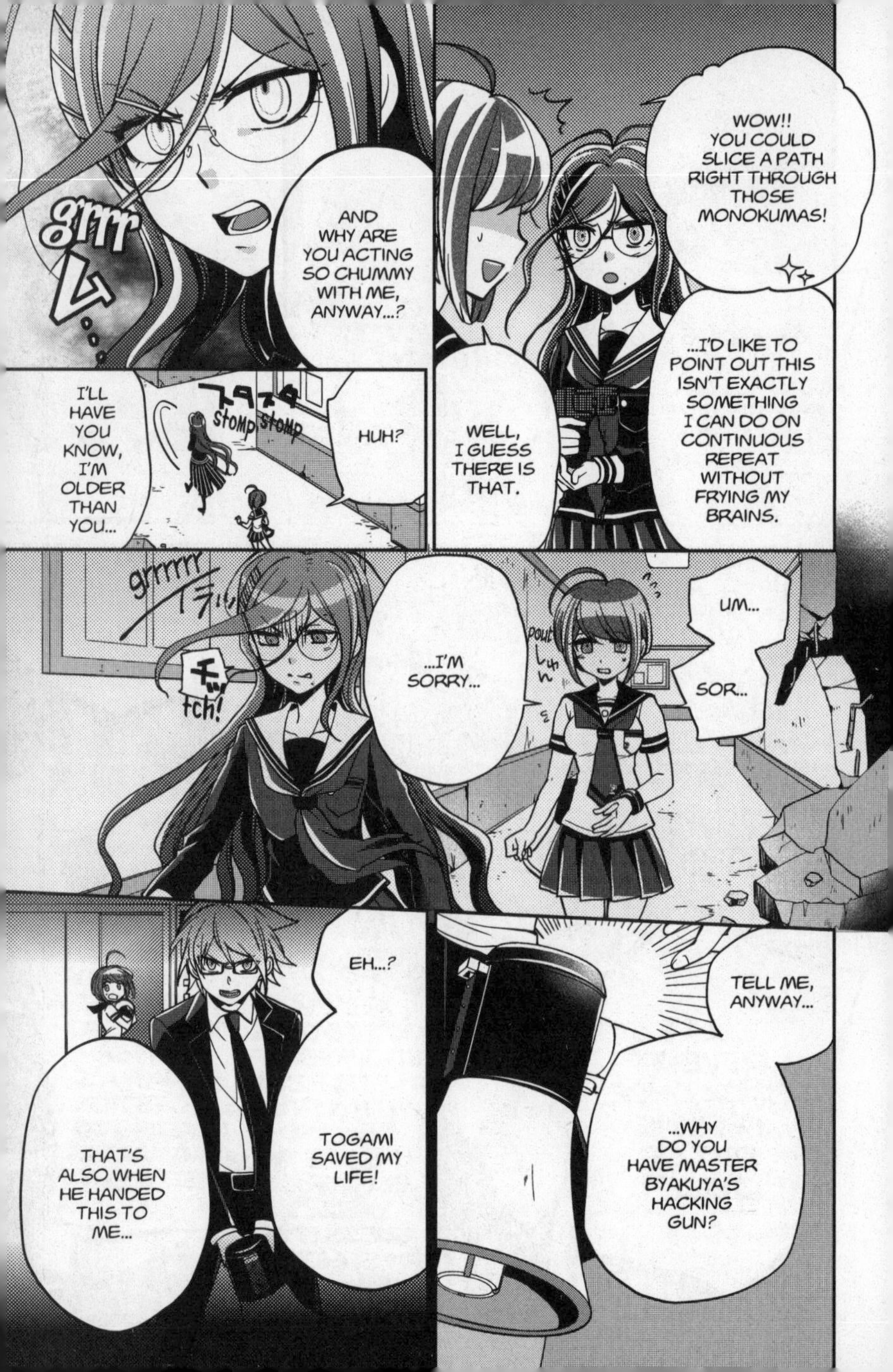
WOW!! YOU COULD SLICE A PATH RIGHT THROUGH THOSE MONOKUMAS!
...I'D LIKE TO POINT OUT THIS ISN'T EXACTLY SOMETHING I CAN DO ON CONTINUOUS REPEAT WITHOUT FRYING MY BRAINS.
WELL, I GUESS THERE IS THAT.
grrr
AND WHY ARE YOU ACTING SO CHUMMY WITH ME, ANYWAY...?
HUH?
stomp stomp
I'LL HAVE YOU KNOW, I'M OLDER THAN YOU...
UM...
SOR...
pout
...I'M SORRY...
grrrrr
tch!
TELL ME, ANYWAY...
...WHY DO YOU HAVE MASTER BYAKUYA'S HACKING GUN?
EH...?
TOGAMI SAVED MY LIFE!
THAT'S ALSO WHEN HE HANDED THIS TO ME...

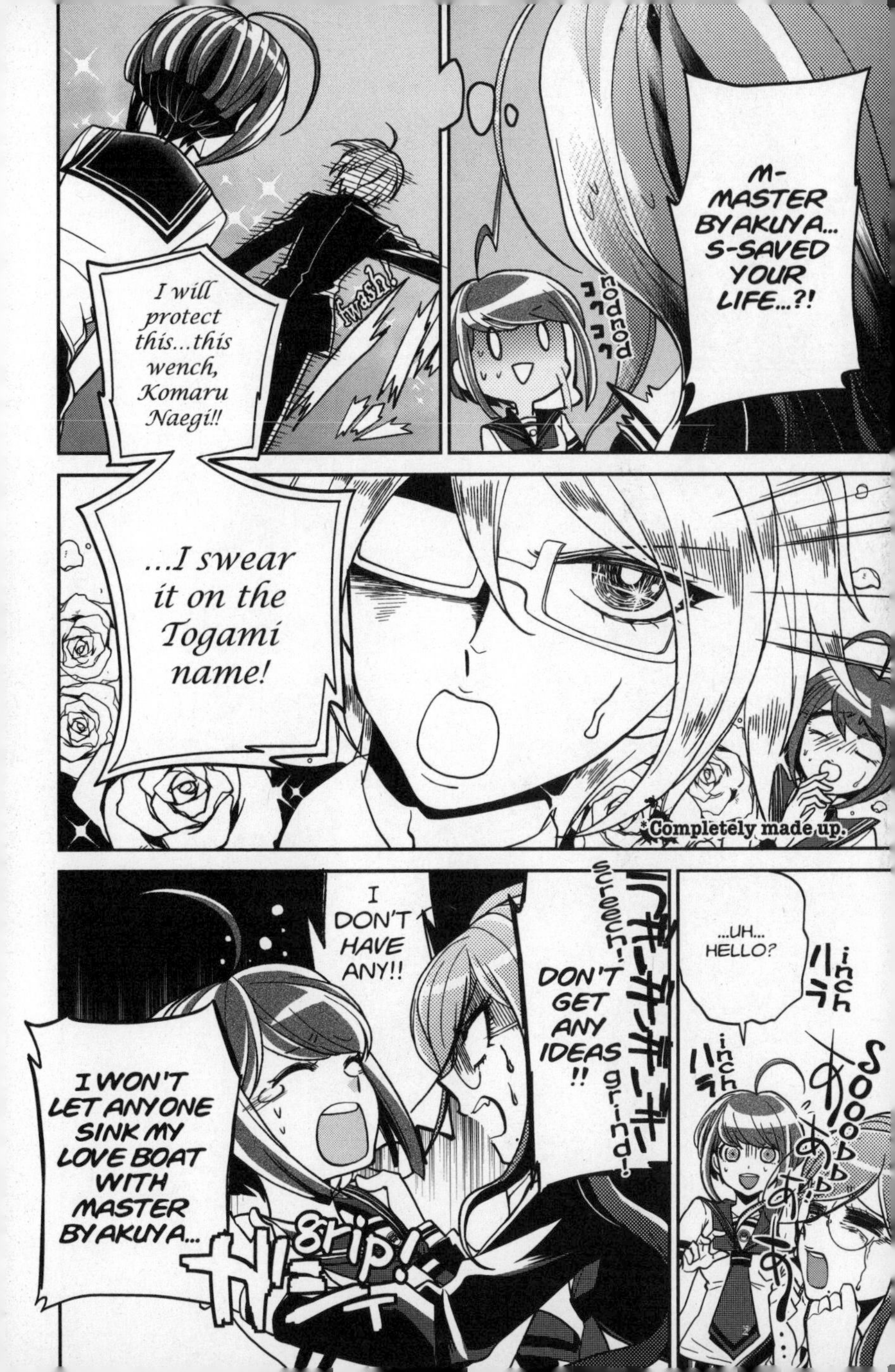

M-MASTER BYAKUYA... S-SAVED YOUR LIFE...?!
nodnod
I will protect this...this wench, Komaru Naegi!!
fwash!
...I swear it on the Togami name!
*Completely made up.
...UH... HELLO?
inch
inch
SOOOBBB
DON'T GET ANY IDEAS!!
screech!
grind!
I DON'T HAVE ANY!!
I WON'T LET ANYONE SINK MY LOVE BOAT WITH MASTER BYAKUYA...
grip!

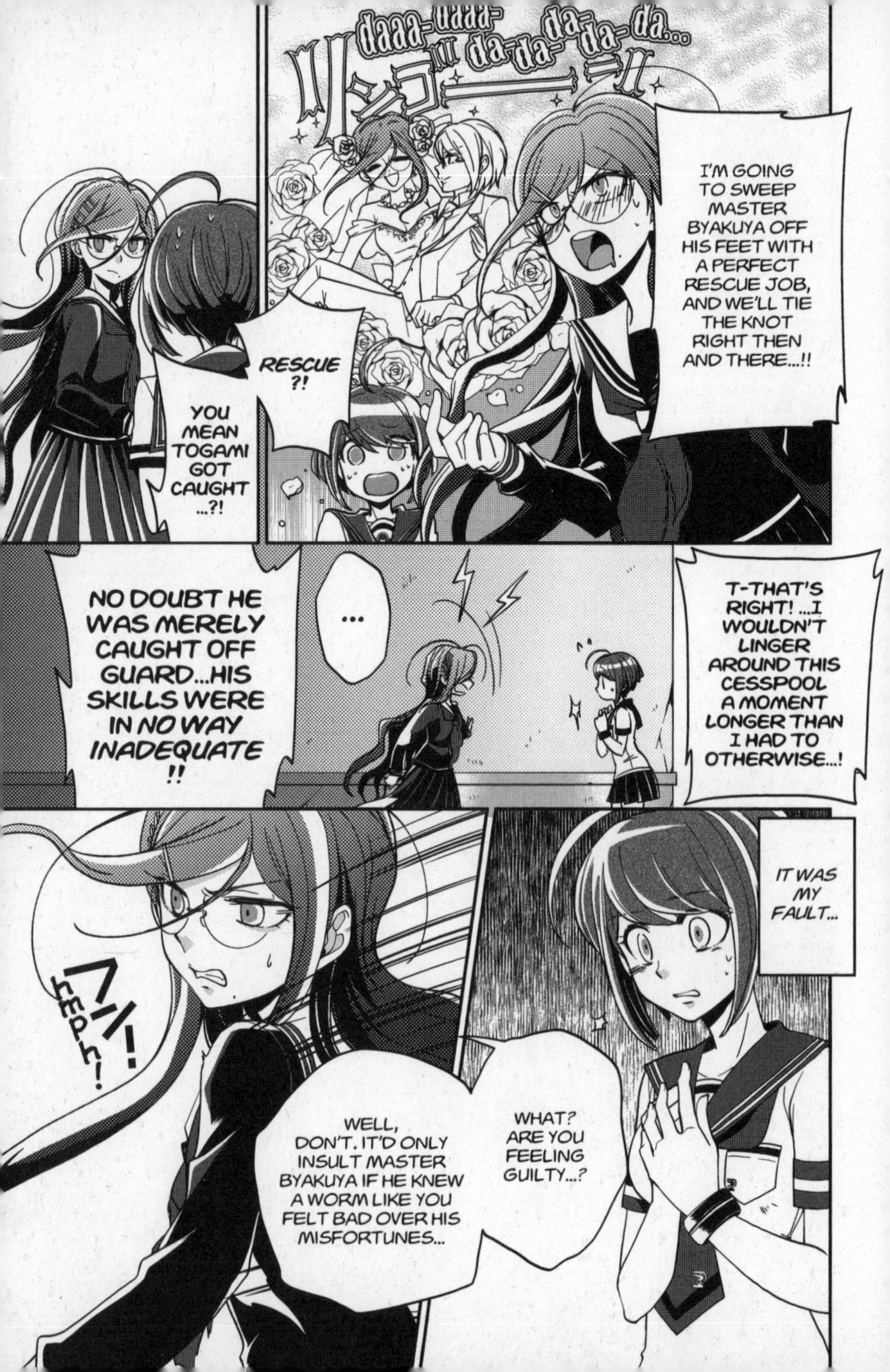
daaa-daaa-da-da-da-da...
I'M GOING TO SWEEP MASTER BYAKUYA OFF HIS FEET WITH A PERFECT RESCUE JOB, AND WE'LL TIE THE KNOT RIGHT THEN AND THERE...!!
RESCUE ?!
YOU MEAN TOGAMI GOT CAUGHT ...?!
T-THAT'S RIGHT! ...I WOULDN'T LINGER AROUND THIS CESSPOOL A MOMENT LONGER THAN I HAD TO OTHERWISE...!
...
NO DOUBT HE WAS MERELY CAUGHT OFF GUARD...HIS SKILLS WERE IN NO WAY INADEQUATE !!
IT WAS MY FAULT...
WHAT? ARE YOU FEELING GUILTY...?
hmph!
WELL, DON'T. IT'D ONLY INSULT MASTER BYAKUYA IF HE KNEW A WORM LIKE YOU FELT BAD OVER HIS MISFORTUNES...

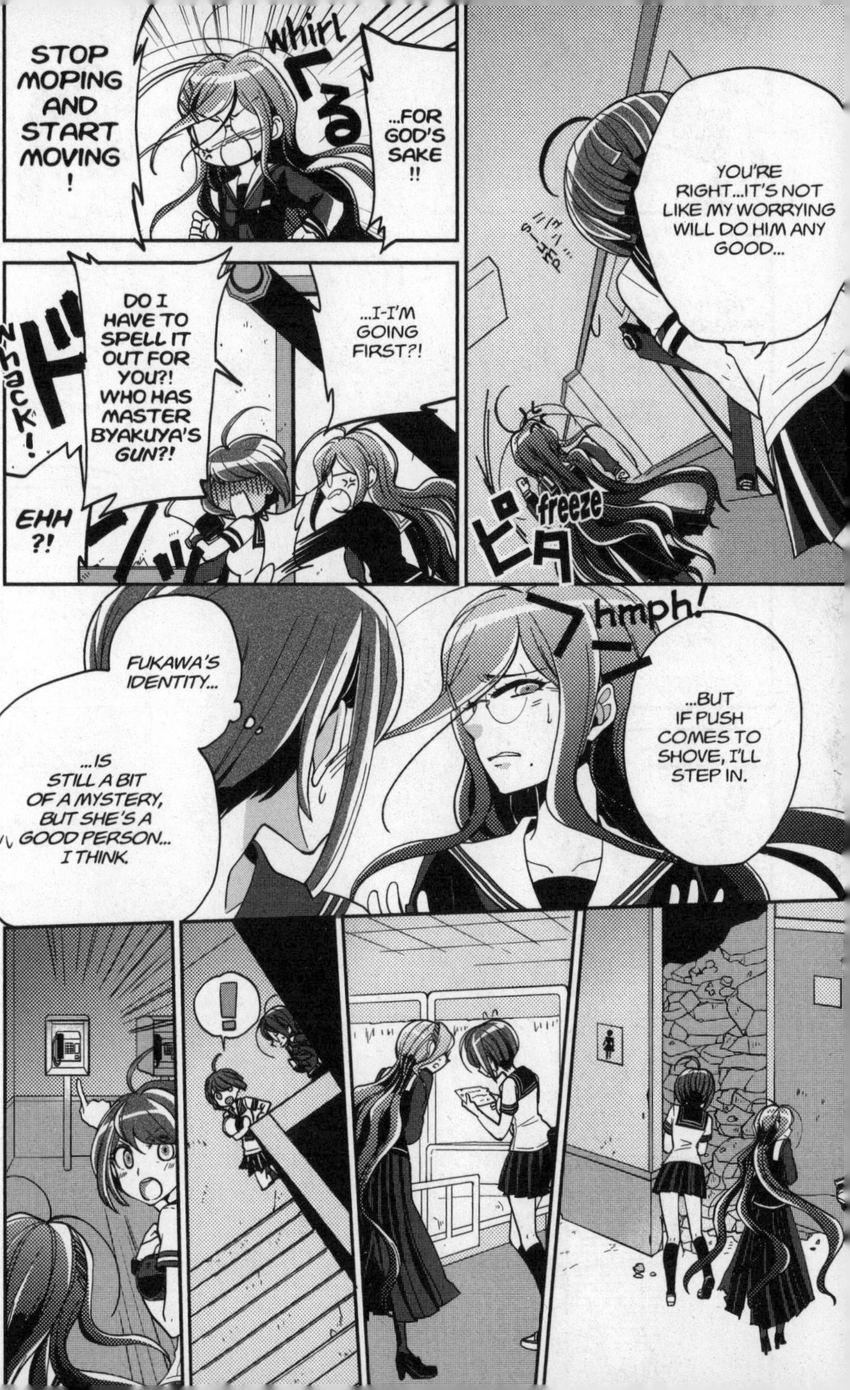
YOU'RE RIGHT...IT'S NOT LIKE MY WORRYING WILL DO HIM ANY GOOD...
freeze
whirl
...FOR GOD'S SAKE !!
STOP MOPING AND START MOVING !
...I-I'M GOING FIRST?!
DO I HAVE TO SPELL IT OUT FOR YOU?! WHO HAS MASTER BYAKUYA'S GUN?!
whack!
EHH ?!
hmph!
...BUT IF PUSH COMES TO SHOVE, I'LL STEP IN.
FUKAWA'S IDENTITY...
...IS STILL A BIT OF A MYSTERY, BUT SHE'S A GOOD PERSON... I THINK.
!

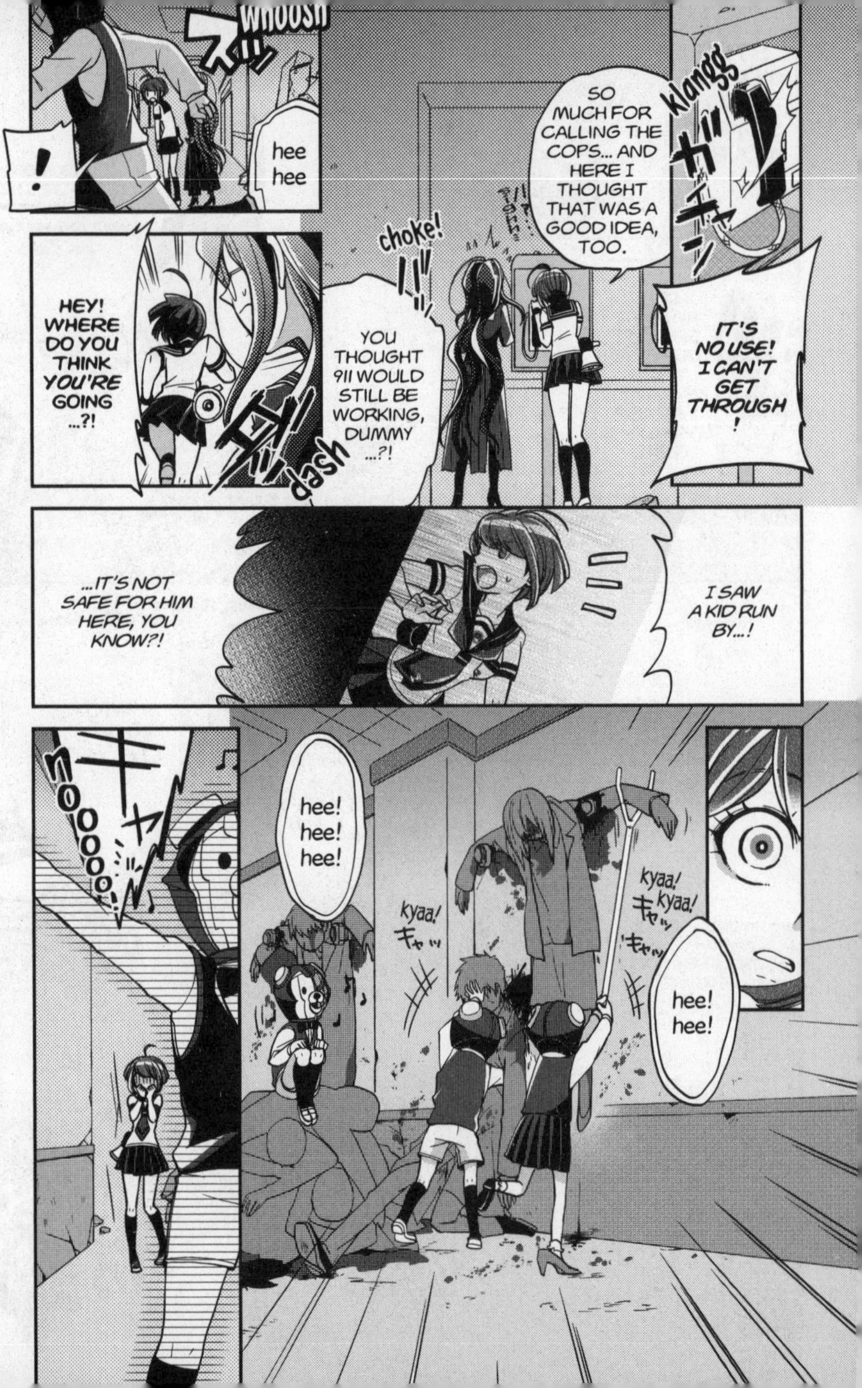
klangg
IT'S NO USE! I CAN'T GET THROUGH!
SO MUCH FOR CALLING THE COPS... AND HERE I THOUGHT THAT WAS A GOOD IDEA, TOO.
choke!
YOU THOUGHT 911 WOULD STILL BE WORKING, DUMMY ...?!
whoosh
!
hee hee
HEY! WHERE DO YOU THINK YOU'RE GOING ...?!
dash
I SAW A KID RUN BY...!
...IT'S NOT SAFE FOR HIM HERE, YOU KNOW?!
kyaa! kyaa!
hee! hee!
hee! hee! hee!
kyaa!
noooooo!

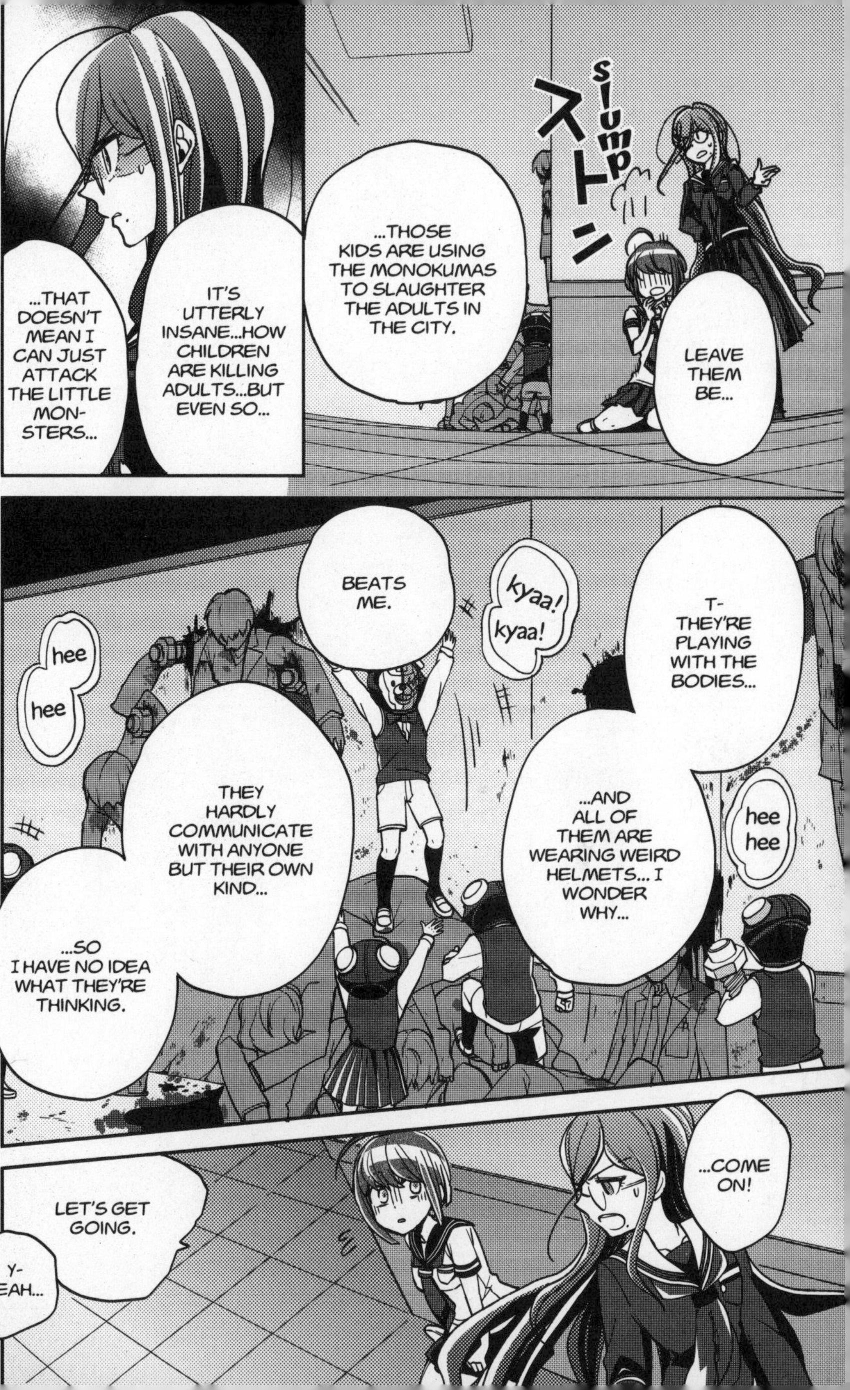
slump ストン
LEAVE THEM BE...
...THOSE KIDS ARE USING THE MONOKUMAS TO SLAUGHTER THE ADULTS IN THE CITY.
IT'S UTTERLY INSANE...HOW CHILDREN ARE KILLING ADULTS...BUT EVEN SO...
...THAT DOESN'T MEAN I CAN JUST ATTACK THE LITTLE MON-STERS...
T-THEY'RE PLAYING WITH THE BODIES...
hee hee
kyaa! kyaa!
...AND ALL OF THEM ARE WEARING WEIRD HELMETS... I WONDER WHY...
BEATS ME.
THEY HARDLY COMMUNICATE WITH ANYONE BUT THEIR OWN KIND...
...SO I HAVE NO IDEA WHAT THEY'RE THINKING.
hee hee
...COME ON!
LET'S GET GOING.
Y-YEAH...

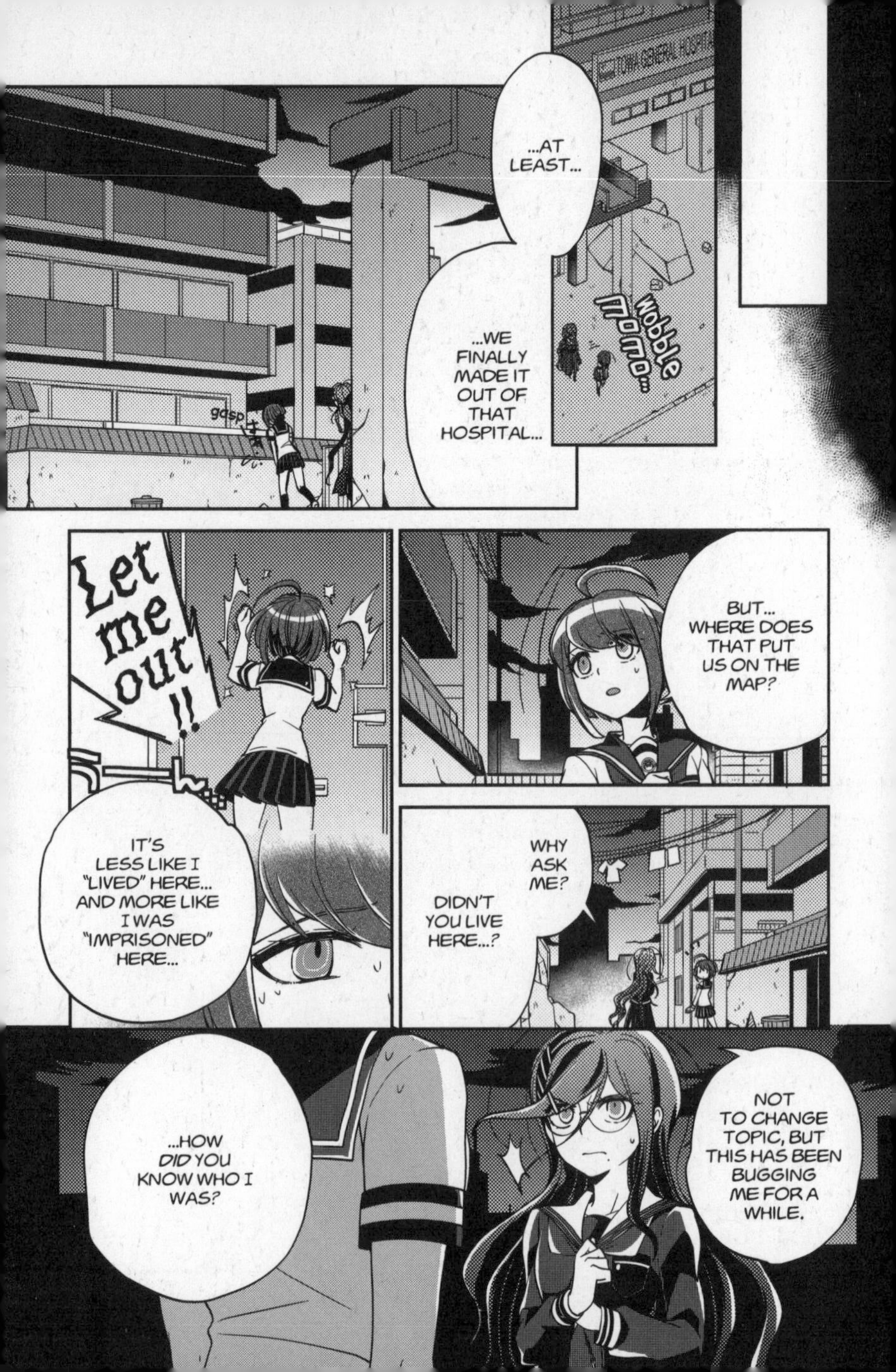
TOWA GENERAL HOSPITA
...AT LEAST...
...WE FINALLY MADE IT OUT OF THAT HOSPITAL...
wobble
gasp
BUT... WHERE DOES THAT PUT US ON THE MAP?
WHY ASK ME?
DIDN'T YOU LIVE HERE...?
Let me out!!
IT'S LESS LIKE I "LIVED" HERE... AND MORE LIKE I WAS "IMPRISONED" HERE...
NOT TO CHANGE TOPIC, BUT THIS HAS BEEN BUGGING ME FOR A WHILE.
...HOW *DID* YOU KNOW WHO I WAS?

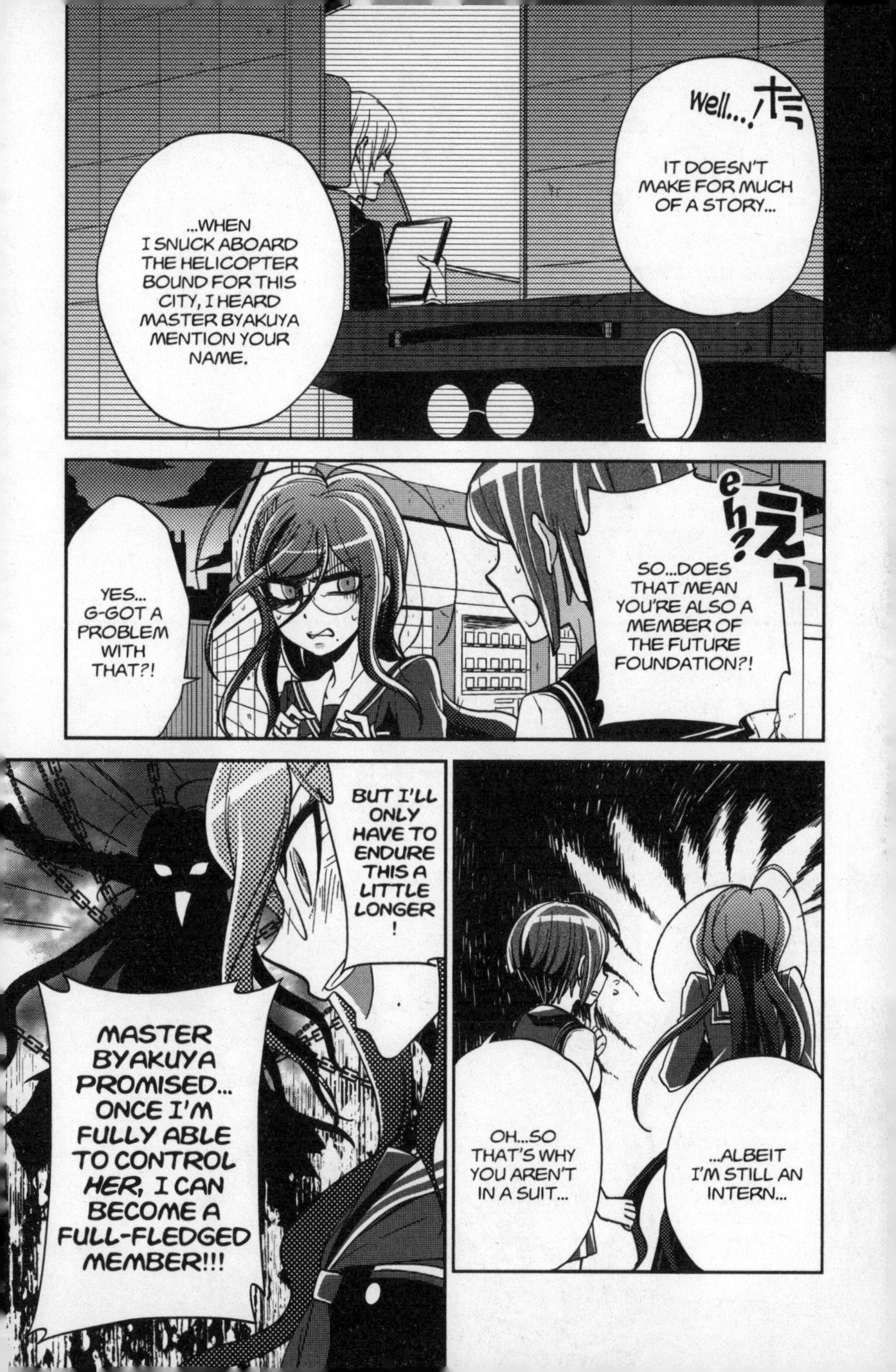
Well...!
IT DOESN'T MAKE FOR MUCH OF A STORY...
...WHEN I SNUCK ABOARD THE HELICOPTER BOUND FOR THIS CITY, I HEARD MASTER BYAKUYA MENTION YOUR NAME.
eh?!
SO...DOES THAT MEAN YOU'RE ALSO A MEMBER OF THE FUTURE FOUNDATION?!
YES... G-GOT A PROBLEM WITH THAT?!
...ALBEIT I'M STILL AN INTERN...
OH...SO THAT'S WHY YOU AREN'T IN A SUIT...
BUT I'LL ONLY HAVE TO ENDURE THIS A LITTLE LONGER!
MASTER BYAKUYA PROMISED... ONCE I'M FULLY ABLE TO CONTROL HER, I CAN BECOME A FULL-FLEDGED MEMBER!!!

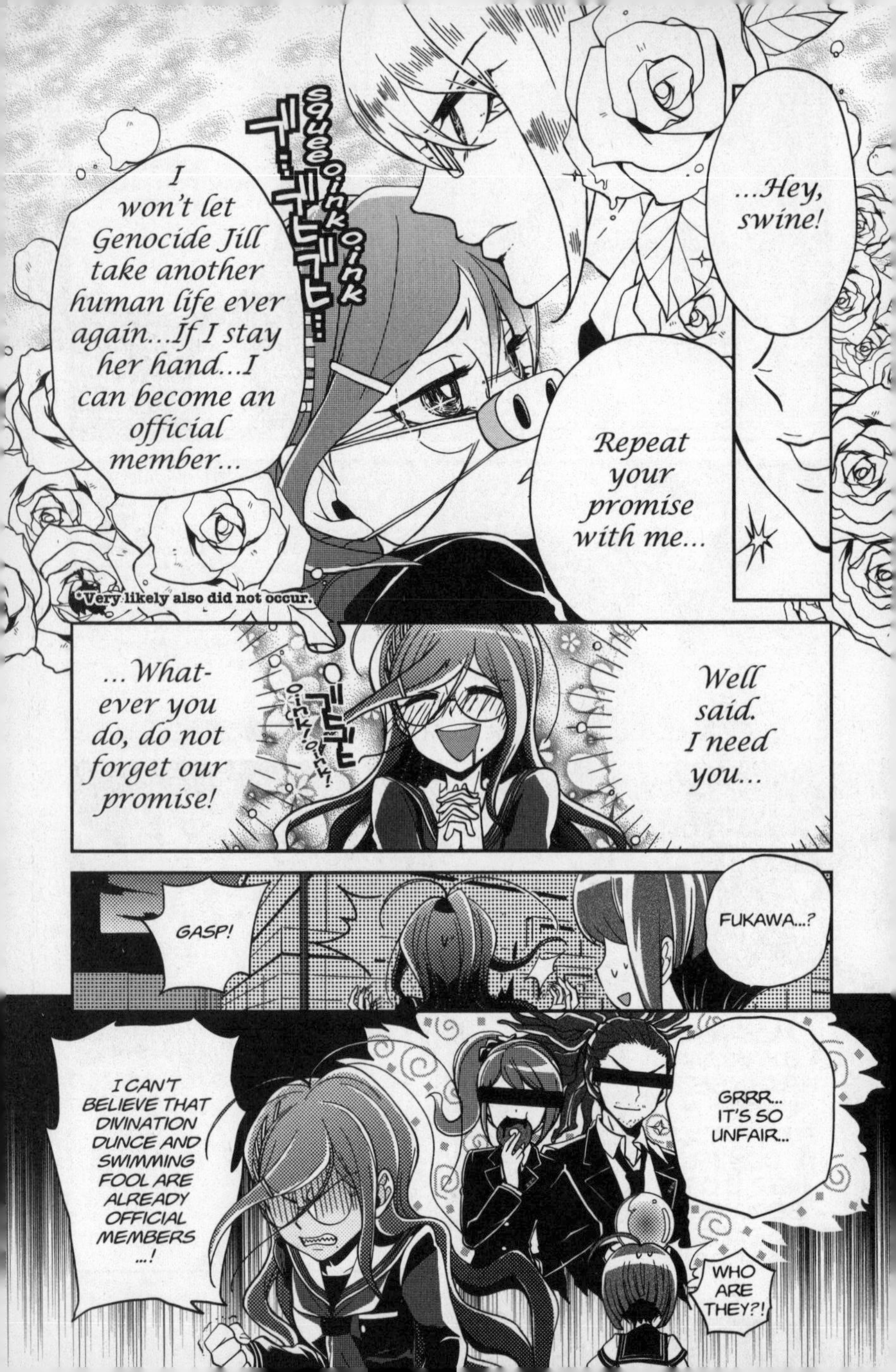
...Hey, swine!
Repeat your promise with me...
squee oink oink
I won't let Genocide Jill take another human life ever again...If I stay her hand...I can become an official member...
*Very likely also did not occur.
Well said. I need you...
oink! oink!
...Whatever you do, do not forget our promise!
FUKAWA...?
GASP!
GRRR... IT'S SO UNFAIR...
I CAN'T BELIEVE THAT DIVINATION DUNCE AND SWIMMING FOOL ARE ALREADY OFFICIAL MEMBERS ...!
WHO ARE THEY?!

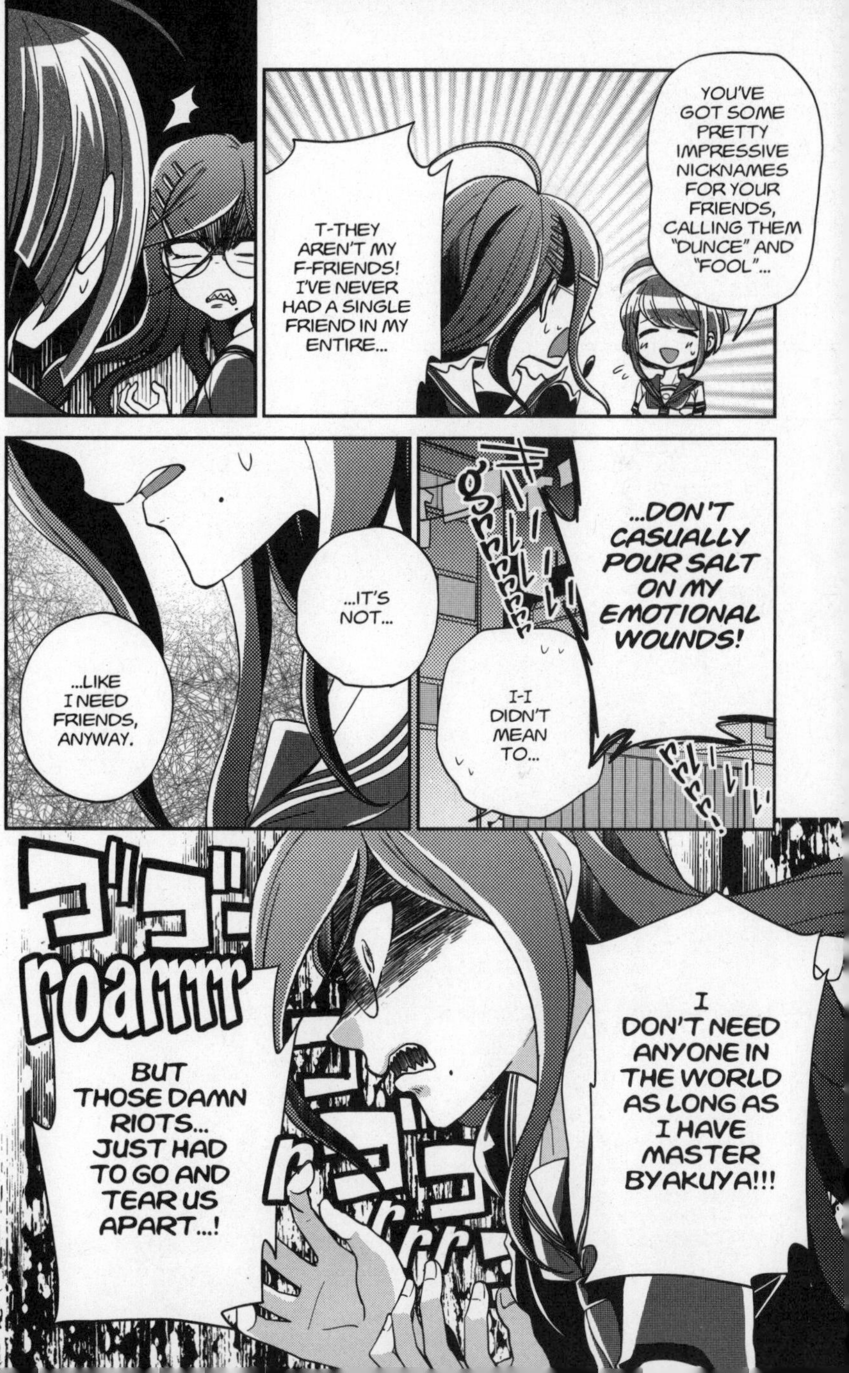
YOU'VE GOT SOME PRETTY IMPRESSIVE NICKNAMES FOR YOUR FRIENDS, CALLING THEM "DUNCE" AND "FOOL"...
T-THEY AREN'T MY F-FRIENDS! I'VE NEVER HAD A SINGLE FRIEND IN MY ENTIRE...
grrrrrrr
...DON'T CASUALLY POUR SALT ON MY EMOTIONAL WOUNDS!
I-I DIDN'T MEAN TO...
rrrrr-
...IT'S NOT...
...LIKE I NEED FRIENDS, ANYWAY.
I DON'T NEED ANYONE IN THE WORLD AS LONG AS I HAVE MASTER BYAKUYA!!!
roarrrr
BUT THOSE DAMN RIOTS... JUST HAD TO GO AND TEAR US APART...!
rrrr

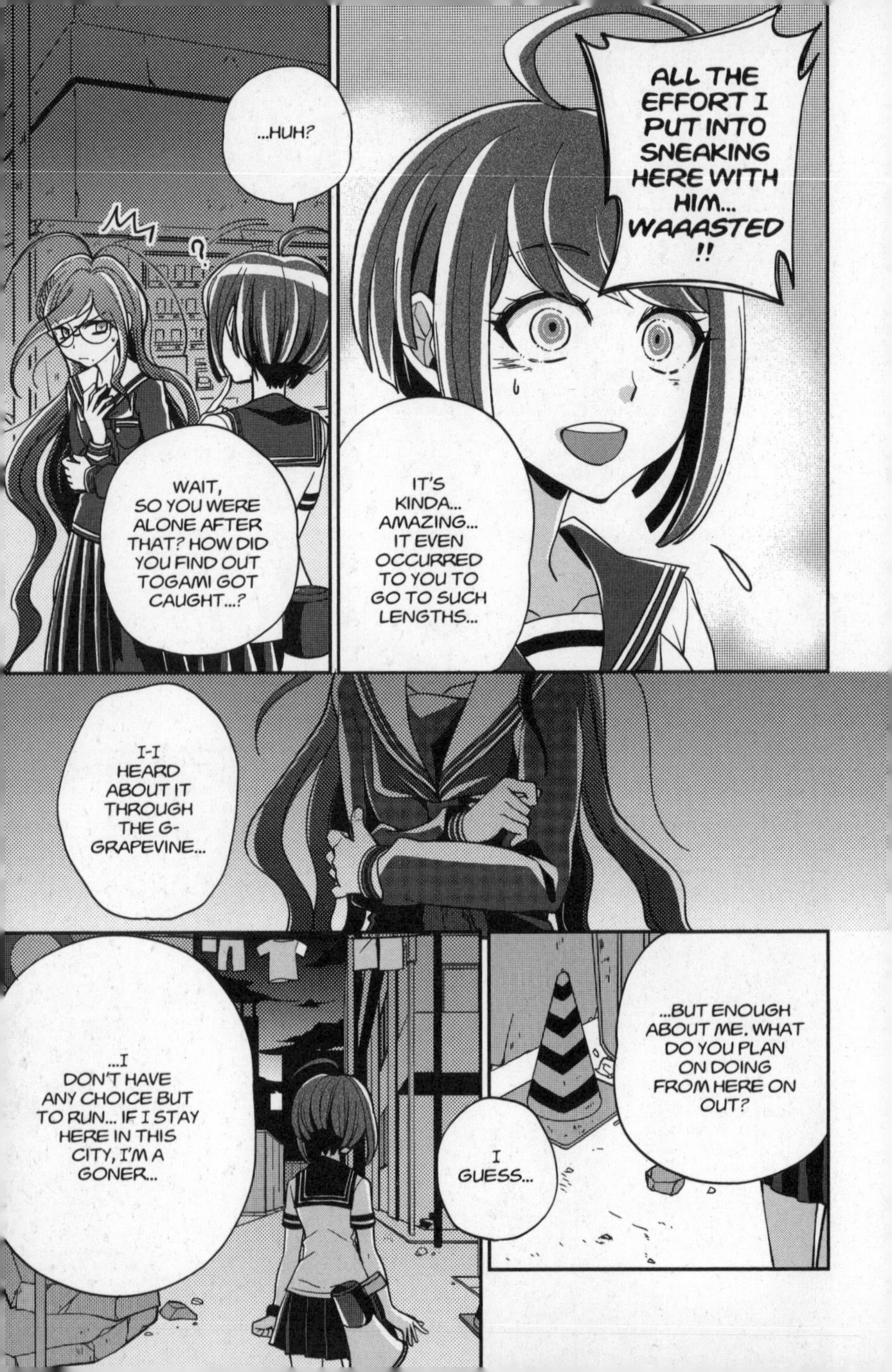
ALL THE EFFORT I PUT INTO SNEAKING HERE WITH HIM... WAAASTED!!
IT'S KINDA... AMAZING... IT EVEN OCCURRED TO YOU TO GO TO SUCH LENGTHS...
...HUH?
?
WAIT, SO YOU WERE ALONE AFTER THAT? HOW DID YOU FIND OUT TOGAMI GOT CAUGHT...?
I-I HEARD ABOUT IT THROUGH THE G-GRAPEVINE...
...BUT ENOUGH ABOUT ME. WHAT DO YOU PLAN ON DOING FROM HERE ON OUT?
...I DON'T HAVE ANY CHOICE BUT TO RUN... IF I STAY HERE IN THIS CITY, I'M A GONER...
I GUESS...

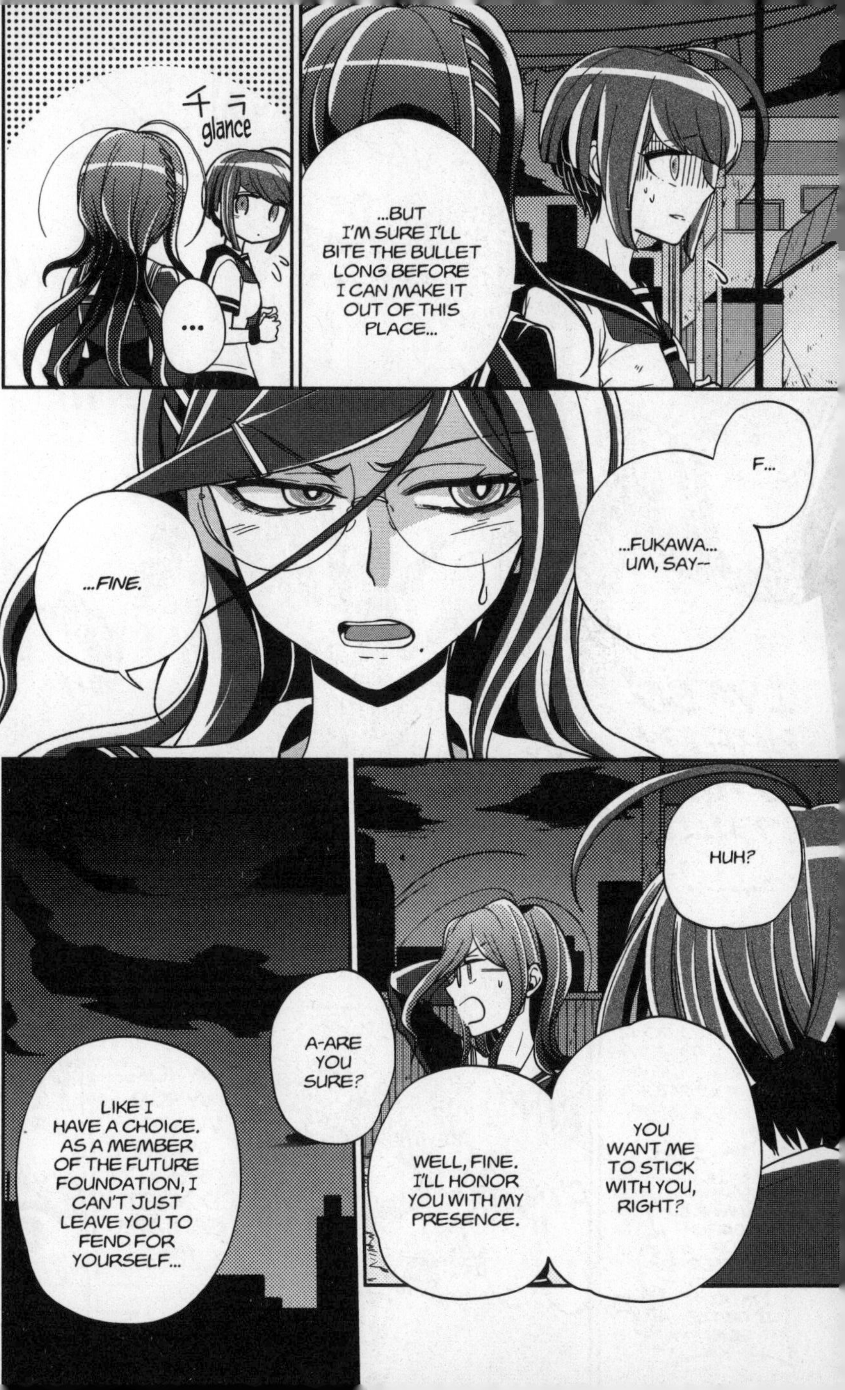
...BUT I'M SURE I'LL BITE THE BULLET LONG BEFORE I CAN MAKE IT OUT OF THIS PLACE...
チラ glance
...
F...
...FUKAWA... UM, SAY--
...FINE.
HUH?
YOU WANT ME TO STICK WITH YOU, RIGHT?
WELL, FINE. I'LL HONOR YOU WITH MY PRESENCE.
A-ARE YOU SURE?
LIKE I HAVE A CHOICE. AS A MEMBER OF THE FUTURE FOUNDATION, I CAN'T JUST LEAVE YOU TO FEND FOR YOURSELF...

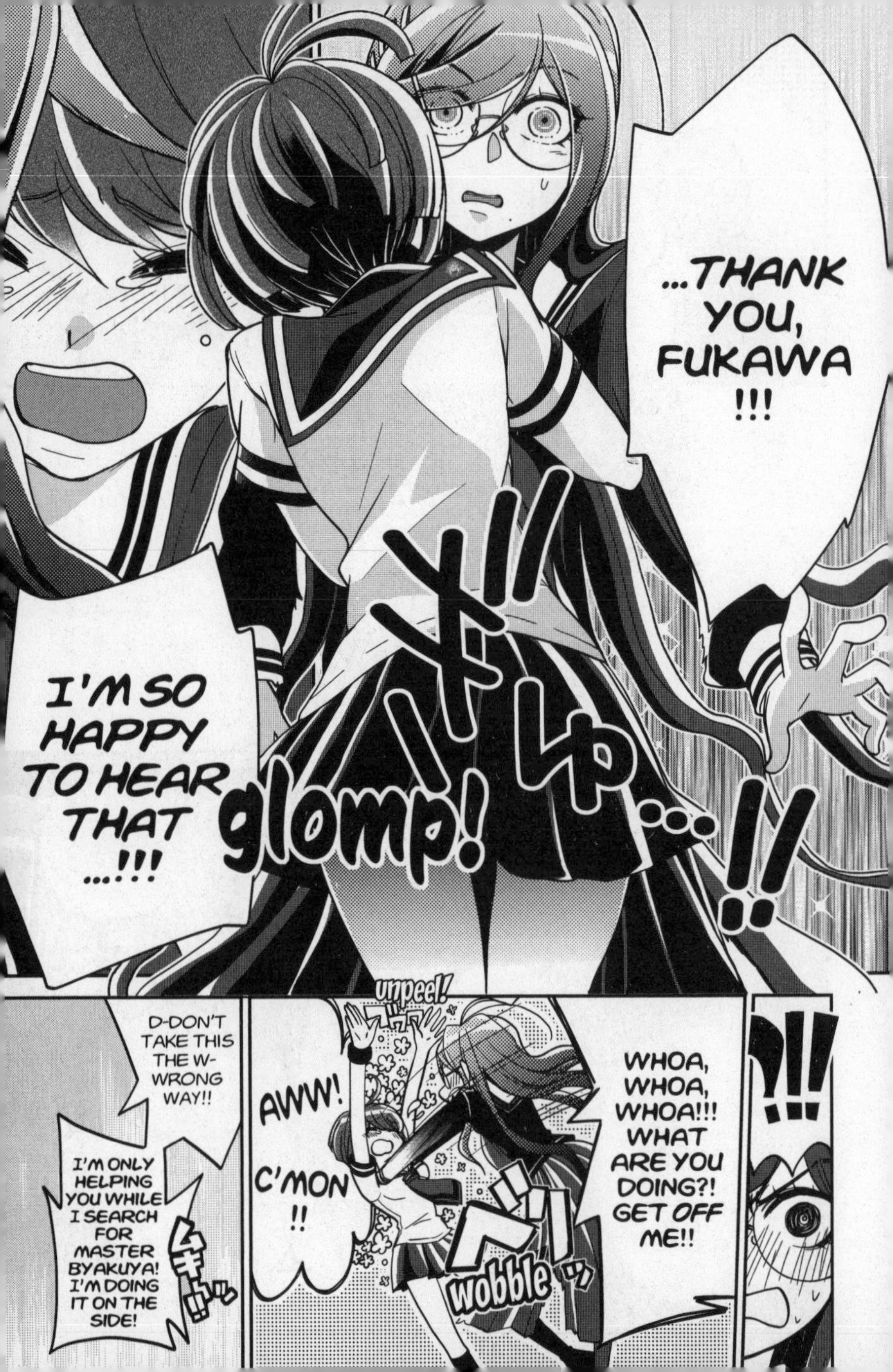
...THANK YOU, FUKAWA !!!
I'M SO HAPPY TO HEAR THAT ...!!!
glomp!
?!!
WHOA, WHOA, WHOA!!! WHAT ARE YOU DOING?! GET OFF ME!!
unpeel!
AWW!
C'MON !!
wobble
D-DON'T TAKE THIS THE W-WRONG WAY!!
I'M ONLY HELPING YOU WHILE I SEARCH FOR MASTER BYAKUYA! I'M DOING IT ON THE SIDE!

Danganronpa Another Episode:
Ultra Despair Girls

CHAPTER 4

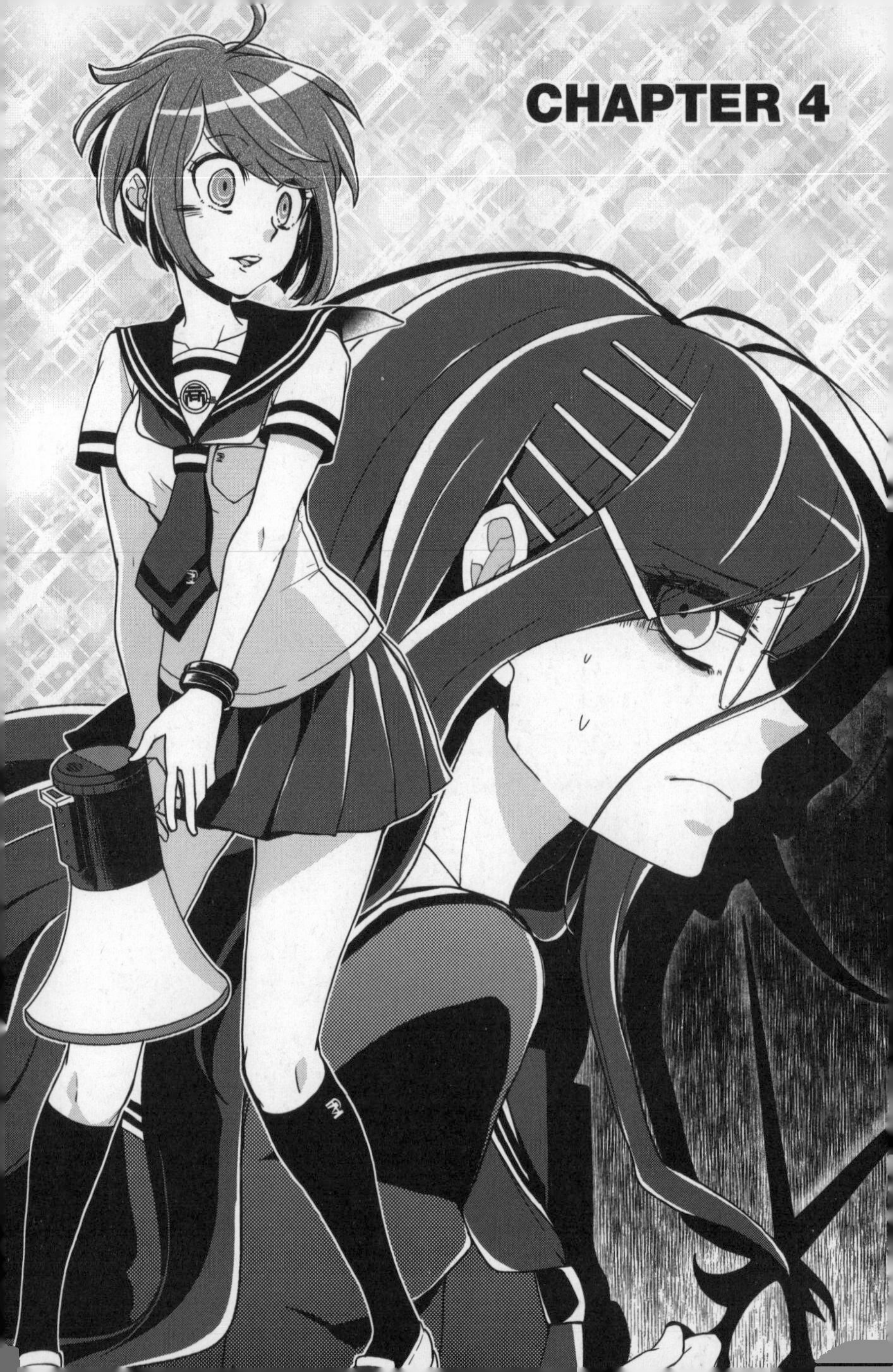

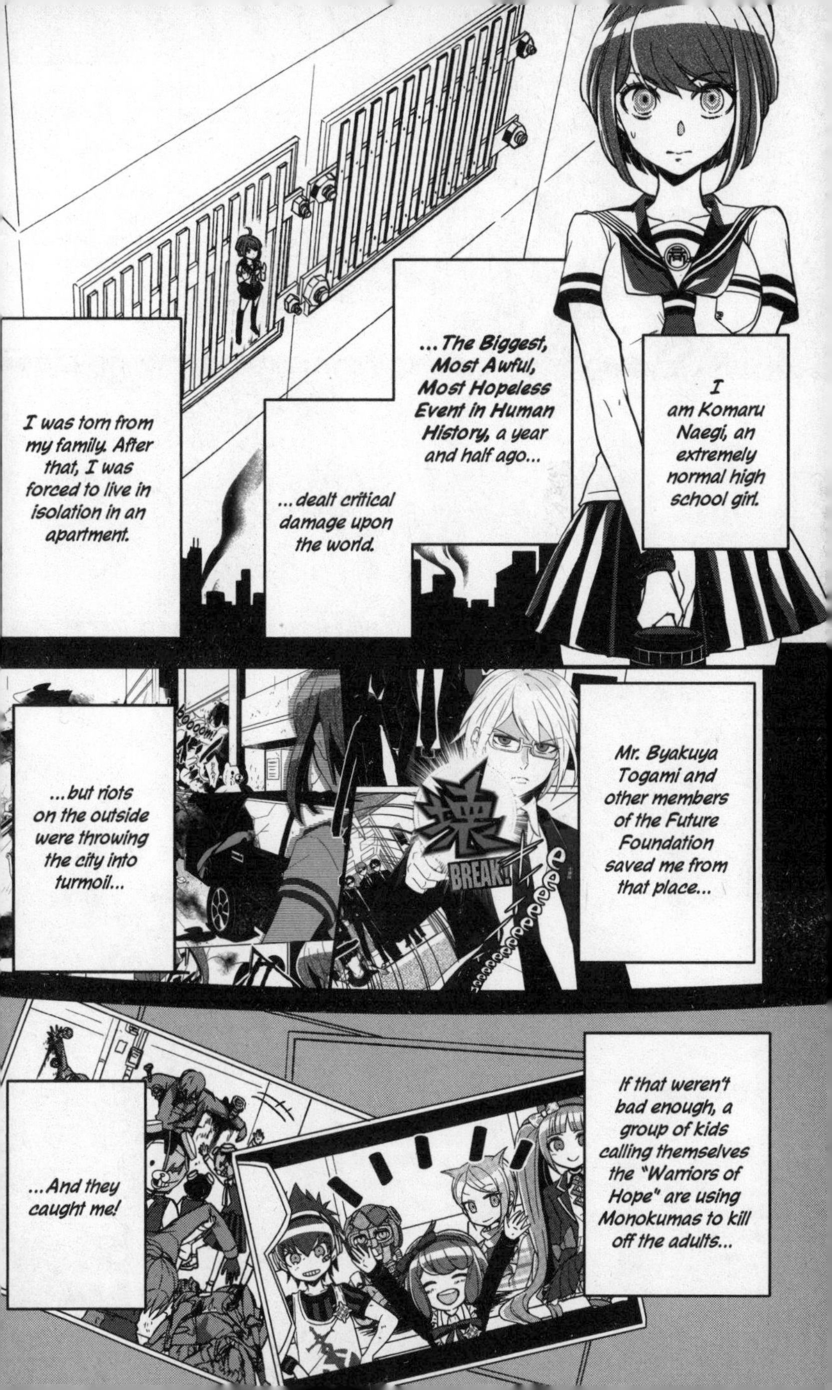
I am Komaru Naegi, an extremely normal high school girl.
...The Biggest, Most Awful, Most Hopeless Event in Human History, a year and half ago...
...dealt critical damage upon the world.
I was torn from my family. After that, I was forced to live in isolation in an apartment.
Mr. Byakuya Togami and other members of the Future Foundation saved me from that place...
BREAK!
...but riots on the outside were throwing the city into turmoil...
If that weren't bad enough, a group of kids calling themselves the "Warriors of Hope" are using Monokumas to kill off the adults...
...And they caught me!

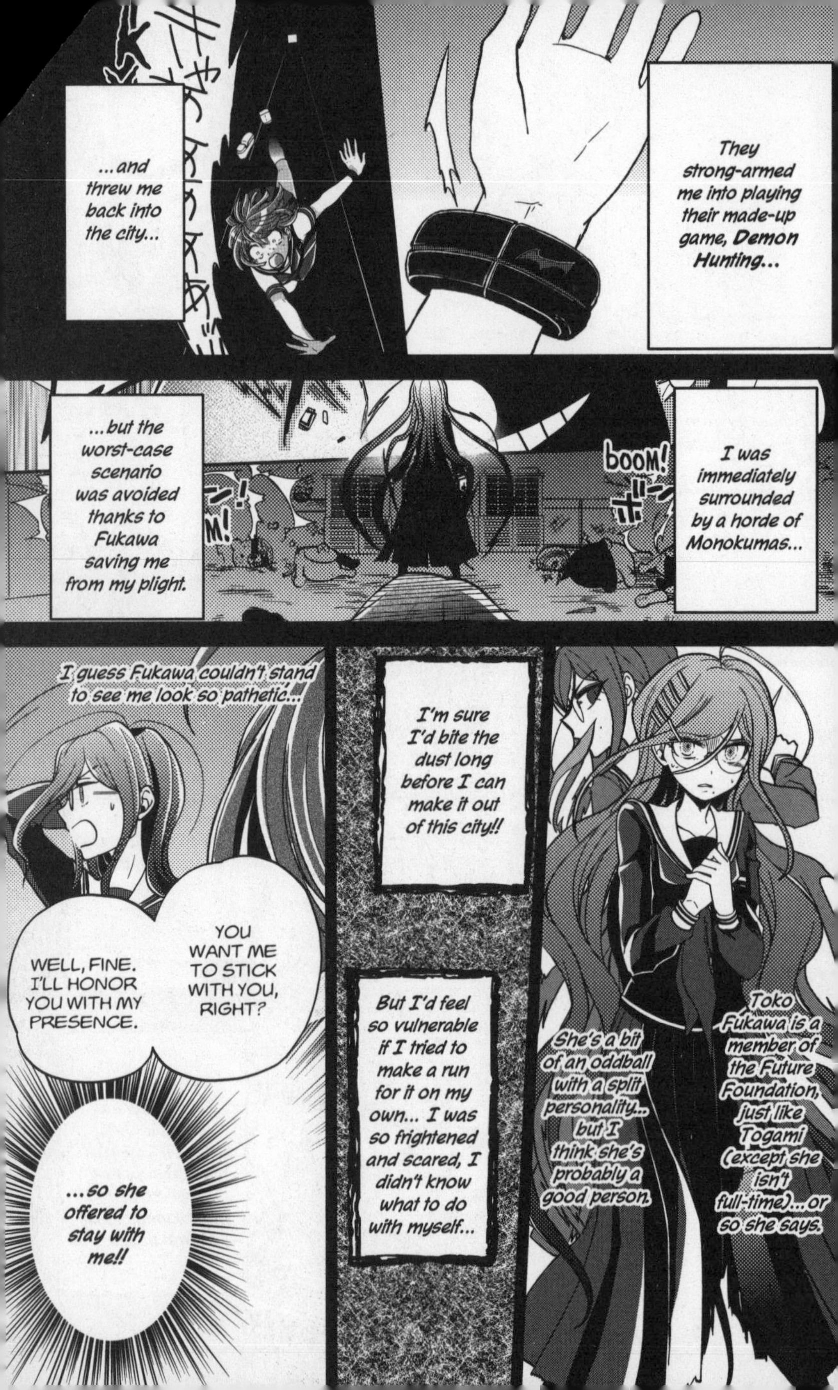
They strong-armed me into playing their made-up game, Demon Hunting...
...and threw me back into the city...
I was immediately surrounded by a horde of Monokumas...
BOOM!
...but the worst-case scenario was avoided thanks to Fukawa saving me from my plight.
Toko Fukawa is a member of the Future Foundation, just like Togami (except she isn't full-time)... or so she says.
She's a bit of an oddball with a split personality... but I think she's probably a good person.
I'm sure I'd bite the dust long before I can make it out of this city!!
But I'd feel so vulnerable if I tried to make a run for it on my own... I was so frightened and scared, I didn't know what to do with myself...
I guess Fukawa couldn't stand to see me look so pathetic...
YOU WANT ME TO STICK WITH YOU, RIGHT?
WELL, FINE. I'LL HONOR YOU WITH MY PRESENCE.
...so she offered to stay with me!!

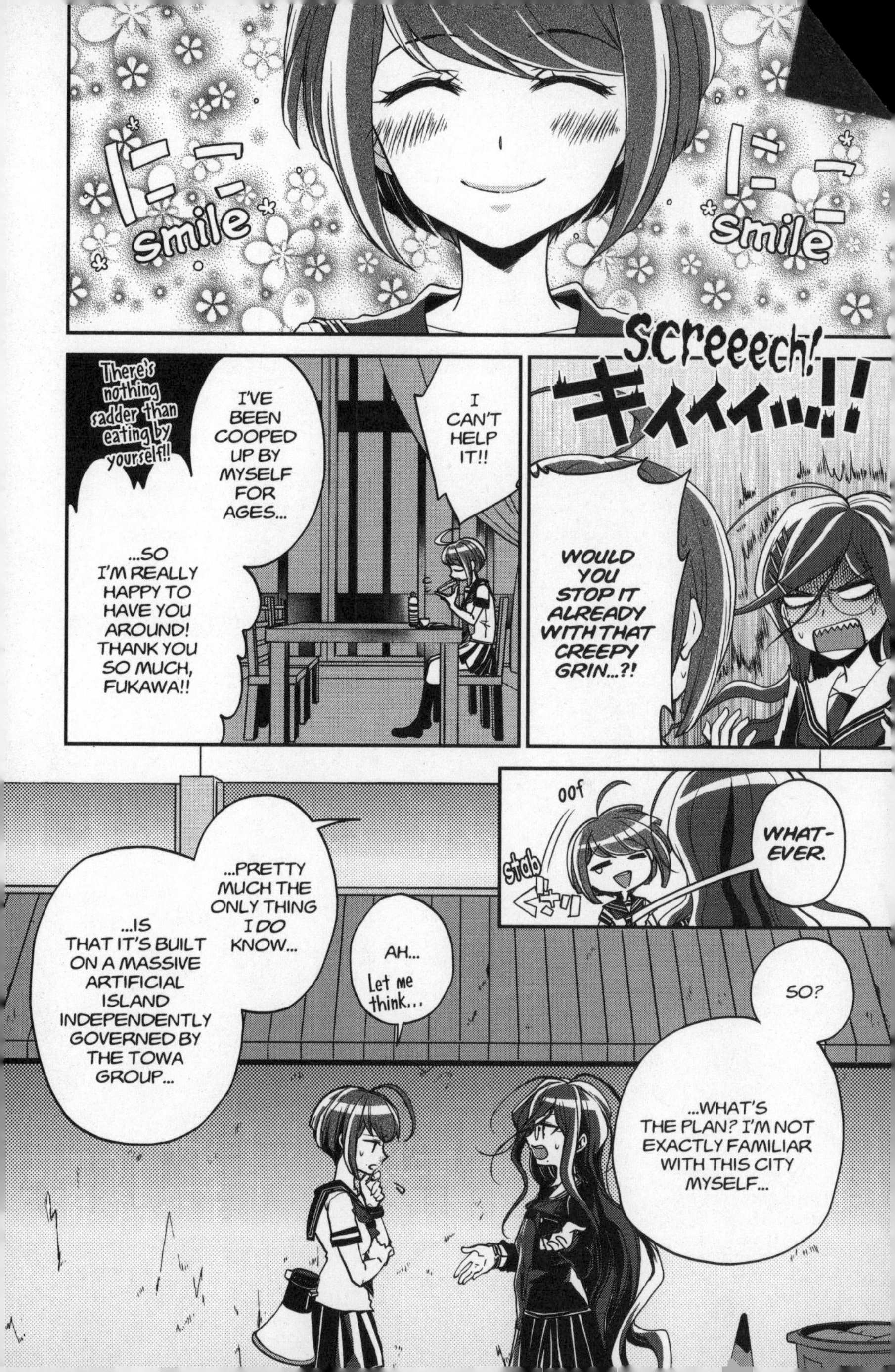
ニコー
smile
ニコー
smile
Screeech!
キイイ…!!
WOULD YOU STOP IT ALREADY WITH THAT CREEPY GRIN...?!
I CAN'T HELP IT!!
I'VE BEEN COOPED UP BY MYSELF FOR AGES...
There's nothing sadder than eating by yourself!!
...SO I'M REALLY HAPPY TO HAVE YOU AROUND! THANK YOU SO MUCH, FUKAWA!!
WHAT-EVER.
oof
stab
ぐさり
SO?
...WHAT'S THE PLAN? I'M NOT EXACTLY FAMILIAR WITH THIS CITY MYSELF...
AH...
Let me think...
...PRETTY MUCH THE ONLY THING I DO KNOW...
...IS THAT IT'S BUILT ON A MASSIVE ARTIFICIAL ISLAND INDEPENDENTLY GOVERNED BY THE TOWA GROUP...

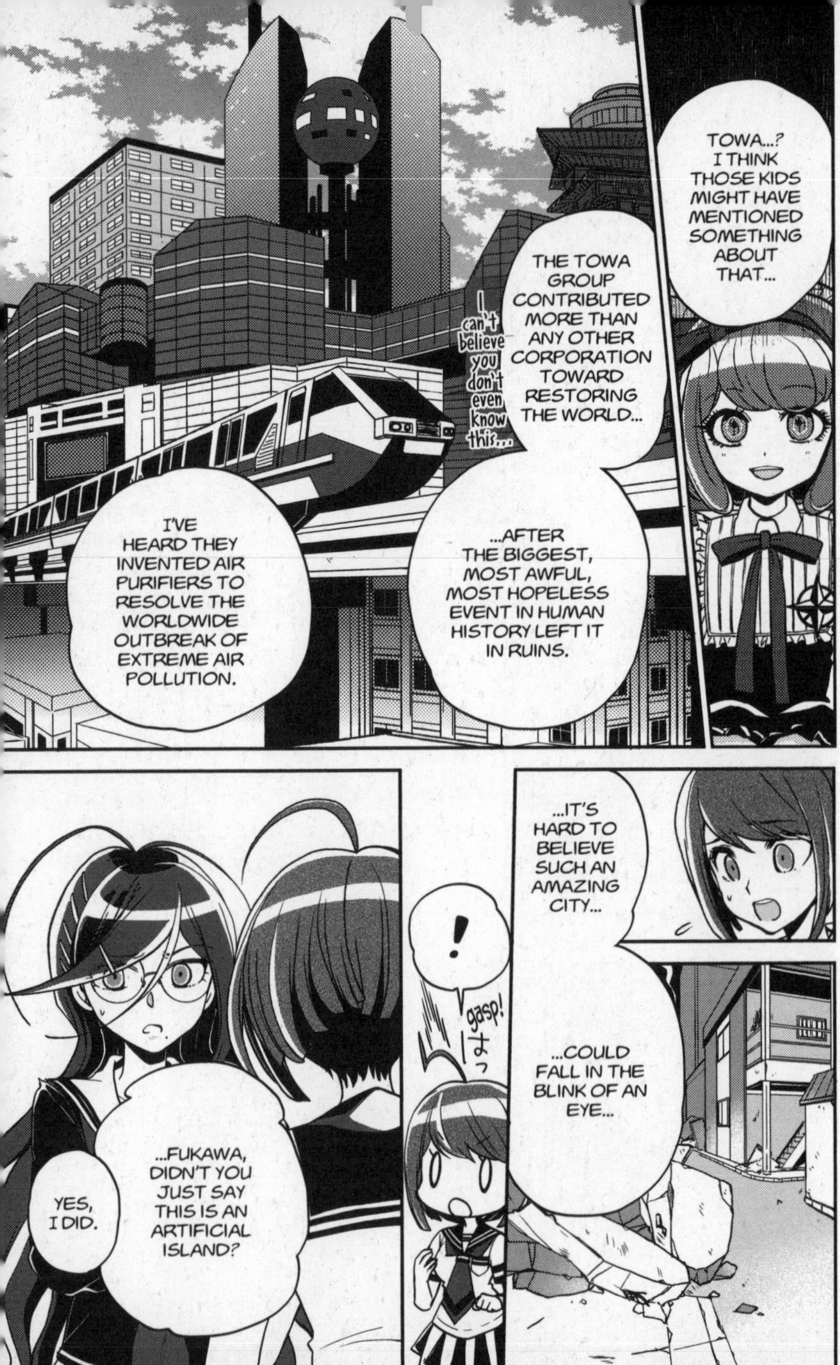
TOWA...? I THINK THOSE KIDS MIGHT HAVE MENTIONED SOMETHING ABOUT THAT...
THE TOWA GROUP CONTRIBUTED MORE THAN ANY OTHER CORPORATION TOWARD RESTORING THE WORLD...
I can't believe you don't even know this...
...AFTER THE BIGGEST, MOST AWFUL, MOST HOPELESS EVENT IN HUMAN HISTORY LEFT IT IN RUINS.
I'VE HEARD THEY INVENTED AIR PURIFIERS TO RESOLVE THE WORLDWIDE OUTBREAK OF EXTREME AIR POLLUTION.
...IT'S HARD TO BELIEVE SUCH AN AMAZING CITY...
...COULD FALL IN THE BLINK OF AN EYE...
!
gasp!
はっ
...FUKAWA, DIDN'T YOU JUST SAY THIS IS AN ARTIFICIAL ISLAND?
YES, I DID.

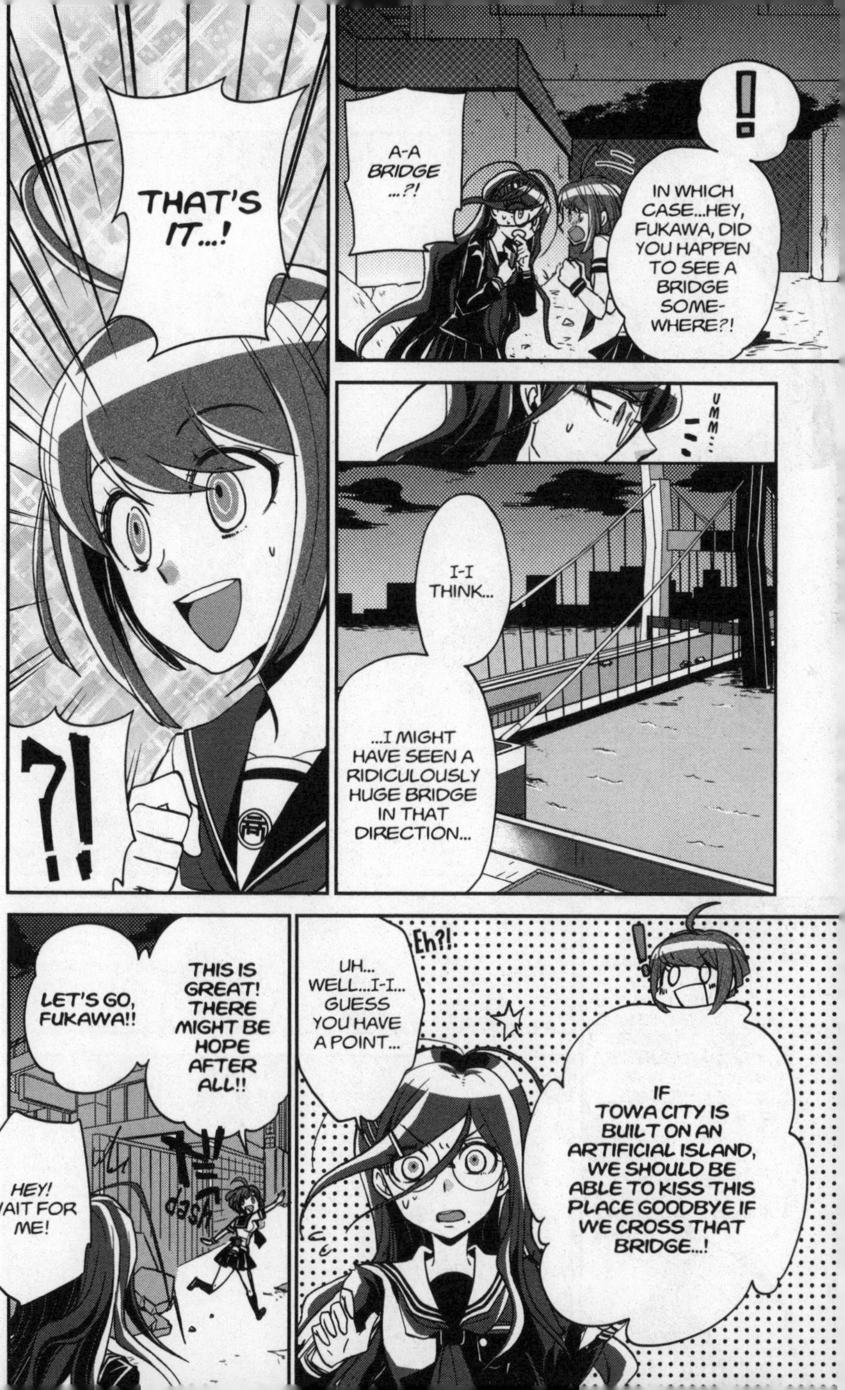
!
IN WHICH CASE...HEY, FUKAWA, DID YOU HAPPEN TO SEE A BRIDGE SOME-WHERE?!
A-A BRIDGE ...?!
UMM...
I-I THINK...
...I MIGHT HAVE SEEN A RIDICULOUSLY HUGE BRIDGE IN THAT DIRECTION...
THAT'S IT...!
?!
!
IF TOWA CITY IS BUILT ON AN ARTIFICIAL ISLAND, WE SHOULD BE ABLE TO KISS THIS PLACE GOODBYE IF WE CROSS THAT BRIDGE...!
Eh?!
UH... WELL...I-I... GUESS YOU HAVE A POINT...
THIS IS GREAT! THERE MIGHT BE HOPE AFTER ALL!!
LET'S GO, FUKAWA!!
dash
HEY! WAIT FOR ME!

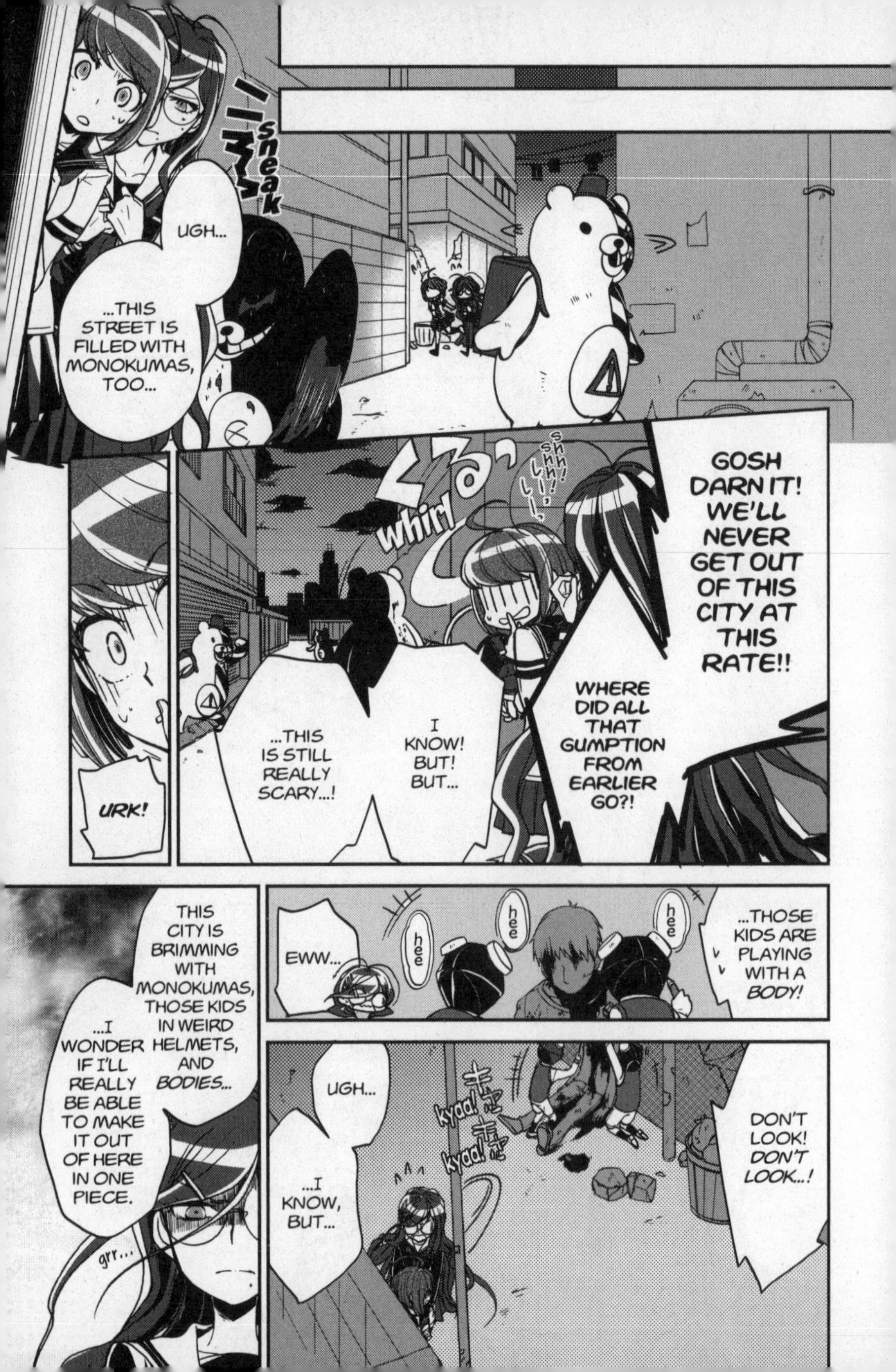
sneak
UGH...
...THIS STREET IS FILLED WITH MONOKUMAS, TOO...
GOSH DARN IT! WE'LL NEVER GET OUT OF THIS CITY AT THIS RATE!!
shh! shh!
whirl
WHERE DID ALL THAT GUMPTION FROM EARLIER GO?!
I KNOW! BUT! BUT...
...THIS IS STILL REALLY SCARY...!
URK!
...THOSE KIDS ARE PLAYING WITH A *BODY!*
hee
hee
hee
EWW...
DON'T LOOK! *DON'T LOOK...!*
kyaa!
kyaa!
UGH...
...I KNOW, BUT...
THIS CITY IS BRIMMING WITH MONOKUMAS, THOSE KIDS IN WEIRD HELMETS, AND *BODIES...*
...I WONDER IF I'LL REALLY BE ABLE TO MAKE IT OUT OF HERE IN ONE PIECE.
grr...

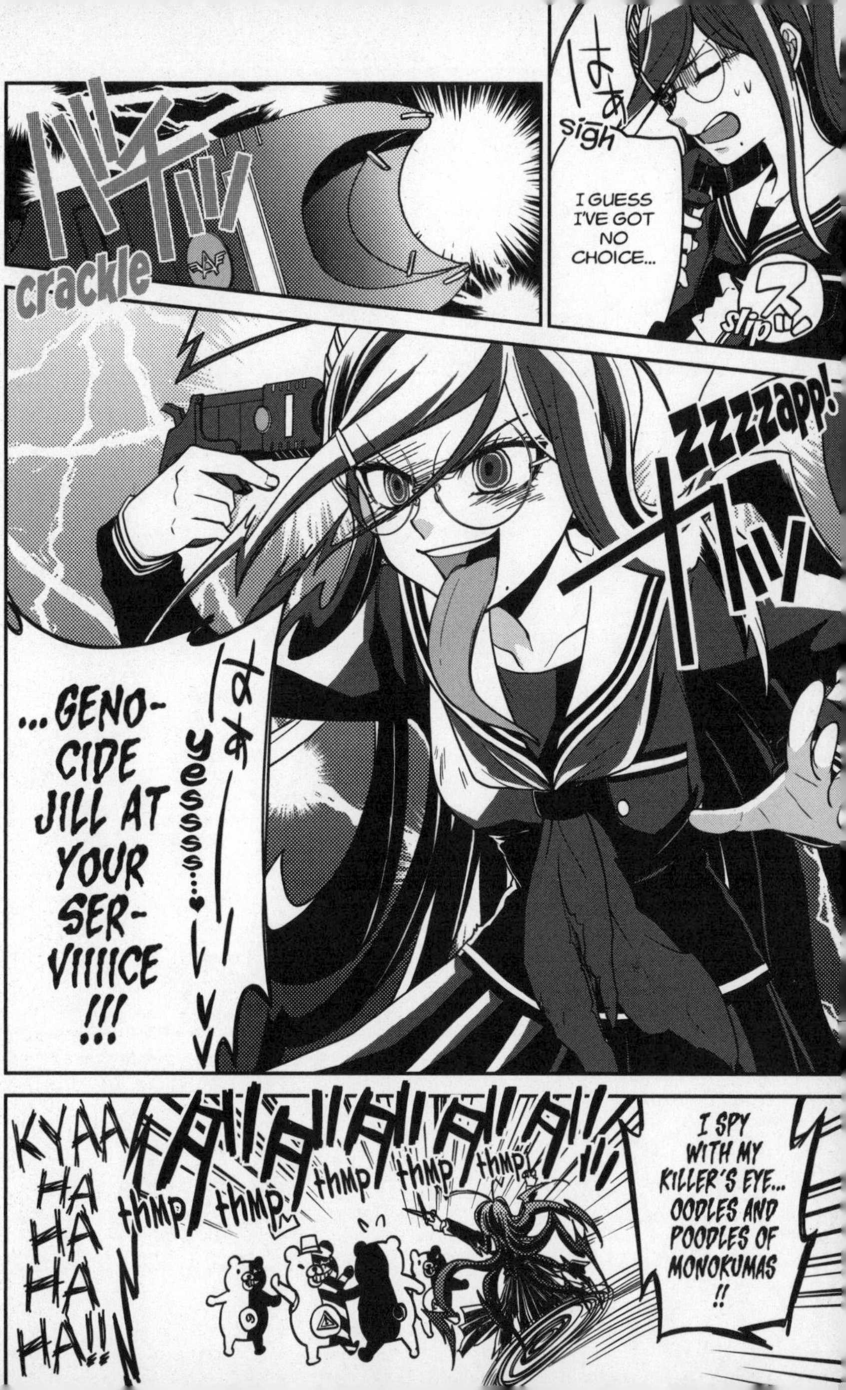

はあ
sigh
I GUESS I'VE GOT NO CHOICE...
ス
slip
crackle
ZZZZAPP!
...GENO-CIDE JILL AT YOUR SER-VIIIICE!!!
yessss...♥
I SPY WITH MY KILLER'S EYE... OODLES AND POODLES OF MONOKUMAS!!
KYAAHA HA HA HA HA!!!
thmp thmp thmp thmp thmp

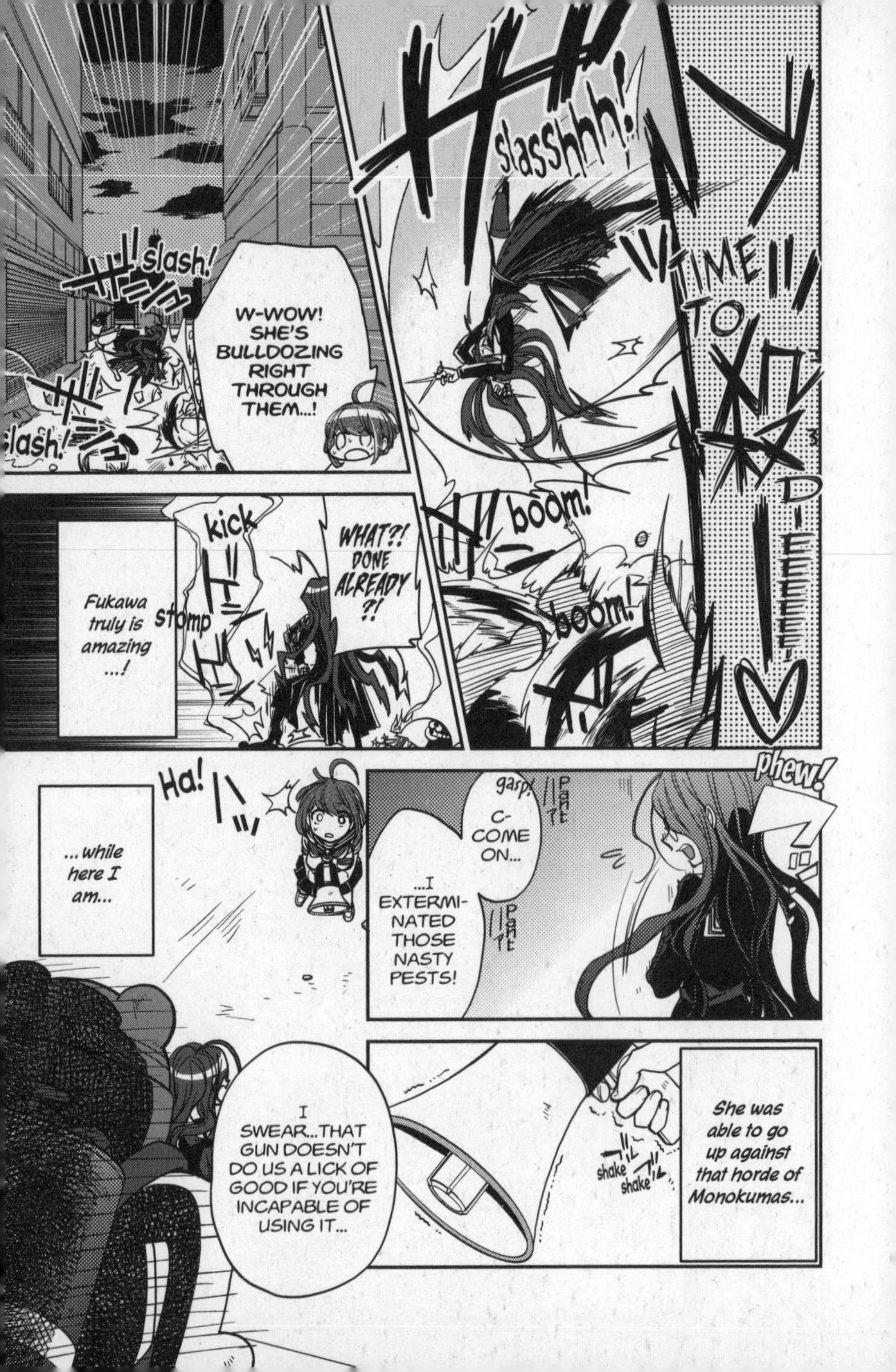
slasshhh!
TIME TO DIE♥
boom!
boom!
slash!
slash!
W-WOW! SHE'S BULLDOZING RIGHT THROUGH THEM...!
WHAT?! DONE ALREADY?!
kick
stomp
Fukawa truly is amazing...!
phew!
gasp!
pant
C-COME ON...
...I EXTERMINATED THOSE NASTY PESTS!
pant
Ha!
...while here I am...
She was able to go up against that horde of Monokumas...
shake
shake
I SWEAR...THAT GUN DOESN'T DO US A LICK OF GOOD IF YOU'RE INCAPABLE OF USING IT...

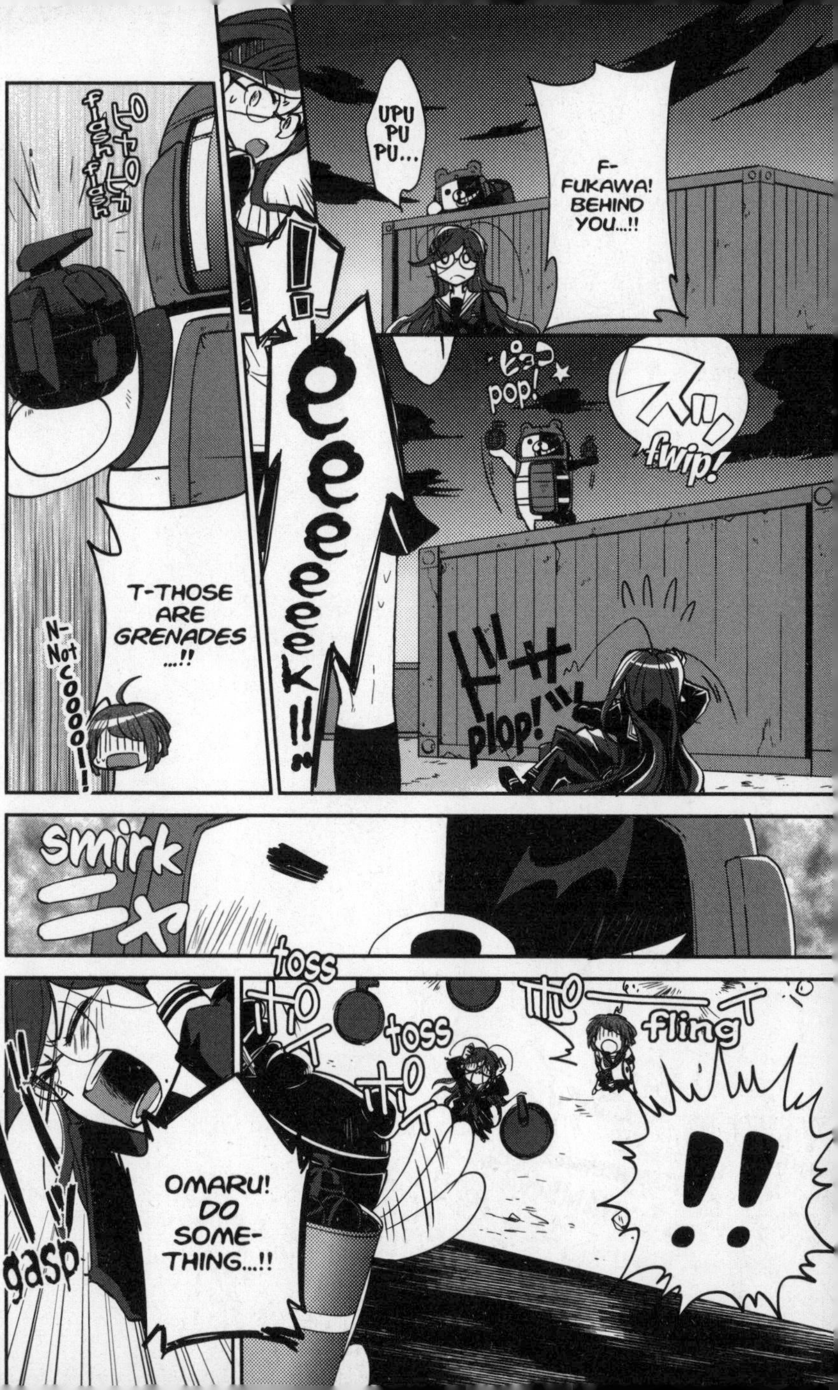

F-FUKAWA! BEHIND YOU...!!
UPU PU PU...
pop!
fwip!
plop!
!
eeeeeeek!!
flash flash
T-THOSE ARE GRENADES ...!!
N-Not cooool!!
smirk
toss
toss
fling
!!
gasp
OMARU! DO SOME-THING...!!

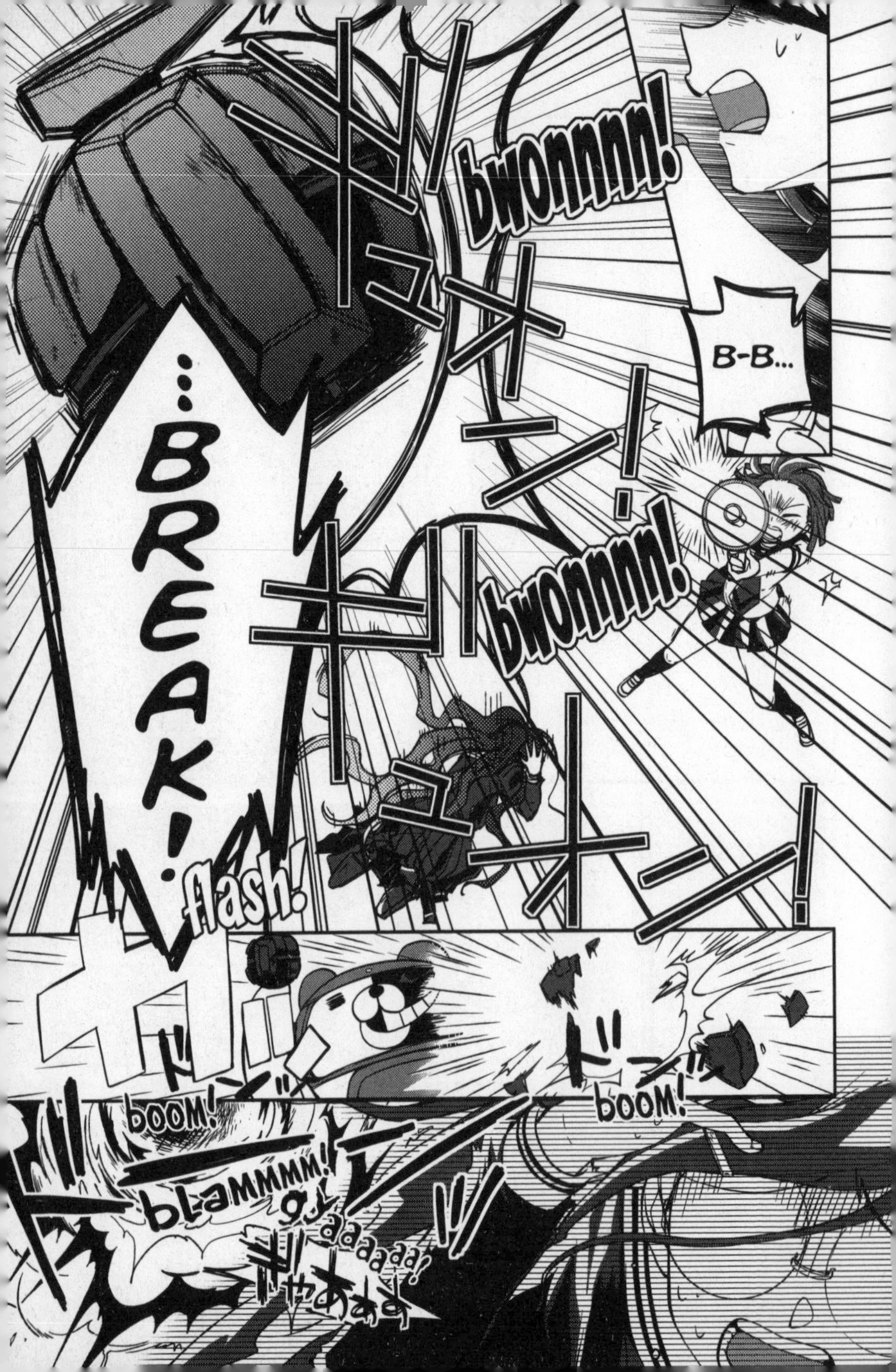
B-B...
bwonnnn!
bwonnnn!
...BREAK!
flash.
boom!
boom!
blammmm!
gyaaaaaa!

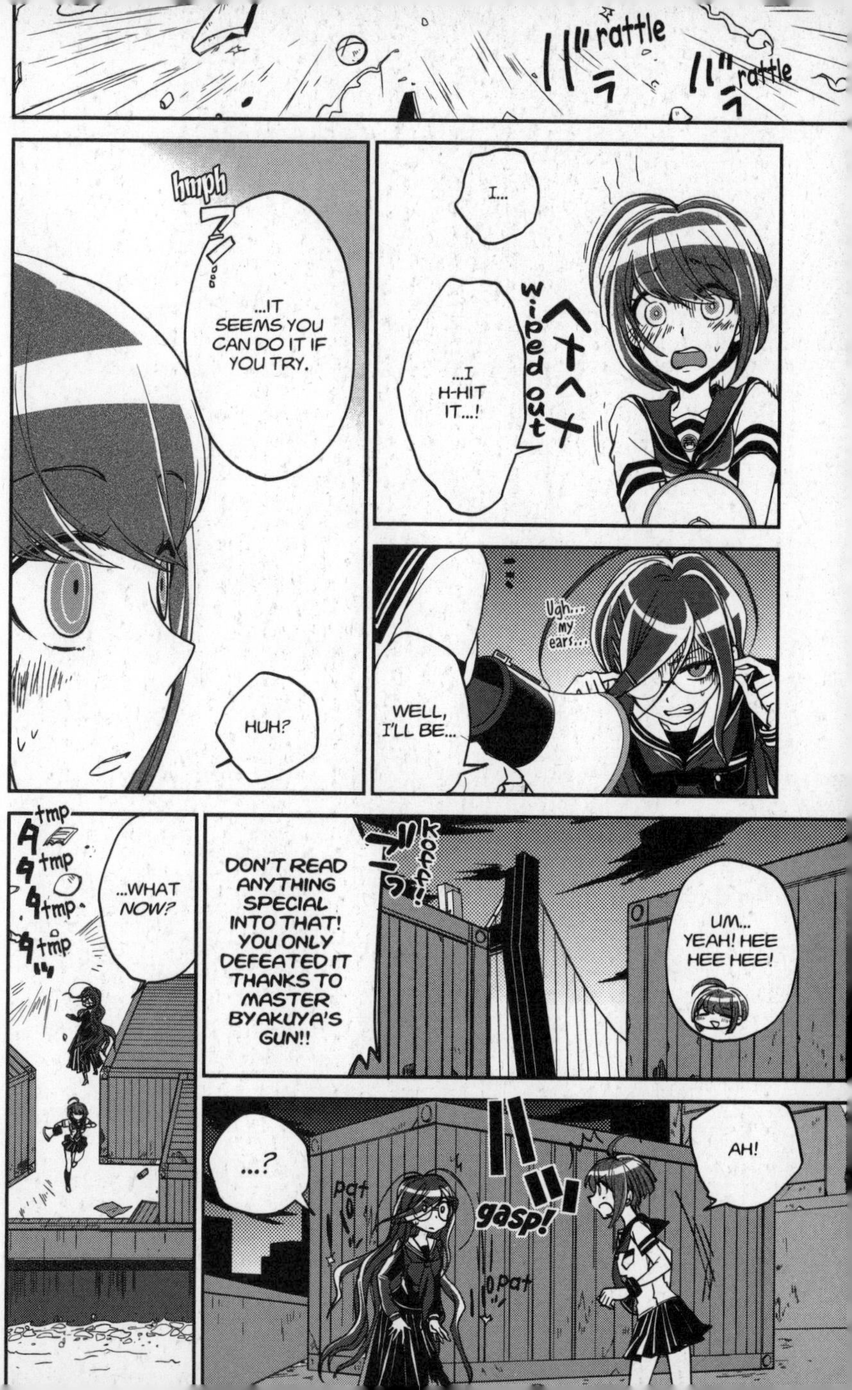
rattle
rattle
I...
...I H-HIT IT...!
wiped out
Ugh... my ears...
WELL, I'LL BE...
...
hmph
...IT SEEMS YOU CAN DO IT IF YOU TRY.
HUH?
UM... YEAH! HEE HEE HEE!
koff!
DON'T READ ANYTHING SPECIAL INTO THAT! YOU ONLY DEFEATED IT THANKS TO MASTER BYAKUYA'S GUN!!
AH!
gasp!
...?
pat
pat
tmp
tmp
tmp
tmp
...WHAT NOW?

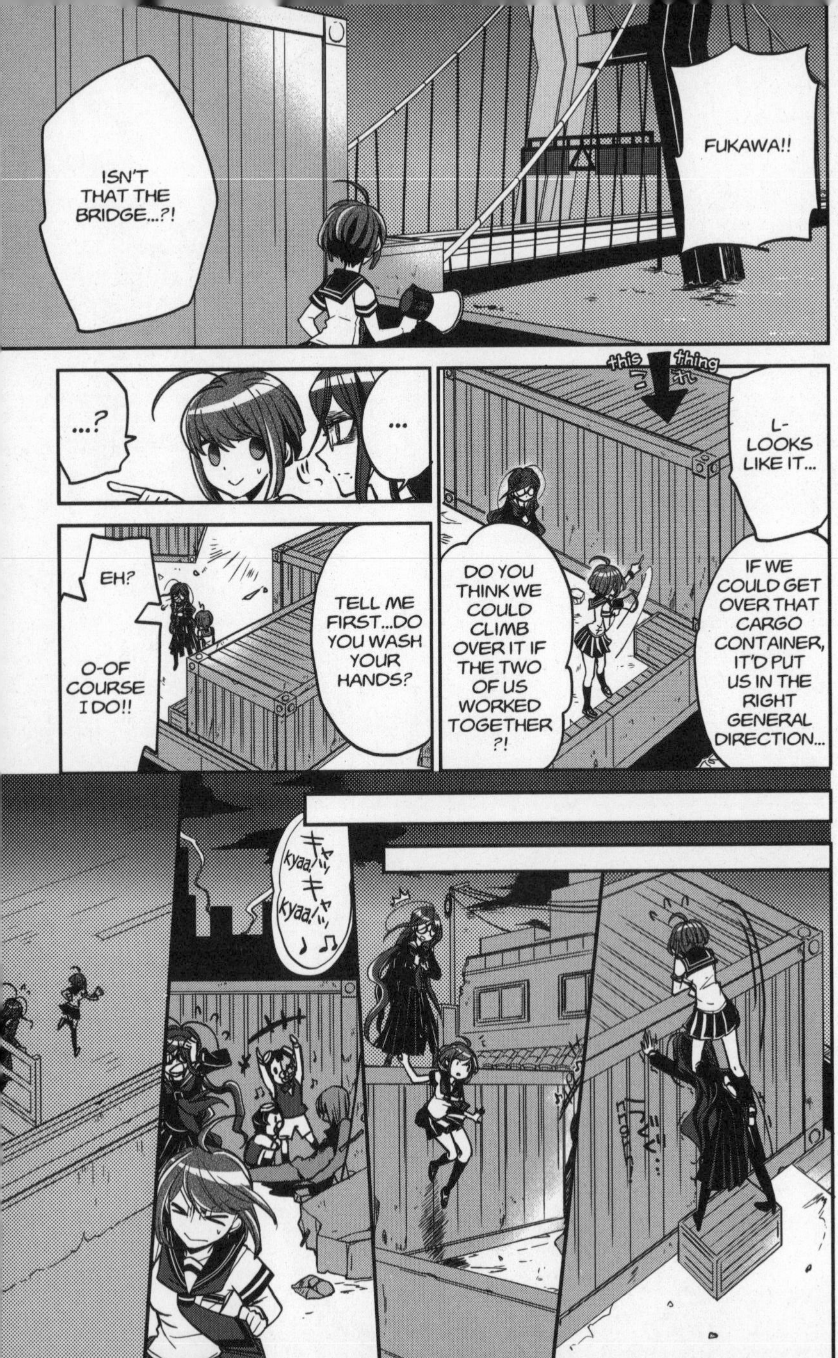
FUKAWA!!
ISN'T THAT THE BRIDGE...?!
this thing
L-LOOKS LIKE IT...
IF WE COULD GET OVER THAT CARGO CONTAINER, IT'D PUT US IN THE RIGHT GENERAL DIRECTION...
DO YOU THINK WE COULD CLIMB OVER IT IF THE TWO OF US WORKED TOGETHER?!
...
...?
TELL ME FIRST...DO YOU WASH YOUR HANDS?
EH?
O-OF COURSE I DO!!
kyaa! kyaa!

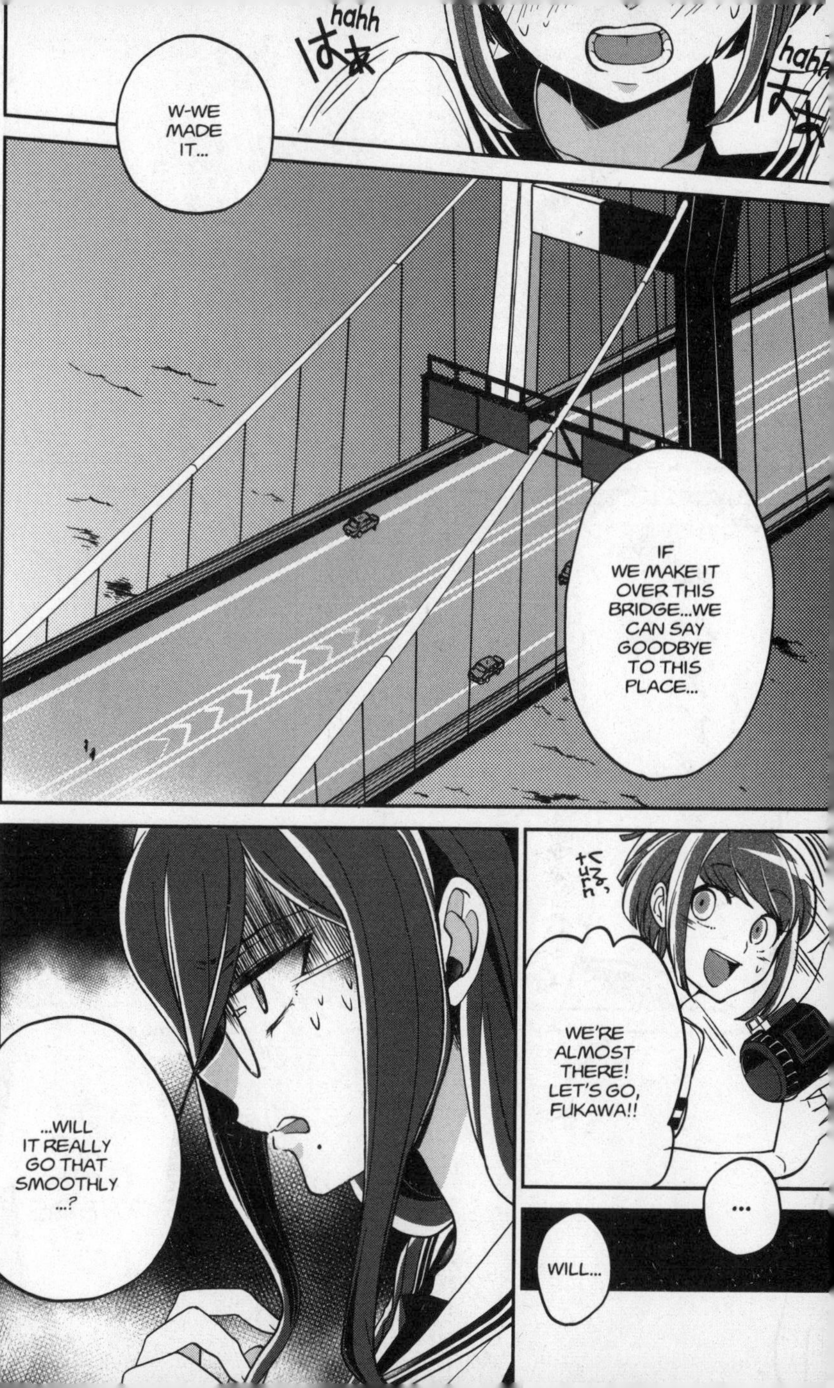
hahh
はぁ
hahh
はぁ
W-WE MADE IT...
IF WE MAKE IT OVER THIS BRIDGE...WE CAN SAY GOODBYE TO THIS PLACE...
turn
WE'RE ALMOST THERE! LET'S GO, FUKAWA!!
...
WILL...
...WILL IT REALLY GO THAT SMOOTHLY...?

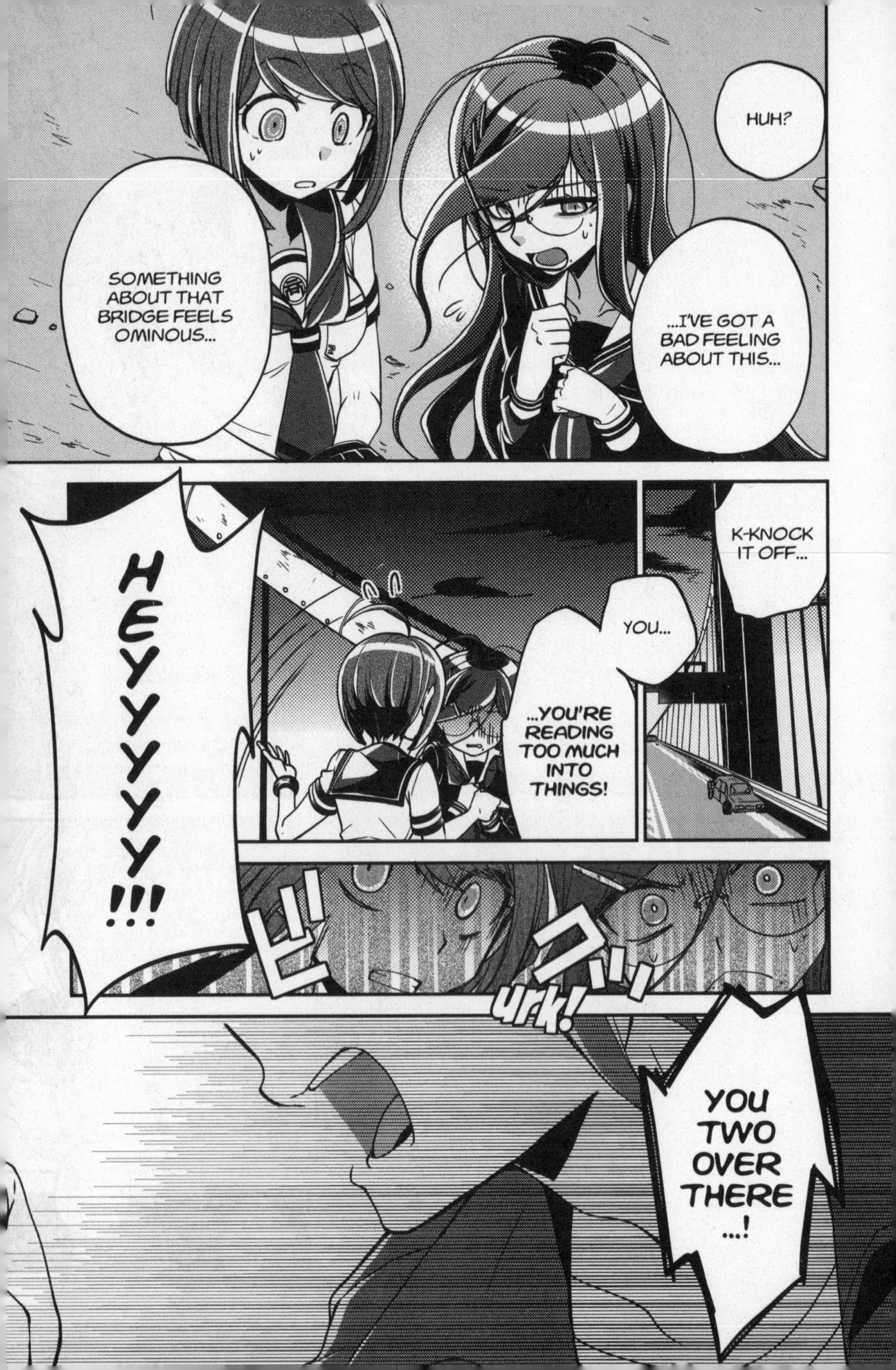
HUH?
...I'VE GOT A BAD FEELING ABOUT THIS...
SOMETHING ABOUT THAT BRIDGE FEELS OMINOUS...
K-KNOCK IT OFF...
YOU...
...YOU'RE READING TOO MUCH INTO THINGS!
HEYYYYY!!!
ビクッ
urk!
YOU TWO OVER THERE ...!

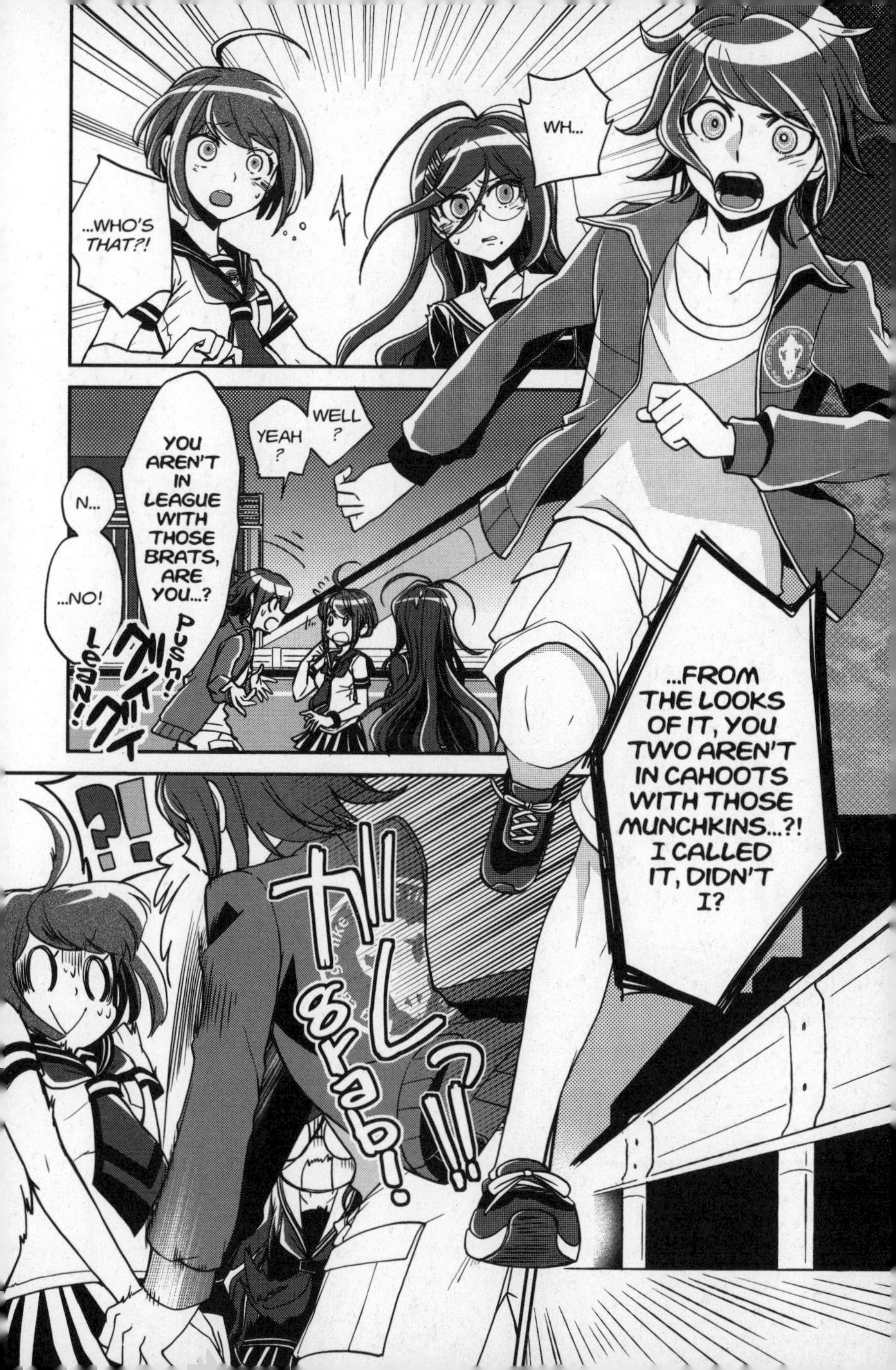
WH...
...WHO'S THAT?!
WELL?
YEAH?
YOU AREN'T IN LEAGUE WITH THOSE BRATS, ARE YOU...?
N...
...NO!
PUSH!
LEAN!
...FROM THE LOOKS OF IT, YOU TWO AREN'T IN CAHOOTS WITH THOSE MUNCHKINS...?! I CALLED IT, DIDN'T I?
?!!

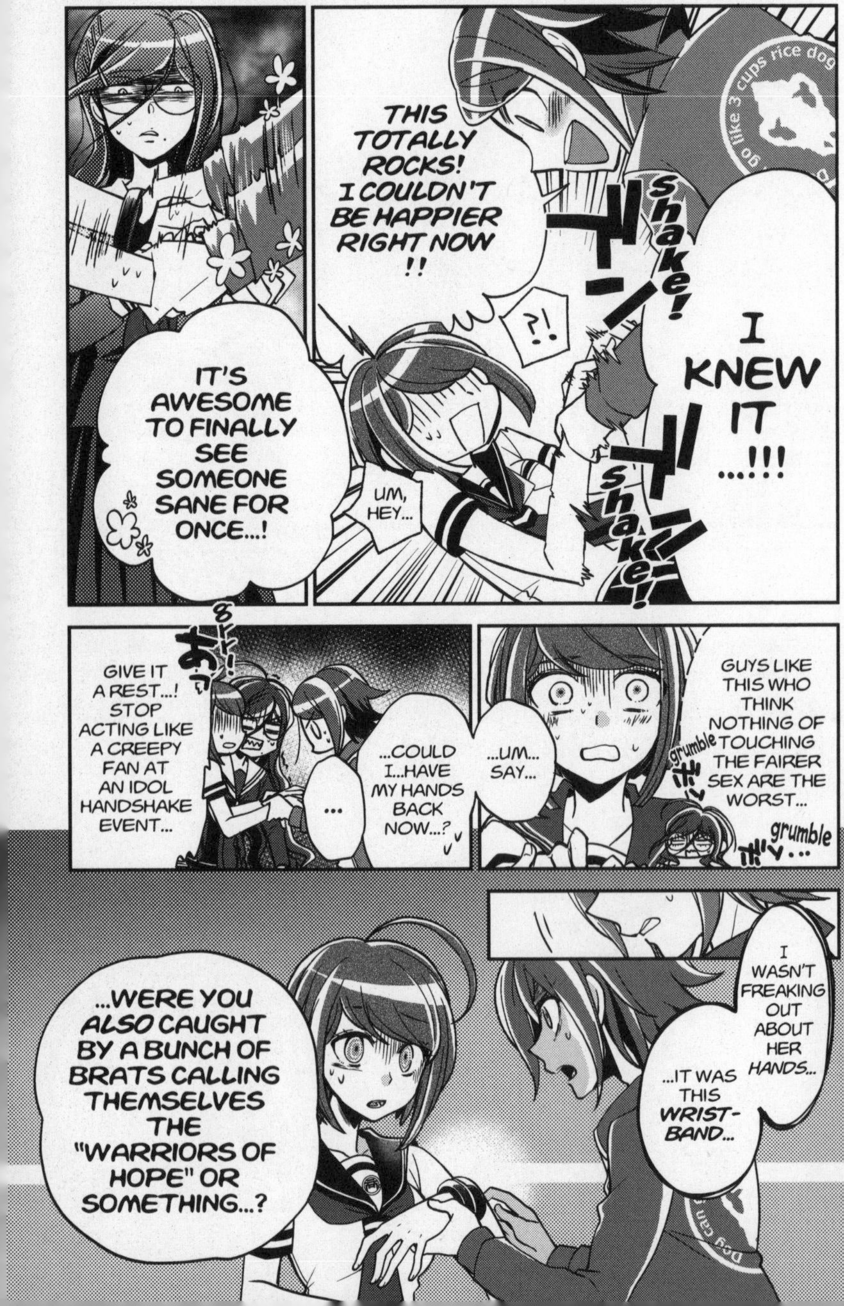

I KNEW IT ...!!!
THIS TOTALLY ROCKS! I COULDN'T BE HAPPIER RIGHT NOW !!
shake!
shake-shake!
?!
UM, HEY...
IT'S AWESOME TO FINALLY SEE SOMEONE SANE FOR ONCE...!
GUYS LIKE THIS WHO THINK NOTHING OF TOUCHING THE FAIRER SEX ARE THE WORST...
grumble
grumble...
...UM... SAY...
...COULD I...HAVE MY HANDS BACK NOW...?
...
GIVE IT A REST...! STOP ACTING LIKE A CREEPY FAN AT AN IDOL HANDSHAKE EVENT...
I WASN'T FREAKING OUT ABOUT HER HANDS...
...IT WAS THIS WRIST-BAND...
...WERE YOU ALSO CAUGHT BY A BUNCH OF BRATS CALLING THEMSELVES THE "WARRIORS OF HOPE" OR SOMETHING...?

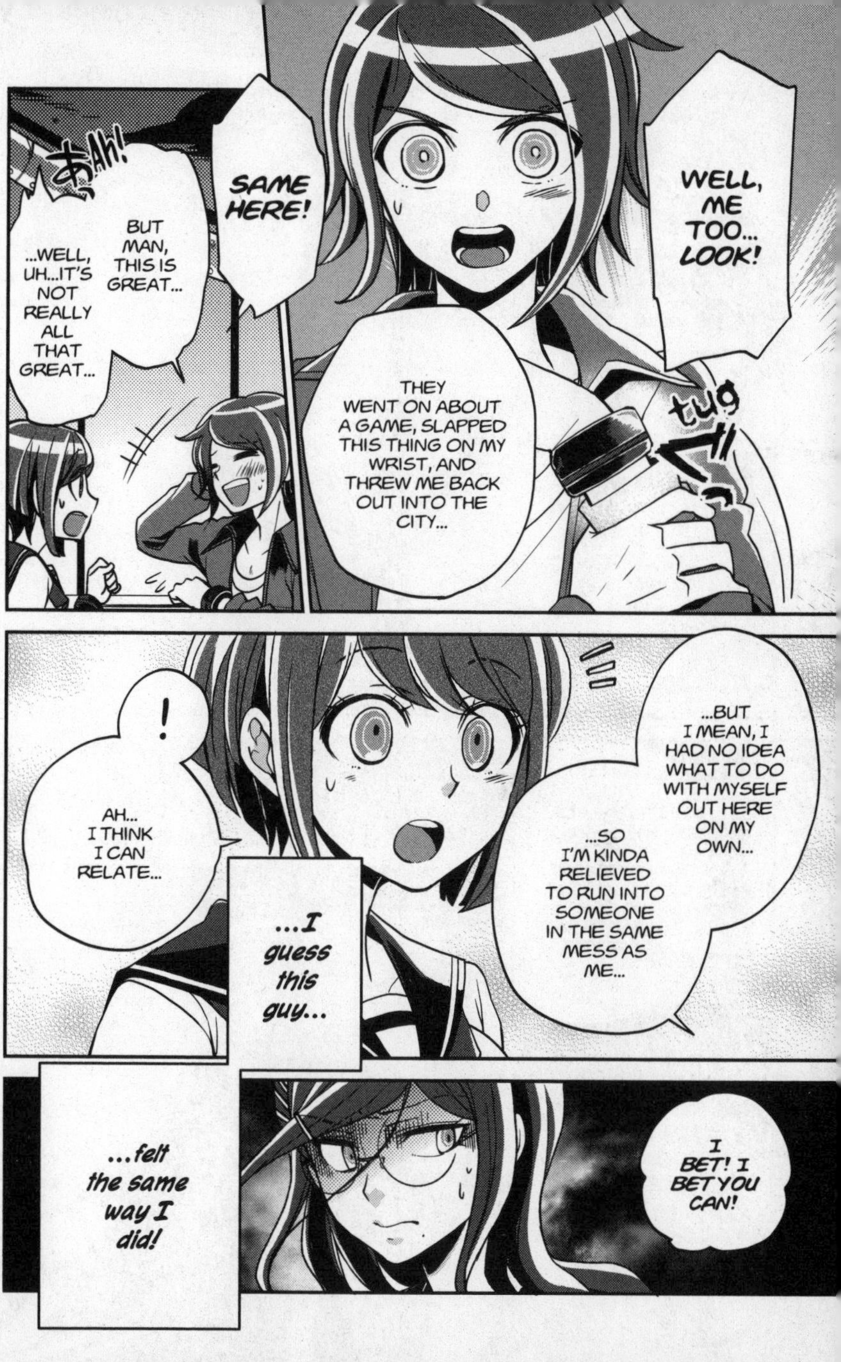
WELL, ME TOO... LOOK!
tug
THEY WENT ON ABOUT A GAME, SLAPPED THIS THING ON MY WRIST, AND THREW ME BACK OUT INTO THE CITY...
SAME HERE!
あ Ah!
BUT MAN, THIS IS GREAT...
...WELL, UH...IT'S NOT REALLY ALL THAT GREAT...
...BUT I MEAN, I HAD NO IDEA WHAT TO DO WITH MYSELF OUT HERE ON MY OWN...
...SO I'M KINDA RELIEVED TO RUN INTO SOMEONE IN THE SAME MESS AS ME...
...I guess this guy...
!
AH... I THINK I CAN RELATE...
I BET! I BET YOU CAN!
...felt the same way I did!

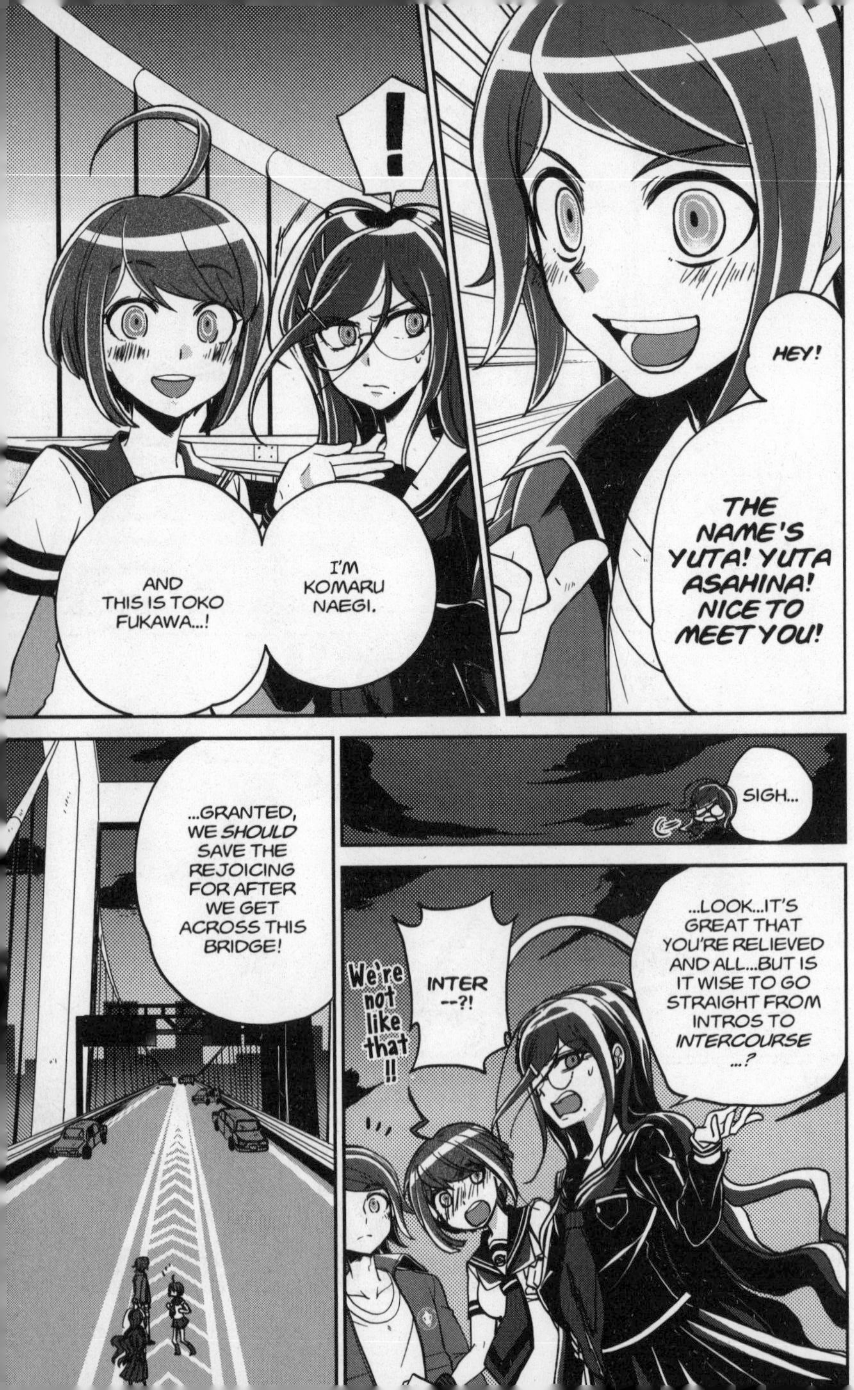
HEY!
THE NAME'S YUTA! YUTA ASAHINA! NICE TO MEET YOU!
I'M KOMARU NAEGI.
AND THIS IS TOKO FUKAWA...!
SIGH...
...LOOK...IT'S GREAT THAT YOU'RE RELIEVED AND ALL...BUT IS IT WISE TO GO STRAIGHT FROM INTROS TO INTERCOURSE ...?
INTER --?!
We're not like that!!
...GRANTED, WE SHOULD SAVE THE REJOICING FOR AFTER WE GET ACROSS THIS BRIDGE!

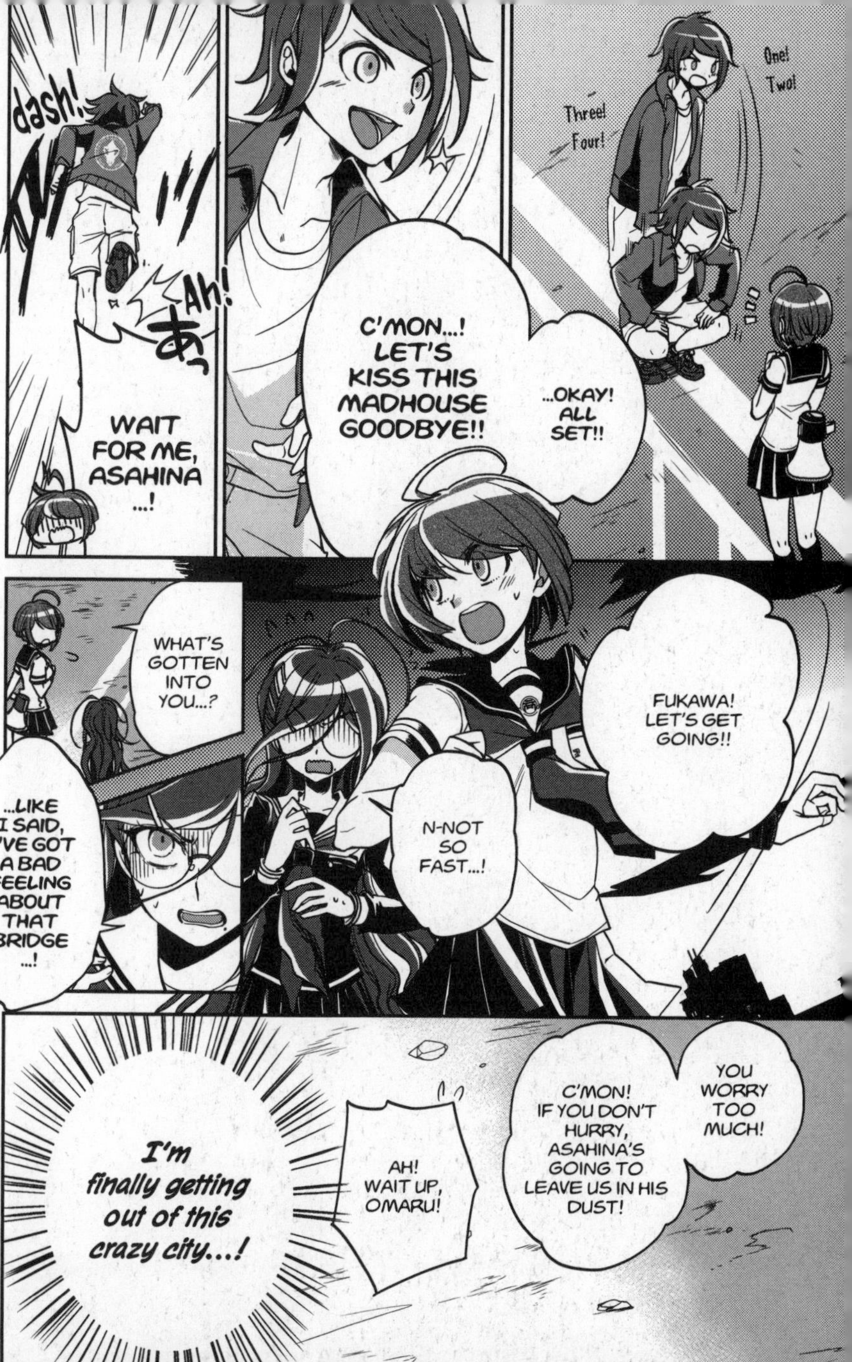
One! Two!
Three! Four!
...OKAY! ALL SET!!
C'MON...! LET'S KISS THIS MADHOUSE GOODBYE!!
dash!
Ah!
あ
WAIT FOR ME, ASAHINA ...!
FUKAWA! LET'S GET GOING!!
N-NOT SO FAST...!
WHAT'S GOTTEN INTO YOU...?
...LIKE I SAID, I'VE GOT A BAD FEELING ABOUT THAT BRIDGE ...!
YOU WORRY TOO MUCH!
C'MON! IF YOU DON'T HURRY, ASAHINA'S GOING TO LEAVE US IN HIS DUST!
AH! WAIT UP, OMARU!
I'm finally getting out of this crazy city...!

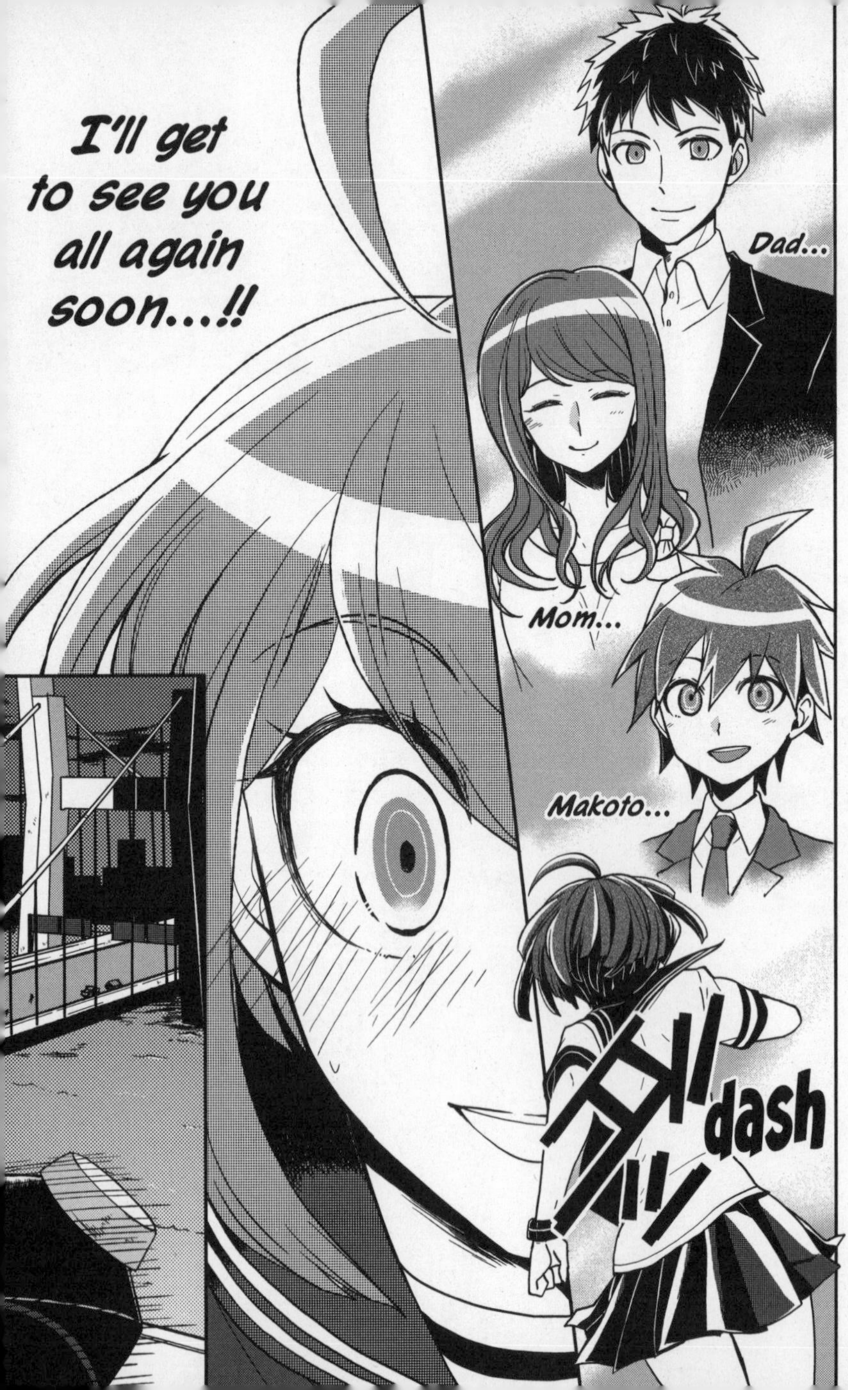
Dad...
Mom...
Makoto...
dash
I'll get to see you all again soon...!!

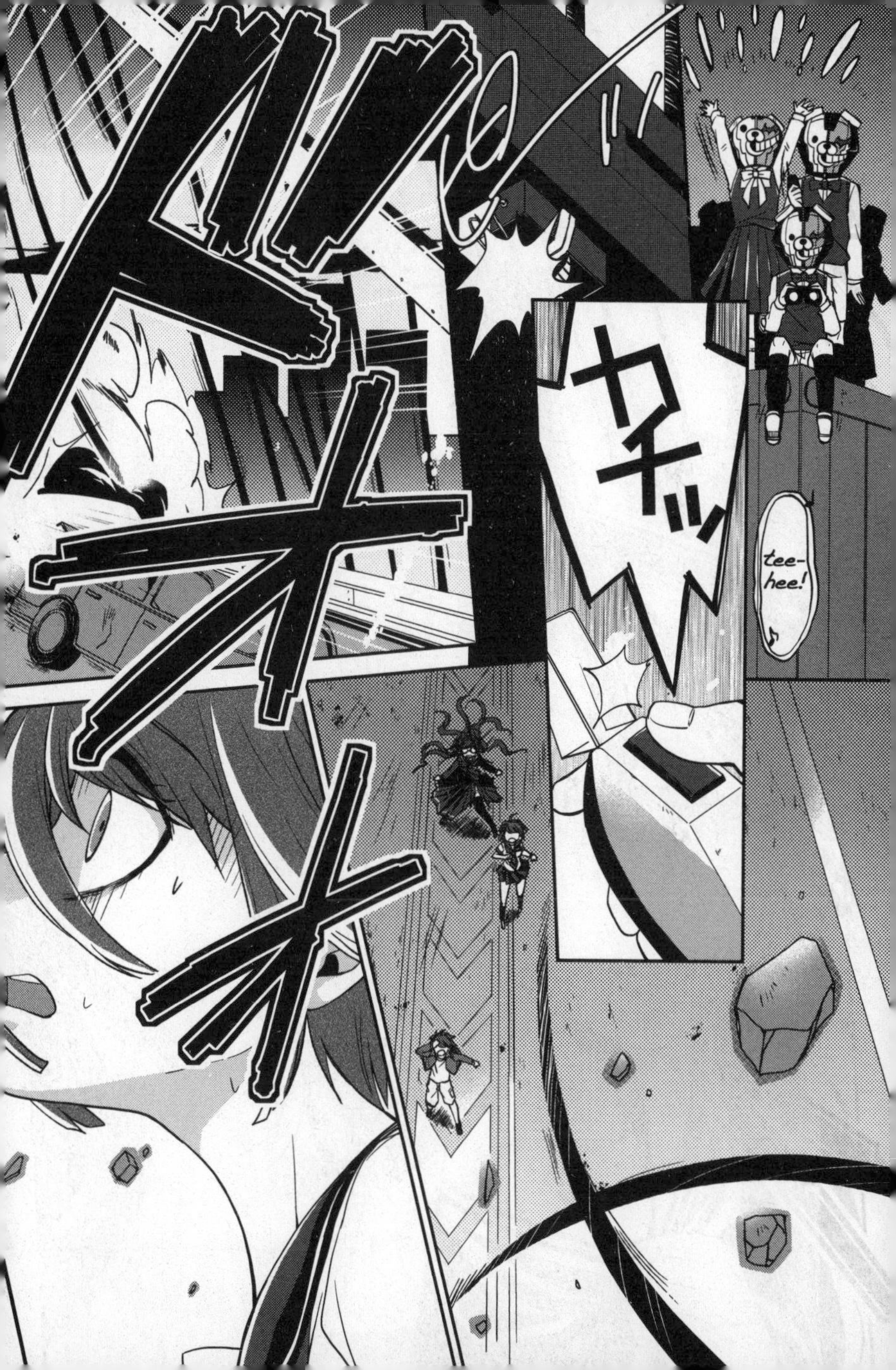
カチッ
tee-hee!

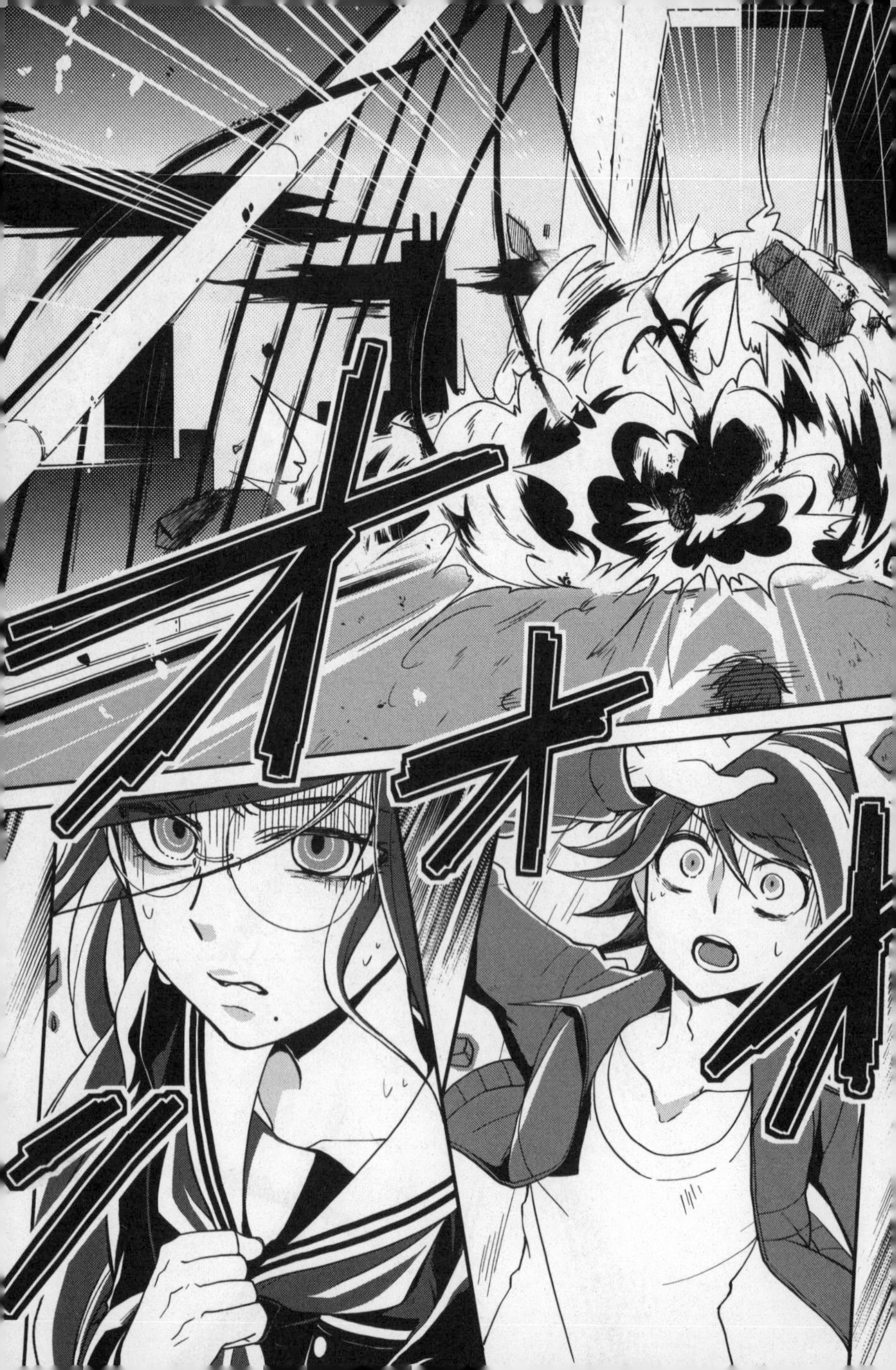

CONTINUED IN VOL. 2 . . .

Danganronpa Another Episode:
Ultra Despair Girls

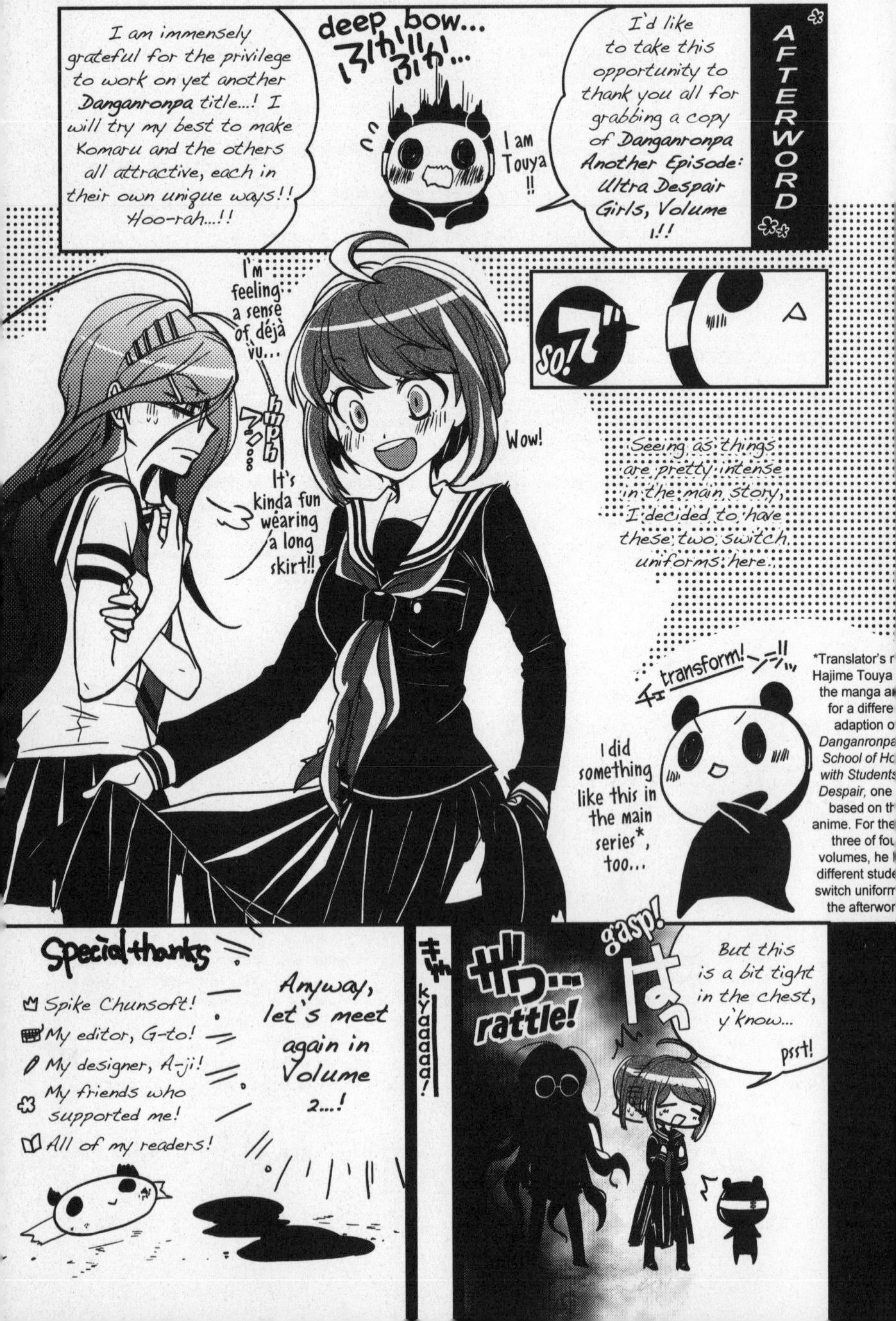
AFTERWORD
I'd like to take this opportunity to thank you all for grabbing a copy of Danganronpa Another Episode: Ultra Despair Girls, Volume 1!!
I am Touya!!
deep bow...
I am immensely grateful for the privilege to work on yet another Danganronpa title...! I will try my best to make Komaru and the others all attractive, each in their own unique ways!! Hoo-rah...!!
so!
Seeing as things are pretty intense in the main story, I decided to have these two switch uniforms here.
Wow!
It's kinda fun wearing a long skirt!!
I'm feeling a sense of déjà vu...
hmph
transform!
I did something like this in the main series*, too...
But this is a bit tight in the chest, y'know...
gasp!
rattle!
psst!
kyaaaaa!
Anyway, let's meet again in Volume 2...!
Special thanks
Spike Chunsoft!
My editor, G-to!
My designer, A-ji!
My friends who supported me!
All of my readers!

*Translator's n Hajime Touya the manga a for a differe adaption o *Danganronpa School of Ho with Students Despair,* one based on th anime. For the three of fou volumes, he different stude switch uniform the afterwor

President and Publisher // **Mike Richardson**

Designer // **Skyler Weissenfluh**

Ultimate Digital Art Technician // **Samantha Hummer**

English-language version produced by Dark Horse Comics

DANGANRONPA ANOTHER EPISODE: ULTRA DESPAIR GIRLS VOLUME 1

Published by
Dark Horse Manga
A division of Dark Horse Comics LLC
10956 SE Main Street
Milwaukie, OR 97222

DarkHorse.com

To find a comics shop in your area, visit comicshoplocator.com

First edition: August 2019
ISBN 978-1-50671-362-5

5 7 9 10 8 6 4

Printed in the United States of America

DESPAIR MAIL

c/o Dark Horse Comics | 10956 SE Main St. | Milwaukie, OR 97222 | danganronpa@darkhorse.com

Welcome back, everyone! As mentioned in the just-concluded Danganronpa 2: Ultimate Luck and Hope and Despair, *we're beginning our next* Danganronpa *manga series now,* Danganronpa Another Episode: Ultra Despair Girls. *And can there be any better way to kick off* **DESPAIR MAIL** *this time than with the Ultra Despair Girls themselves, Toko and Komaru? No, I don't think so. This "wish you were ~~despair~~ here" photo is courtesy of . . . well, check the next page!*

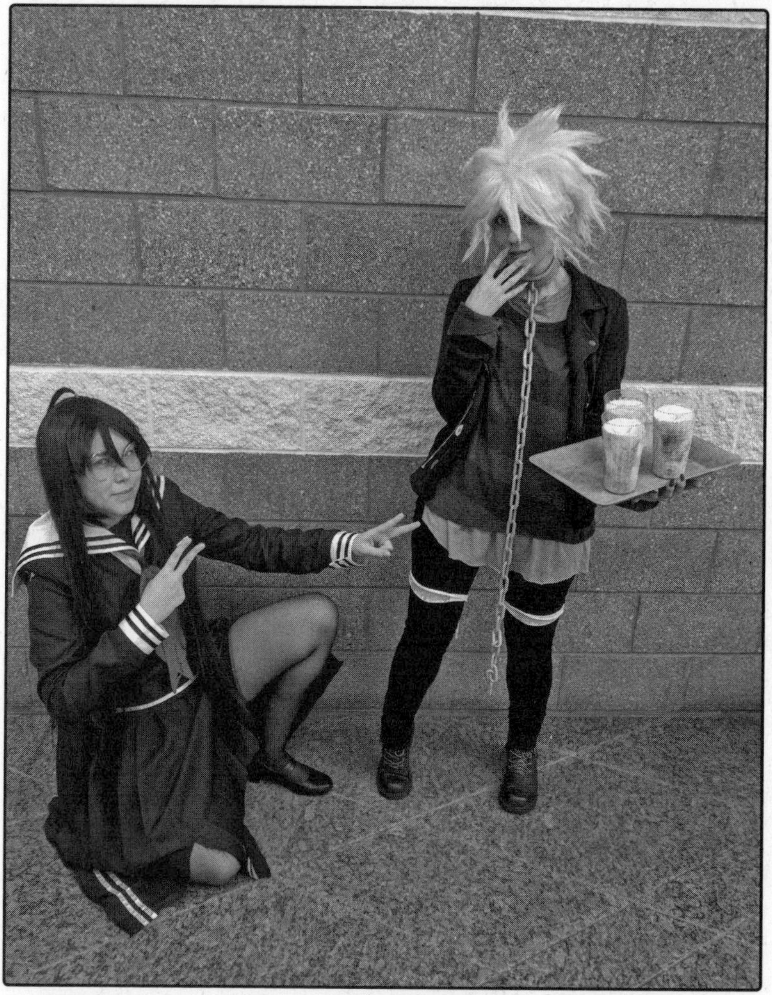

Caitlin/Toko poses with your humble Servant (pay him no mind) and tells **DESPAIR MAIL**, *"Hello! My name is Caitlin, or @komochi.cosplay on Instagram. I have been cosplaying* Danganronpa *since 2014, and this series remains very close to my despair-ridden heart. My latest cosplay is Toko Fukawa as a part of an* Ultra Despair Girls *cosplay group!* Danganronpa *has helped me make so many lifelong friends, so I am so appreciative to Dark Horse for embracing this series as well. Thank you for all that you do! With much love and despair, Caitlin."*

Just a little
chunch of hope,
keeps me going
everyday.

GG.

Yeah! Like Nagi—I mean, Servant says, just pay him no mind. He seems
like a harmless enough fellow, and I'm sure that chain around his neck is
for no particular reason. This drawing is from Grace Grasham, who says,
"Hi, I really love Danganronpa. I played all the games, watch the
animations, and have read all the books so far. I would be so happy if you
added my art, thanks :)" We're happy to do so!

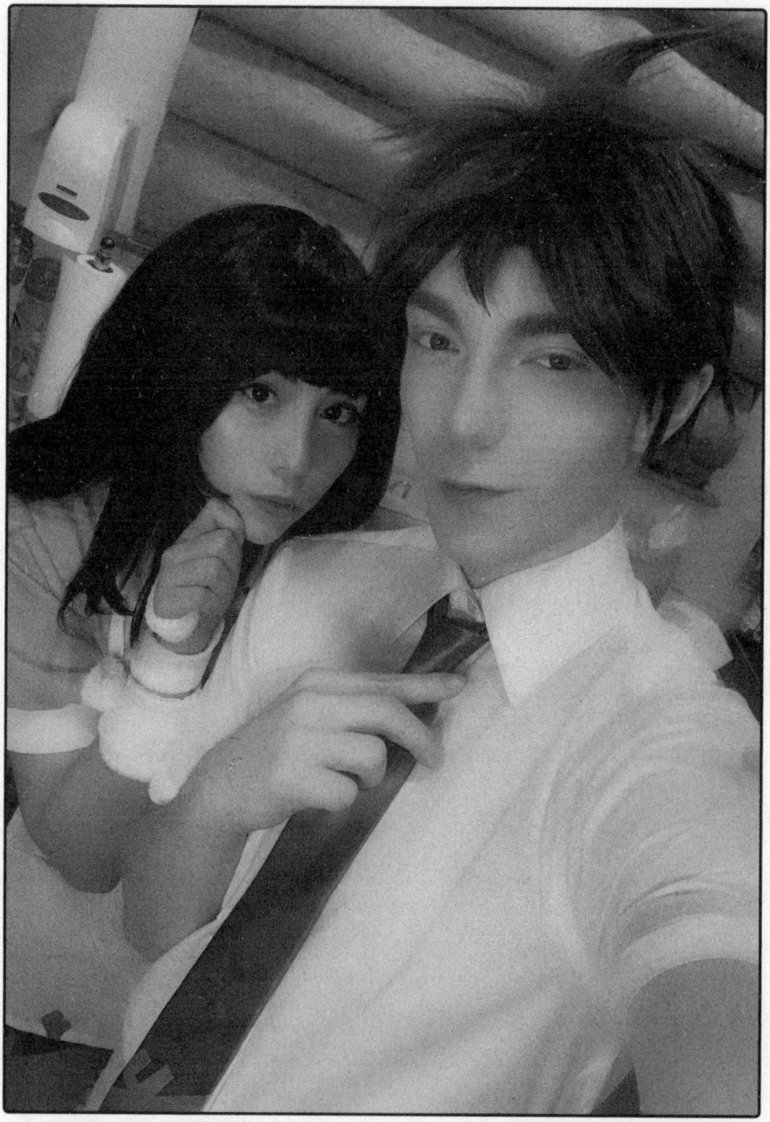

"Hello, my name is Garret. I really love Danganronpa, *it's such a wonderful series. I love being able to cosplay from it with my girlfriend Jade—we both really love Mikan and Hajime, and Shuichi and Tsumugi."*

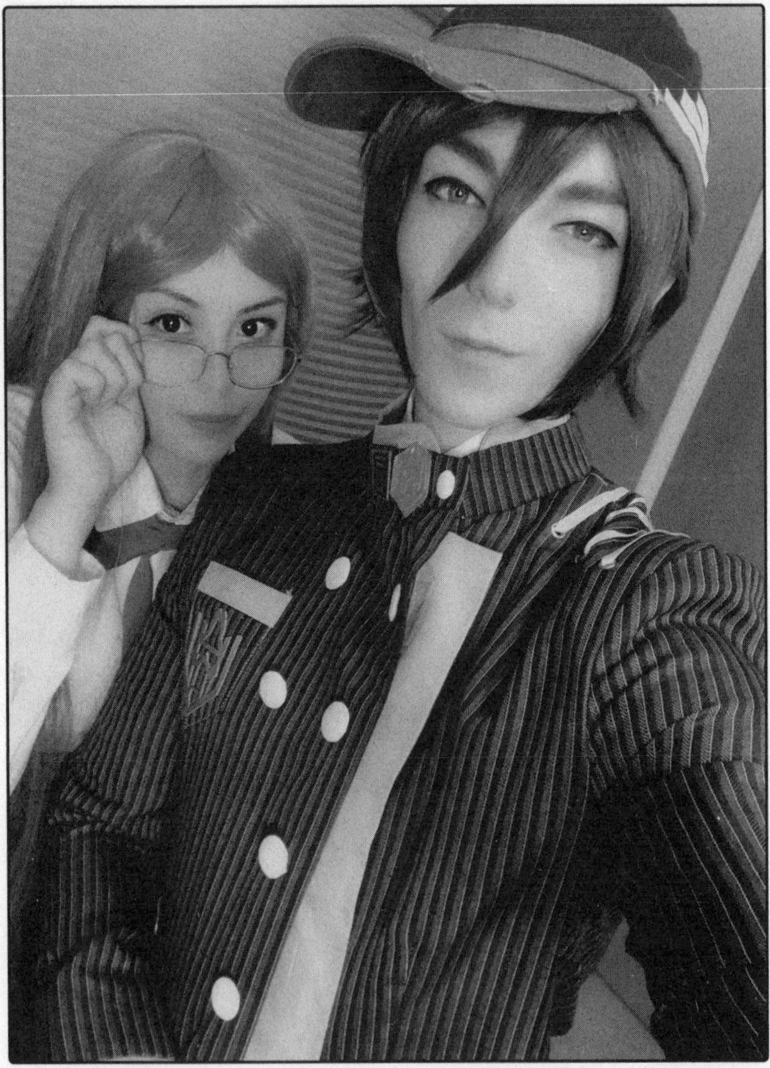

Of course, we just saw Mikan and Hajime in Danganronpa 2: Ultimate Luck and Hope and Despair *(and we'll see them again in our next series,* Danganronpa 2: Goodbye Despair*) but Shuichi Saihara and Tsumugi Shirogane, naturally, lie in the future of the* Danganronpa *storyline, in* Danganronpa 3: Killing Harmony.

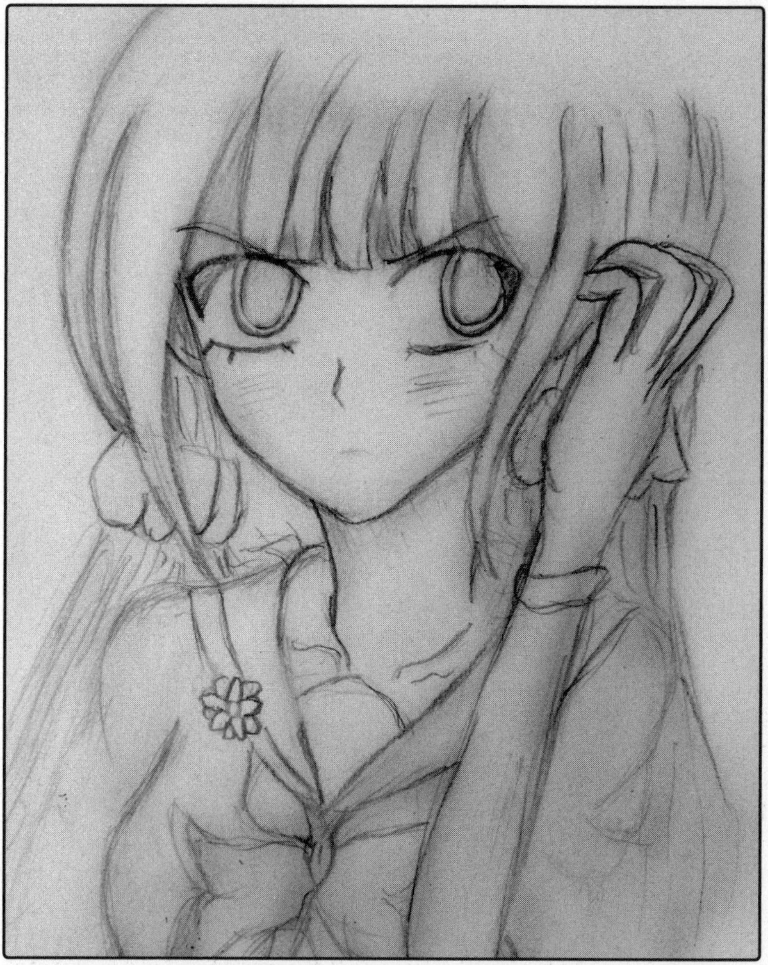

As, of course, is Maki Harukawa, depicted here by Boovaliant, who says, "Hey! I'm kinda nervous sending this, but I want to show my love for this series and the work that has been put into it. Danganronpa *has changed my life pretty dramatically, and it made me more confident, it's hard to explain…regards, Boovaliant!" A lot of people have written in to* **DESPAIR MAIL** *to talk about the positive influence* **Danganronpa** *has had for them. As was pointed out in an earlier* **DESPAIR MAIL**, *someone at Dark Horse found out during a routine check-up that their doctor was a* Danganronpa *fan, so society benefits too ^_^*

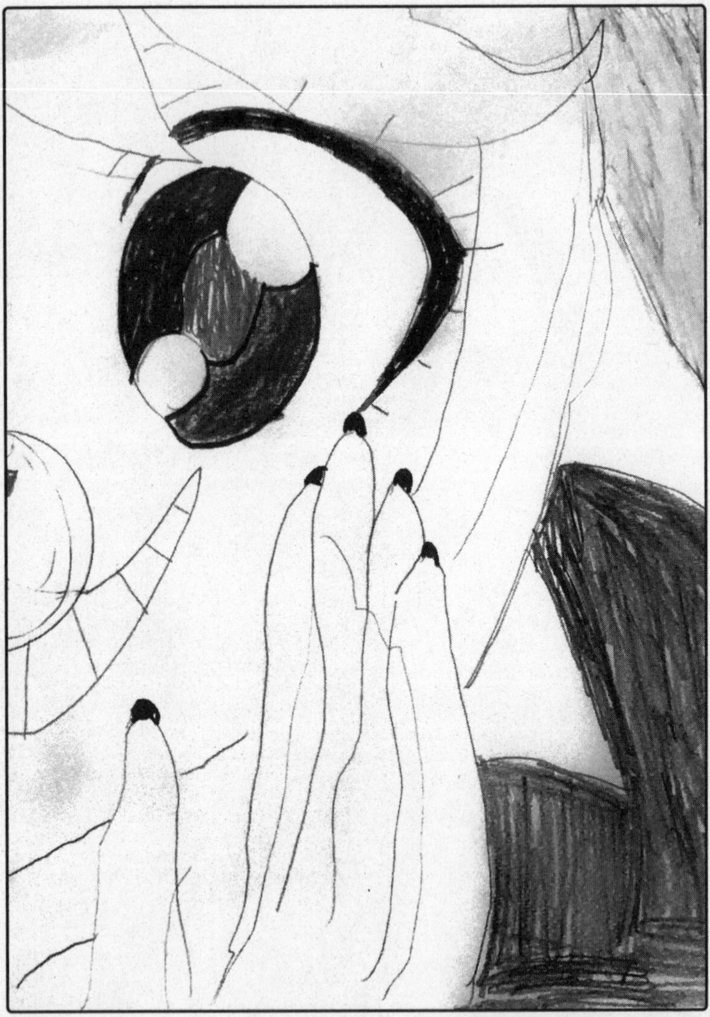

Of course, we're not saying you HAVE to be positive. Maybe sometimes you feel like hurling the world into the depths of profound, sublime despair. Gaze deep into this drawing from Dankcidueye, who says, "I was reading the first series of the Danganronpa *manga, and I saw* **DESPAIR MAIL** *was a thing, and I thought that it would be fun to send a submission, so I have some art here of Enoshima combined with Monokuma. I think I got the quality right, so here ya go. UPUPUPUPUPU."*

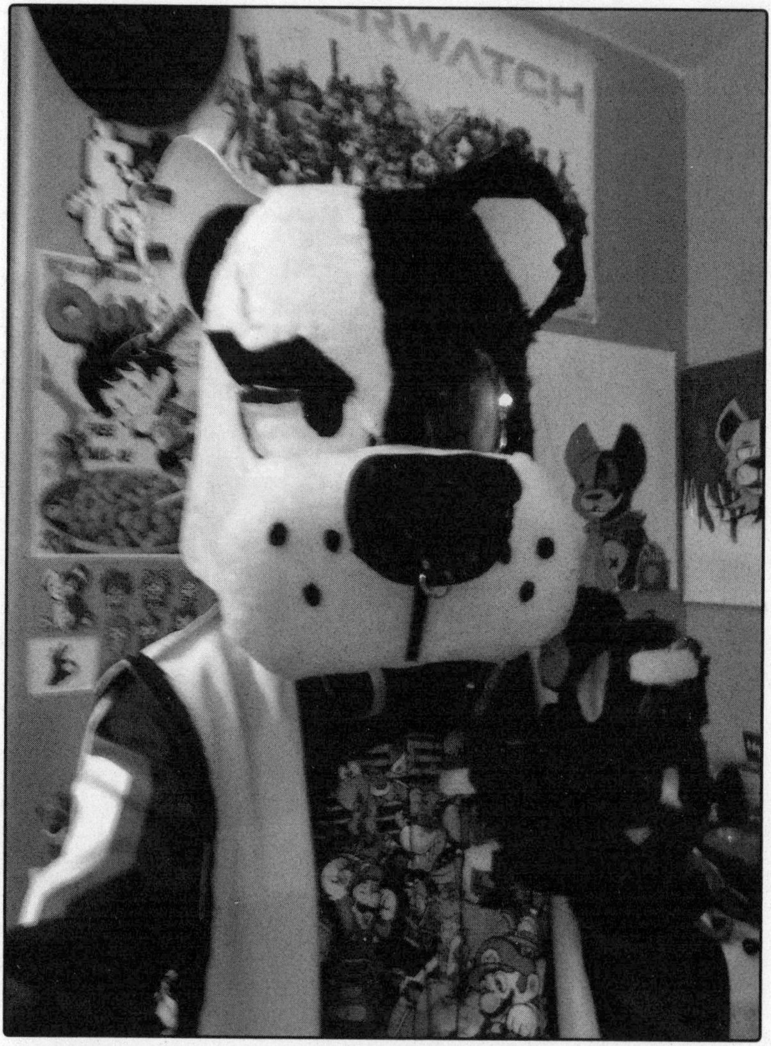

"Hello, my name is Sienna, and I wanted to show you guys my Monokuma mask. I made this when Danganronpa V3 *was released. It was a lot of hard work, but it was worth it. Thank you." You're very welcome, Sienna! By the way, not to boast about Dark Horse :) but looking around the photo I was reminded of the fact that in addition to Danganronpa, we also publish the* Super Mario Encyclopedia *and* The Art of Overwatch.

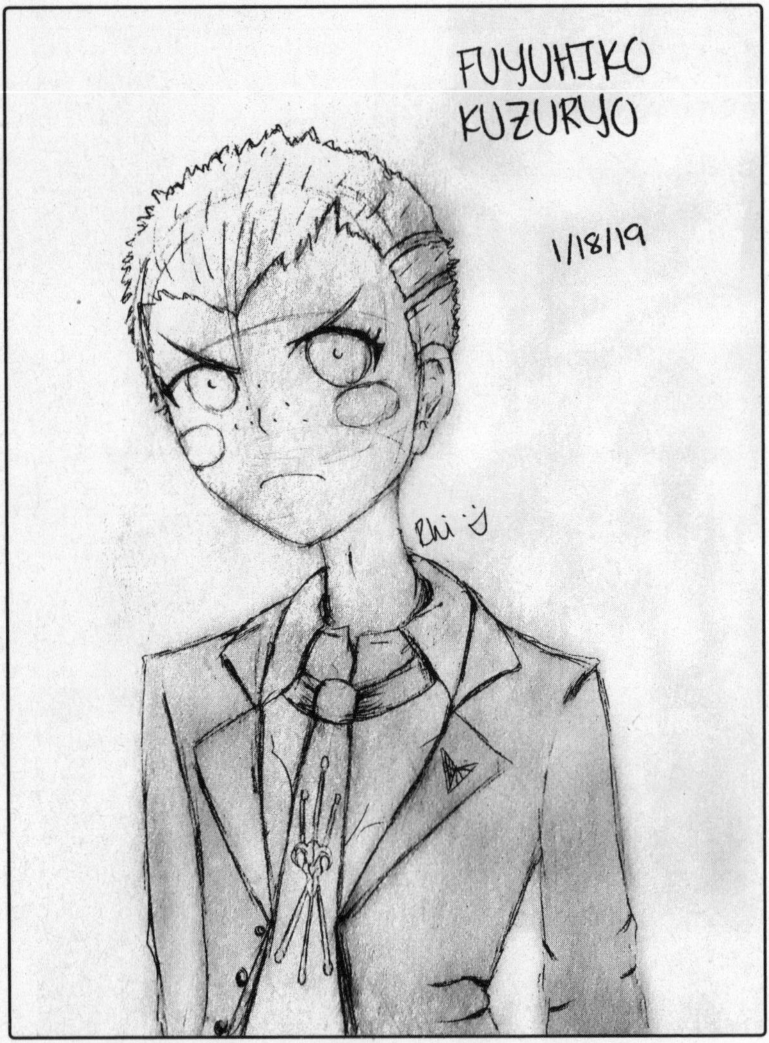
FUYUHIKO
KUZURYO
1/18/19
Rhi

But let's return a moment to Danganronpa 2 *with this drawing of Fuyuhiko Kuzuryu from Rhiannon, who also made a contribution to vol. 3 of* Ultimate Luck *and* Hope and Despair*. Actually, I think this is the first time anyone's drawn* Kuzuryu. *Were people scared to do so just because of his profession (and his bodyguard)? Gangsta, gangsta, that's what they're yellin'—it's not about a salary, it's all about reality!*

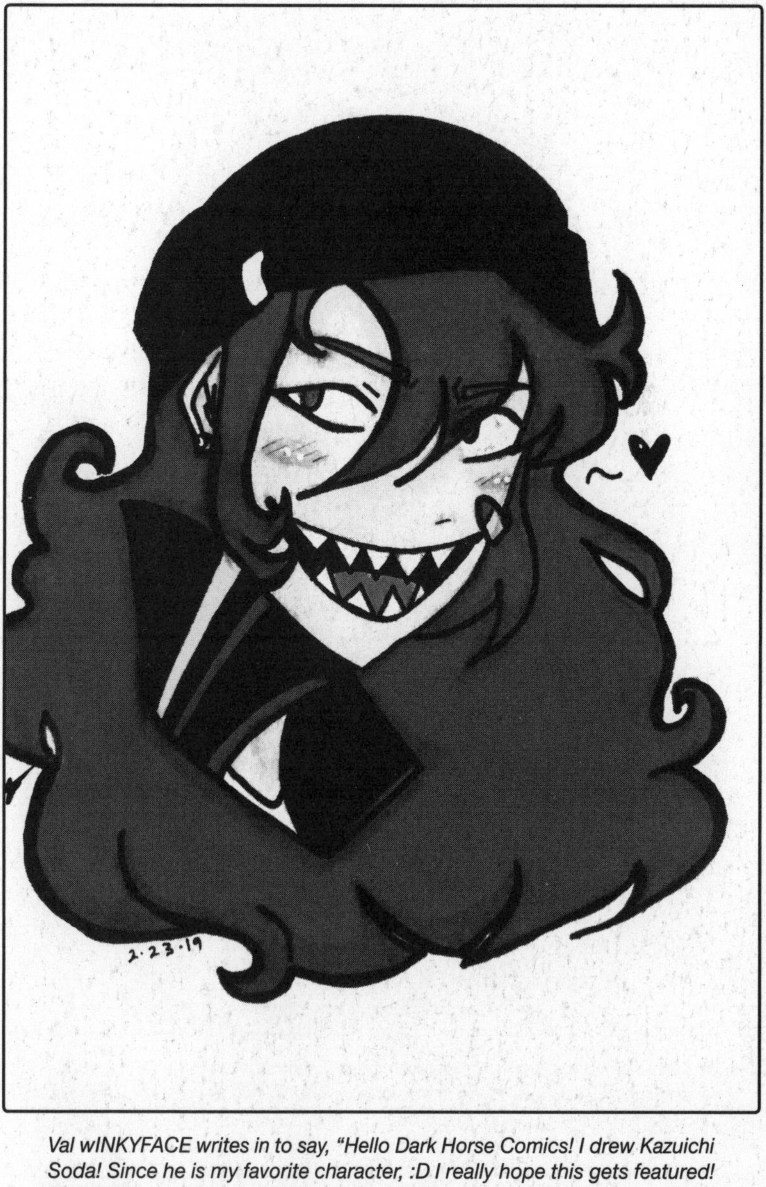
2·23·19

Val wINKYFACE writes in to say, "Hello Dark Horse Comics! I drew Kazuichi Soda! Since he is my favorite character, :D I really hope this gets featured! Thank you, and keep up the good work :))"

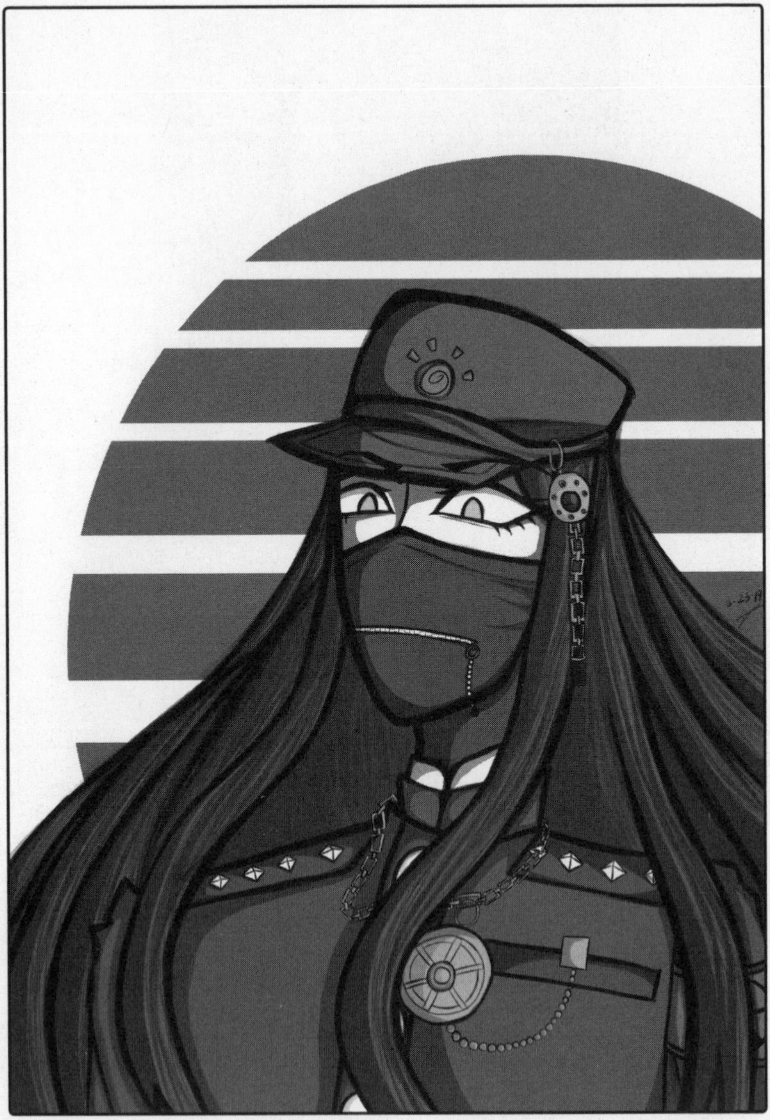

Several weeks later, Val wINKYFACE sent in this drawing of Korekiyo Shinguji. He's plainly here just to observe, seamlessly blend in, and not interfere with your normal lives, as befits the Ultimate Anthropologist.

Ultimate Pianist
Kaede Akamatsu

The Ultimate Pianist wants to know what an anthropologist is. Beth the Cat writes in to say, "Just recently got Danganronpa 2 vols. 1 & 2, they're really great! :D Hopefully they'll make Killing Harmony serialized. In the meantime, here's one of my favorite characters from the third game, Kaede Akamatsu." Hmm, another Killing Harmony contribution. Yes, maybe we should look into doing a manga!

At first I was a little thrown at the sight of three people together in similar school uniforms—in Danganronpa *it's usually more like everyone's trying to dress as different from each other as possible (and succeeding ^_^), but the translator pointed out this great illustration by Kristen Goepfert is from the anime* Danganronpa 3: The End of Hope's Peak High School *(but the rest of you all knew that :-))— Kyosuke Munakata, Chisa Yukizome, and Juzo Sakakura.*

And finally, we'll finish this time right where we began—with Toko and Komaru, this time sent to us from Aylin: "Hi! We are two cosplayers from Mexico :)! We are big fans of the Danganronpa series, all the games and animations, and now the manga as well, ha ha. Saludos desde México!!" Thank you so much for sending these photos of the Ultra Despair Girls to **DESPAIR MAIL!** A Venezolano Danganronpa fan, Eduardo Albarran, put it very well: "Sin lugar a dudas si quieres conocer mas a estas personajes te recomiendo totalmente el manga." ^_^

As always, we'd love to receive more of your thoughts, fan art, cosplay, etc., on all things Danganronpa! Remember to use high resolution if possible (300 dpi or better) for your photos or images, so it'll look its best in print. See you in vol. 2 of Ultra Despair Girls...and don't forget, we're also starting a <u>fourth</u> Danganronpa manga series in November—this time going back to many people's favorite with Danganronpa 2: Goodbye Despair. Well, you didn't think we were just going to trust Nagito-kun's view of events, did you...?

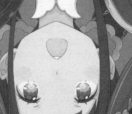

As a manga, *Danganronpa Another Episode: Ultra Despair Girls* reads right-to-left, so this page is actually the back of the book. Sometimes, you've got to look the other way to keep moving forward. See, Toko's doing it. Take life lessons from a serial killer!

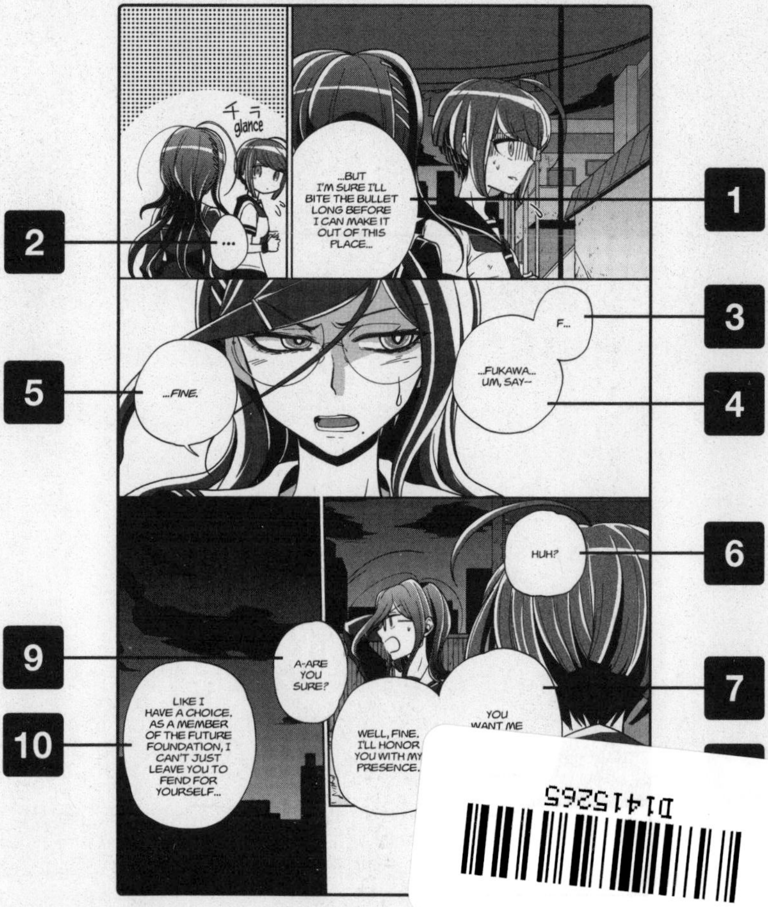
1
...BUT I'M SURE I'LL BITE THE BULLET LONG BEFORE I CAN MAKE IT OUT OF THIS PLACE...
チラ
glance
2
...
3
F...
4
...FUKAWA... UM, SAY--
5
...FINE.
6
HUH?
7
YOU WANT ME
WELL, FINE. I'LL HONOR YOU WITH MY PRESENCE.
9
A-ARE YOU SURE?
10
LIKE I HAVE A CHOICE. AS A MEMBER OF THE FUTURE FOUNDATION, I CAN'T JUST LEAVE YOU TO FEND FOR YOURSELF...